Praise for

Ordinary Injustice

"One of the best portrayals I've read of the everyday, mundane, and yet utterly paralyzing weaknesses of state criminal justice systems . . . Sobering, and important."

—Emily Bazelon, Slate.com

"A highly readable and balanced look at a variety of criminal justice problems in America's courts . . . With compassion and an open mind, Bach has created a work capable of broadening even the sophisticated lawyer-reader's perspective on where injustice is found."

— Alyson Palmer, *Fulton County Daily Report* (Atlanta)

"It takes an attorney to investigate state county courtrooms, and *Ordinary Injustice* reveals the sorry condition of certain state county courtrooms. Amy Bach is a hero to the faceless numbers who have stood before them, alone, convicted, without the guaranteed benefit of a zealous defense."

—Mandy Twaddell, *The Providence Journal*

"Exemplary legal writing."

—Green Bag awards, 2009

"Amy Bach sets out to uncover and, more important, explain widespread failures of the legal process. That she achieves this is reason enough to read and respect *Ordinary Injustice*. But she does it in a way that turns a necessary study into a hard-to-put down narrative that sometimes reads like a screenplay."

—Steven Brill,
founder of Court TV and
The American Lawyer

ORDINARY INJUSTICE

ORDINARY INJUSTICE

HOW AMERICA HOLDS COURT

AMY BACH

A HOLT PAPERBACK

METROPOLITAN BOOKS / HENRY HOLT AND COMPANY

NEW YORK

Holt Paperbacks
Henry Holt and Company, LLC
Publishers since 1866
175 Fifth Avenue
New York, New York 10010
www.henryholt.com

Library of Congress Cataloging-in-Publication Data

Bach, Amy, 1968–
   Ordinary injustice : how America holds court / Amy Bach.—1st ed.
     p. cm.
   Includes bibliographical references and index.
   ISBN: 978-0-8050-9227-1
   1. Criminal justice, Administration of—United States.   2. Judicial error—
United States.   I. Title.
   KF9223.B23 2009
   345.73'05—dc22   2008027484

Originally published in hardcover in 2009 by Metropolitan Books
First Holt Paperbacks Edition 2010

Designed by Meryl Sussman Levavi

Printed in the United States of America

1 3 5 7 9 10 8 6 4 2

To John Markman

CONTENTS

ORDINARY INJUSTICE

INTRODUCTION

One rainy afternoon in Quitman County, Mississippi, I met with a woman who was certain her granddaughter had been raped. There was plenty of evidence and a likely perpetrator, yet the allegation had never seen the inside of a courtroom. The victim was just eleven years old.

When I was greeted by the grandmother at her door, she asked whether I was from the Justice Department. Her face was lit up with hope. It was, however, a strange question. Just the day before, I had explained that I was working on a book about America's criminal justice system and wanted to talk about her family's case. We sat at the kitchen table where she produced a worn paper bag filled with the detailed inquiries she had sent to government officials as well as the form letters she had received in response. She wanted answers: Why had no one taken the case seriously? Did no one care that an adult male had raped an eleven-year-old girl? A prosecutor is obliged to evaluate reports and decide whom to charge. Why wasn't the prosecutor doing his job?

It turned out that the grandmother was not the only one frustrated with the courts. As soon as word got out that there was a reporter in town, my phone started ringing. People from all over the area wanted to tell their stories; most were victims of crimes that had never been investigated, let alone prosecuted. They were happy to talk to me—relieved even—though also incredulous. Why was I so interested? Even the county's prosecutor was surprised. He had resolved these cases ages ago, why was I bothering with them? "Let me ask you this," he said. "Who is complaining?" He knew the answer, of course. It was no one—no official, no one he could hear.

The grandmother's questions were more difficult to address. Like so many citizens, she wanted to hold someone responsible for the lapse in justice that had left her granddaughter's rapist uncharged. She was right to mistrust the prosecutor, though he was but a small cog in a very large and malfunctioning wheel. He lived and worked in a community where legal professionals, local officials, and citizens had known about ongoing problems in the criminal courts for years but had done nothing to fix them.

This book examines how state criminal trial courts regularly permit basic failures of legal process, such as the mishandling of a statutory rape allegation. Ordinary injustice results when a community of legal professionals becomes so accustomed to a pattern of lapses that they can no longer see their role in them. There are times when an alarming miscarriage of justice does come to light and exposes the complacency within the system, but in such instances the public often blames a single player, be it a judge, a prosecutor, or a defense attorney. The point of departure for each chapter in this book is the story of one individual who has found himself condemned in this way. What these examples show, however, is that pinning the problem on any one bad apple fails to indict the tree from which it fell. While it is convenient to isolate misconduct, targeting an individual only obscures what is truly going on from the scrutiny change requires. The system involves too many players to hold only one accountable for the routine injustice happening in courtrooms across America.

■ ■ ■

This book is based on the premise that it takes a community of legal professionals to let a sleeping lawyer sleep. Over the years, there have been quite a few reports of lawyers who literally dozed off during trial, but the one that made international headlines featured Joe Frank Cannon. His client, Calvin Burdine, was convicted of murder for shooting a man during a convenience-store robbery in Texas; for the crime, he was sentenced to death. In 2001, a panel of federal appellate judges vigorously debated whether Cannon had violated the Constitution by falling asleep repeatedly during the trial (with his head nodding and tilting down to his chest for minutes at a time). The panel considered whether a sleeping lawyer can adequately represent someone at trial, as if the problem was about setting an appropriate legal standard and a particular lawyer whose performance had been subpar. Although the panel reviewed the issue through a narrow legal appellate lens, it gave commentators an opening to condemn the state's vigorous use of the death penalty in such an obviously flawed system. But this criticism missed the crucial point: How was it possible that a defense lawyer could fall asleep during a murder trial, and yet no judge, defendant, juror, or member of the bar sitting in the courtroom, no witness, not even the prosecutor, objected?[1]

The prosecutor claimed he was too focused on the witnesses to notice what was happening at the defense table. The judge said he was busy watching the witnesses testify, taking notes, and drafting the charge to the jury. But the jury foreperson saw Cannon dozing and so did two other jurors. The court clerk, whose job is to assist the judge, said she had seen the lawyer sleep on other occasions, too, not just during long portions of this trial. "I knew that he had this problem," the clerk testified when the sleeping became an issue on appeal. Another attorney, who had worked with Cannon before on a capital murder trial, said as much. So at least one court official knew what was happening, although no one in the trial had bothered to wake the lawyer.[2]

4 ■ ORDINARY INJUSTICE

I often thought of Joe Frank Cannon during the winter of 2001 when I found myself sitting in court on a daily basis. I had made a career as a journalist writing about law and later went to law school myself. Working on a series of magazine articles about civil rights, I was intrigued by the routine violations of constitutional law that no one with legal training (or even an avid fan of the many legal dramas on prime-time TV) could fail to notice. With great regularity, I saw citizens have their rights flouted. Many of these people had no idea what they had been denied. And the attorneys looking on never protested.

This pattern of inaction was only the surface of what I began to notice in courts across the country. What was more startling, and what launched this project, was a sense that many of the lawyers involved, often talented and dedicated professionals, couldn't see their own role in perpetuating bad behavior. They didn't seem able in any way to connect their conduct to the courts' worst outcomes. For example, while researching this book I met a New York judge who had stopped notifying many defendants of their right to have an attorney. He also repeatedly failed to assign lawyers to the indigent, as he was obliged to under the Constitution. Twice he recorded guilty pleas for a man without the man's knowledge. In another instance, he refused to assign a lawyer to a seventeen-year-old girl charged with assault; she wanted an attorney but ended up conducting her own trial, alone against a prosecutor (she lost). When the state eventually charged the judge with misconduct, he told me that his response was to ask, "Where is the serious stuff?"

This example may seem extreme, but the effects of less spectacular denials of due process are just as damaging to the system. They happen regularly and create an environment in which more grievous incidents can take place. Ordinary injustice seems to occur in a blind spot. Of course, the ideal (the laws, principles, theories) and the actual (the practitioners and the contingencies they face) never match each other perfectly. But the way legal professionals strike the balance between the two ultimately determines what criminal justice actually amounts to on any given day.

■ ■ ■

America has an adversary system of justice. A trial is a contest between the prosecutor, who represents the state, and the defense attorney, who represents the accused. The facts of the case or an appreciation of the truth at the heart of it arises from the combat between these two sides. The role of the judge is to oversee what happens, impartially enforcing rules of evidence and procedure.

This adversarial model is most evident in countries where the practice of justice is based on English law. Many say the United States has the best system in the world. It is uniquely American in that it is based on regulated competition, much like U.S. markets are supposed to be. One could argue that the American trial process is meritocratic. The best argument and most compelling application of the law wins. Having one set of lawyers that investigates the facts and says, "He did it," while another set tests that assertion and says, "He did not" should ideally create a self-checking mechanism. The contest in the courtroom is, in theory, the end result of the tireless work—depicted in so many movies, hit TV shows, and books—of legal troops who scope out crime scenes, pick through garbage, and employ cutting-edge technology to tap a phone or match saliva through DNA evidence. Even if facts get distorted or a lawyer has performed incompetently, each party is assured the opportunity to present its side of the story and focus attention on the evidence and applicable law.

A person accused of a crime is guaranteed certain rights to ensure a fair process that produces a just outcome. Those rights include trial by jury of one's peers, the right to have one's lawyer cross-examine the prosecution's witnesses to test the truthfulness of testimony, and the right to present testimony that may show innocence. In a perfect world, these rights make certain that facts are subjected to tests, which serve to counterbalance the lopsided battle between the state (represented by the prosecutor) and the individual (represented by the defense). The structure aims to protect against foibles such as laziness and the temptation of professionals to collude.

Collegiality and collaboration are considered the keys to success in most communal ventures, but in the practice of criminal justice they are in fact the cause of system failure. When professional alliances trump adversarialism, ordinary injustice predominates. Judges, defense lawyers, and prosecutors, but also local government, police, and even trial clerks who process the paperwork, decide the way a case moves through the system, thereby determining what gets treated like a criminal matter and what does not. Through their subtle personal associations, legal players often recast the law to serve what they perceive to be the interest of their wider community or to perpetuate a "we've-always-done-it-this-way" mind-set. Whether through friendship, mutual interest, indifference, incompetence, or willful neglect the players end up not checking each other and thus not doing the job the system needs them to do if justice is to be achieved. This book shows what happens when the theory behind the adversarial system is not realized.

One case at a time, we see in each chapter how daily collaboration within the system can undermine this adversarial mechanism. When a lawyer is forced to choose between performing vigorously in his role as an adversary and maintaining easy and necessary professional and institutional relationships, he often opts for the path of least resistance, which undermines justice for some.

Lax adversarialism, a condition that lets cases and defendants pass through the system unchecked, often begins well before a case gets to court. Prosecutors have crushing workloads; they don't want to waste their time on a matter that might not end in conviction. At times, legal teams develop a shorthand calculus for predicting which cases will end up in the "lost" column on their scorecards. You will never see this formula published in a book or as part of a public record, but it governs the prosecutor's approach to a case in which a win before a jury seems unlikely. The assessment is not based on the actual facts but often on stereotypes or on the stature of the victim. Consequently, entire categories of crime, like domestic violence, might go unpursued for decades.

On the flip side, when everyday cases do get to court, incentives to keep caseloads manageable and moving drive the process. Prosecutors negotiate plea deals without having interviewed the victims or witnesses; instead they rely on a few details scribbled in a police report and hope the defense lawyers will overlook any inaccuracies. Defense attorneys, for their part, are also overwhelmed, and often collude, sometimes unknowingly, with prosecutors to abandon cases that don't seem worth their time. Teamwork like this pushes cases through the system at a rapid clip. The point here is not that every case warrants an extensive trial. Plea bargaining is an accepted, condoned practice, as is exercising the prosecutorial discretion not to bring a case to trial. The concern is that ordinary injustice flourishes in the shadows where these deals are cut and decisions are made.

At times, judges abandon their neutrality and step into the adversarial void, acting like prosecutors, forcing defendants either to take a deal or wait in jail for a trial date. That, or they deny a defendant his rights altogether. During my research, I saw many defendants plead guilty without a lawyer present. In some cases, they had been in jail for months without counsel. In others, they had no idea what they were pleading guilty to or they accepted sentences higher than the legal maximum. Some sentences may seem small at the time, but they can have catastrophic unanticipated consequences for landing a job, obtaining public housing, maintaining an immigration status, or for the punishment of a crime that occurs later.

With little fear of being called out by their peers, the professionals (judges, prosecutors, and defense attorneys) seem at ease. They feel okay about their work. A smooth, non-adversarial, machine process gives the appearance of efficiency: courthouse employees can go home on time; colleagues who run into each other don't have to worry about hurt feelings after an uncomfortable exchange because there has been no struggle to ferret out the truth.

Alongside the easy manner in which such slack justice is carried out is the opposite problem, one of excess adversarialism, in which legal professionals over-prosecute, usually at the insistence of a community that feels threatened by a headline-grabbing crime. A prosecutor wants to show the community that the crime will be redressed and order restored.

It is for these cases, which take on a "show trial" quality, that the system saves its ammunition. The state marshals its forces and will not let up. Defendants who are wrongfully convicted are living proof of the extent to which the state will go to demonstrate the system's vigor, even when presented with evidence that contravenes its case.

Consider Rolando Cruz who was sentenced to death in the 1983 kidnapping, rape, and murder of ten-year-old Jeanine Nicarico in Du-Page County, Illinois. Early on, the lead detective resigned in protest over the way prosecutors were mishandling the case.[3] Two years later, another man, a known sex offender, confessed to committing the rape and murder himself.[4] Nonetheless, prosecutors stuck with Cruz as the perpetrator. In 1992 a young lawyer who was defending the state against Cruz's appeal concluded that he was innocent. She advised the attorney general of her findings—to no avail. Ultimately, she too quit her job, making news. DNA evidence eventually excluded Cruz as the perpetrator and linked the confessed sex offender to the crime, yet still prosecutors refused to drop the case. Why, in the face of overwhelming evidence to the contrary, did the state cling so desperately to its theory?[5]

Legal professionals do sometimes denounce failings but more often they assist them in ways large and small, which then compromises their ability to speak out. Attorneys on both sides become defensive and don't want to admit problems. When challenged, they tend to respond as a unit and place the blame elsewhere. "The defendants are guilty." "The victims deserved it." "The case is minor." "There's nothing to be done." "It's an aberration." "We have the right guy even if DNA says otherwise." These explanations are rampant. They are the stock phrases of ordinary injustice that appear throughout this book.

■ ■ ■

Ordinary injustice is virtually always rooted in an incomplete story. The complete facts of a case, the very stuff that could force a remedy, are usually missing. We assume that competing narratives drive every courtroom drama. But when the contest is short-circuited because every case on a docket is pleaded summarily or because a case never makes it to court in the first place there will be no narrative on record.

This book attempts to fill in the incomplete stories. Each chapter begins with one of the key players in the adversarial model (the defense attorney, the judge, or the prosecutor) and examines the circumstances that have allowed injustice to thrive in his particular court location: Greene County, Georgia; Troy, New York; Quitman County, Mississippi; and Chicago, Illinois. While I chose stories that occurred in state trial courts—because that is where most people experience the criminal justice system—the specific settings matter less than the overarching issue of how America holds court. North or south, rich or poor, urban or rural, black or white, ordinary injustice cannot be explained away by any one variable.

When I began this project, I took a wager that ordinary citizens, most of whom will never face a criminal prosecution, could be roused to engage with what transpires in the nation's courtrooms. Indeed, in nearly every community I visited, I found individuals striving to correct failures in the system: clerks, paralegals, prisoners, family members, as well as journalists, and outside organizations. Even more encouraging was the participation of the four lawyers at the center of this book: Robert Surrency in Georgia, Hank Bauer in New York, Laurence Mellen in Mississippi, and Tom Breen in Illinois. While they were, or had been, mostly blind to the problems they had aided and abetted, they did not attempt to hide them. Were it not for their candor and that of other attorneys in the legal communities I have observed over the past seven years, the cases and patterns identified here might never have come to light. The very people who have helped perpetrate ordinary injustice met with me repeatedly, for countless hours, to talk about their roles and answer questions they might well have preferred to ignore. In their transparency, we can see the outlines for change.

CHAPTER ONE

"WHAT'S A DEFENSE?"

I didn't know I was going to jail," I heard a defendant say as she stood before the judge in Greene County, Georgia. Of course she didn't. No one had told her the consequences of pleading guilty. Most people, educated or not, often have no idea what a guilty plea actually means: the conviction of a crime that subjects them to incarceration, fines, probation, a criminal record with unforeseen future consequences. Many do not even know that a guilty plea is not mandatory or that an appeal after conviction at trial is possible, even though a judge is required to correctly advise defendants before any plea.

I had first come to Greene County in 2001 after hearing about the chaos in its court system which seemed representative of a statewide problem; and I continued to visit for weeks at a time over the next five years. As required by the U.S. Supreme Court precedent, the county was fulfilling the obligation to provide attorneys to those who couldn't afford them. With little state oversight, court-appointed lawyers, for a

variety of reasons, were sacrificing the interests of their most vulnerable and malleable constituency—the defendants they were supposed
to be protecting. In this process, the defense lawyer, the judge, and prosecutor formed a kind of a tag team—charge the accused, assign a lawyer,
prosecute, plead, sentence—with slight regard for the distinctions and
complexities of each case.

Robert E. Surrency was under contract with Greene County to represent poor people accused of crime. He was not employed by the
county full-time; he continued to represent a number of paying clients as
well. Even so, his private work was not lucrative enough, so he needed
the indigent defense contract to support himself. On an annual basis,
his caseload was double the national recommendation for a full-time
attorney.[1]

Surrency was raised in Media, Pennsylvania, where his father, Er-
win C. Surrency, had worked as the law librarian and assistant dean for
Temple Law School. "I grew up in the stacks," he said of his upbringing.
Surrency's father, whom he admired greatly, had been born and married in Georgia. In turn, Surrency attended Mercer University in Macon,
where he had kin. Afterward, he headed back to Temple for law, passed
the Pennsylvania Bar, and landed a clerkship with a state court judge
for whom he helped write opinions. He then hung out a shingle as a
solo practitioner and established a civil-law practice. In the mid-1980s
his father decided to return to Georgia to become the director of the library at the University of Georgia Law School. Surrency, in his thirties,
chose to move as well. He opened a law practice on Main Street in
Watkinsville, Georgia, conveniently located near several other towns,
Madison and Greensboro, and near his father in Athens. But he found
it hard to make a living. Surrency seemed to lack the relationships
those who had grown up there enjoyed. An old-time attorney explained that Georgians born and bred "kind of rule around here" and
that Surrency constantly had to prove himself. "He was a stranger," the
attorney said. Surrency's practice foundered.

One afternoon in 1987, he drove the thirty-five-minute trip to
Greene County's courthouse and ran into Chip Atkins, a longtime local

lawyer. Atkins had been the public defender but no longer wanted the job. He said that the contract to represent poor people was up for "bid," and urged him to apply. Surrency won the contract by offering to handle all the routine cases for fifteen thousand dollars, plus seventy-five dollars an hour for serious cases like murder; his bid, which came in at about twenty thousand dollars total, was slightly lower than anyone else's, he explained. In his first year, he represented forty defendants while maintaining a private practice. "It was a good side job," Surrency said.

In the fourteen years that followed, his public caseload multiplied tenfold, while the amount of time he devoted to each case inevitably shrank. In 2001, the year I first met him, 1,359 people were arrested and held in the Greene County jail. Because the vast majority of criminal defendants nationwide are too poor to afford a lawyer, many of those arrested in Greene County would become his clients.[2] During the same fourteen years, Surrency's pay rose only to $42,150.

Nonetheless, Surrency claimed to have achieved good results. He settled a large number of cases through plea-bargaining, which he called "a uniquely productive way to do business." It got his clients in and out of the system quickly, which, he maintained, was what they wanted; and it saved him from having to defend clients whose cases he did not have time to try. Holding onto his contract depended on, among other things, expediting the process. If he got stuck on one client, he couldn't push the rest through. The judges expected him to perform—one had a motto, "Slow justice is no justice"—and could complain to the county commissioners, who had a lot of influence with the committee that awarded Surrency's contract.

Outsiders and a few insiders, such as the head clerk and Surrency's former paralegal, saw him as the quintessential "meet 'em, greet 'em, and plead 'em lawyer" who met his defendants minutes before they would face the judge and who, by then, had few options but to plead guilty. Even so, Surrency insisted he was helping people. He saw himself as a man of experience who was defending the poor. He helped extract the innocent from the system and shepherd the guilty through an imperfect and unjust world.

When I arrived at the Greene County courthouse just before nine in the morning to watch Surrency in action, he was trudging up the stairs to the courtroom. He had red tousled hair and wore a loose grey suit. The old courtroom, with its ceiling fans and creaky floors, was packed. Those who didn't have a seat overflowed into the hallways outside. Surrency looked distracted and then defeated as he saw the crowd that awaited him. Some, waving papers, laid into him with frustrated questions. Many had phoned him about their cases but had not heard back, or had spoken with him briefly and been told to meet with him before court. They were swarming around him like gnats. "Everybody back up. Back up," he said. "I'll try to get to talk to all of you before you go to the judge."

I had come on the first day of "trial week," the term of court when this rural court attempts to resolve cases that have built up over the previous quarter with jury trials. The label is a misnomer. In four years, Surrency had taken only fourteen cases to trial out of 1,493; he won five. The rest of the cases he managed during that period—more than 99 percent—he plea-bargained. In this particular session no cases went to trial. People either pleaded guilty or had their cases rescheduled, a drill that took only two days. There were 142 defendants on the court calendar and 89 were Surrency's. In a flash, it seemed, forty-eight of his clients rose from the rickety dark wooden benches, one after the other, to plead guilty. After the first day I spent in court observing him, he announced, "We have successfully done a ten-page calendar in one day!" For Surrency, speed meant success.

In court, he would yell out a client's name, like the hostess at a restaurant clearing the wait list. "Mr. Jones, are you here?" Then he would peruse the list of plea offers the prosecutor had given him and tell his defendant how much he or she would have to pay in fines or serve in jail time. If the defendant didn't want to plead, the matter was held over until the next trial week. Surrency theorized that the longer a case dragged on, the more likely it was that incriminating witnesses might forget what had happened. His job had devolved into this: Plead guilty or come back another day.

Can a defense lawyer plead virtually all his cases and still be doing a decent job? In assessing the quality of a lawyer's work, the number of cases he pleads out is less significant than the amount of attention he gives to each one. What is required of him is not necessarily research in law books, but investigation and client contact: initial interviews about what led to the arrest or the charge; discussions, for example, with the prosecutor's witnesses to assess their strength, or with the arresting police officer; perhaps a review of any forensic reports or psychiatric evaluations. What's needed is a range of basic inquiries involving phone calls or brief meetings that go toward deciding strategy for everything from bail setting to finding evidence.

Surrency had little time to talk in detail to his clients, and so he often had limited information to use in their favor. It was thus difficult for him to bargain with prosecutors to secure a more lenient sentence, nor could he produce the ultimate trump card: a willingness to go to trial when his clients claimed innocence. Many of them risked losing their homes, children, and livelihoods if they pleaded guilty, and yet his actions remained the same: His caseload often made it hard for him to clarify the facts—for example, whether his client had been the ringleader or had acted without intent or was guilty of a lesser crime—which is the kind of information that can mitigate the severity of a sentence or get charges dropped in negotiation.

Part of Surrency's problem was that his contract did not fund investigations or expert witnesses. For these, Surrency would have to ask the judge to provide funds or just lay out the money and then ask for reimbursement, which he didn't like to do. He didn't want to get people riled up about spending the county's money. Moreover, he claimed not to need these resources, anyway, because most of his cases were "pretty open and shut." Under the weight of too many clients to represent, he seemed to have lost the ability both to decide which cases required attention and to care one way or the other.

Defendants, of course, didn't like Surrency's way of doing things. The then-clerk of the court, Marie Boswell, had received many complaints, but none had been formally filed. Instead, those accused of crimes banded together as if they were on one team and their lawyer on another, at times passing around advice, and a few proclaiming that the best solution was to represent themselves. I spoke with one woman, in her mid-twenties, smoking with her friends outside court, who was there on charges of selling cocaine. She dug into her savings to hire her own lawyer. "He meets with me. He talks with me about the case," she said, as if this were exceptional.

H,§ another defendant, twenty-eight years old, a heavily built black man with a shaved head, was sitting in the back row of the courtroom, charged with aggravated assault and battery of his boyfriend. He said he had never been in trouble with the law before. The crime, which he did not dispute, involved hitting his lover with his car after he learned that the victim had knowingly exposed him to HIV and now H had tested positive. "I guess I panicked," H says. "A lot of emotions were going through me."

H's explanation constituted a defense. But Surrency never returned H's phone calls. "I bet if [his clients] all lined up in a lineup he couldn't pick a person out," H said.

Surrency, I found, was resolute in his defense of himself. He did not allow for the prospect of having ill-treated his clients. "Nobody was treated bad," he said. "Nobody could say that they didn't have their day in court." But in his mind, it hardly mattered since most defendants wanted to plead guilty from the outset, whether they had or had not committed the exact crime with which they were charged. And if he went to trial rather than taking the plea, he risked a judge giving the maximum sentence. Plus, pragmatically, he said, people wanted to move on. The employed wanted to avoid missing work (which could mean days if the case was postponed over and over), while the unemployed found coming to court burdensome. Many didn't have cars, and there was no public transportation in Greene County. "A car don't run by itself," said one woman I met, who had been charged with committing aggravated assault with a heavy meat grinder. She had paid a friend ten dollars for a ride.

§ "H" asked to be called by a single initial to maintain his privacy.

More often than not, what a defendant really wants is what Harvard Law School professor Charles Fried calls "a special-purpose friend," an attorney who, perhaps with a hand on the client's shoulder, "acts in your interests, not his own; or rather he adopts your interests as his own," guiding a client through the process and defending him against injury.[3]

This was not Surrency. Witness a conversation between him and a client, a woman in an orange prison jumpsuit.

"I know I'm pleading guilty," she said. "But I don't know why."

"Well, we talked about that," he said.

She shook her head. No, they hadn't.

"Don't you remember when we talked?" said Surrency, as he flipped through a file.

"We *never* talked," she said, calm and resigned, mocking her lawyer as if she knew she would get nothing from him and just wanted him to admit as much.

Rejecting this complaint, Surrency told me that he talked to all his clients at some point, but that the average defendant would usually protest that he or she didn't get enough time. Clients seemed bottomless in their need for attention. "You have to draw the line somewhere," he said.

It seemed that after seventeen years, he was exhausted—by the job and the system. As Surrency put it, the local governing agency that hired him, the Greene County Board of Commissioners, "didn't want these people"—indigent defendants—"to get an even break just to start with. 'They are guilty anyway, what do they need a lawyer for?'— that is their attitude today. There is really a consensus among the local people paying their taxes that these people don't need any defense, much less a quality legal defense."

And so it went. Frequently, Surrency was not even in court when his defendants pled. He'd stand in the hallway talking to other clients. Another lawyer, Rick Weaver, who knew even less about the cases, would often take his place. Surrency regularly paid Weaver, a former prosecutor, six hundred dollars for one day of work, which allowed Surrency the freedom to communicate plea deals to his clients while

Weaver stood before the judge. Surrency would talk to the prosecutor to receive the plea offer, then he would pass it on to the client, often on the day of court. The next step was sending the client, with his file, to see Weaver, who would accompany the accused as the plea occurred before the judge.

An attorney who is present in court and armed with specific information about a case stands a good chance of influencing the outcome for his client. Nevertheless, Surrency, in a letter that recapped his work load to the local government budget committee, wrote that there were times "when an attorney needs to be in two places at one time and Mr. Weaver has solved that problem." He maintained that "the trial judge and the District Attorney were very pleased with the addition of Mr. Weaver to the business of the day."[4]

Weaver stood up awkwardly beside Terrical Lashay Porter, who was in court on drug charges. Porter, in her early twenties, came from a family in which two of her uncles, as well as her brother and her mother, had served time for drug crimes, including trafficking or selling. On a search warrant based on her brother's conduct, the police had found a bag of marijuana that Porter admitted was hers. "It was in my bedroom," she told me; a friend had given it to her after a party. She was charged with possessing more than an ounce of marijuana with intent to sell—a felony for which the law mandates a maximum of ten years in prison. Porter had never been arrested for a crime before.

After the charge, she had heard nothing about her case for two years until the day before her appearance in court, when a neighbor brought her a subpoena sent to an old address. Porter raced to court early, but Surrency had too many people around him to talk to her. When their turn came to meet, she learned that the prosecution was offering her five years of probation on "conditional discharge"—a special, one-time deal for people charged with drug possession as a first offense that resembles the "first offender" law in which a felony record is dismissed and discharged—with no conviction, if the "terms or conditions" of probation, such as paying a fine and seeing a probation officer once a month, are met. If, however, Porter got convicted of another crime—*any* crime—during the probation period, a judge could nail her with the maximum sentence for her original offense. Given that her family was clearly on the police radar, Porter might well get arrested, even for something as minor as driving without a license and she could conceivably end up getting sentenced to a full ten years. The risk seemed not worth it to Porter. She said she told Surrency she would rather accept the five years of probation, but without the conditional discharge, even if it meant a permanent record instead.

Soon after the meeting with him, Porter stood before the judge. She looked nervous. Her foot was twitching. She was sweating. Rick Weaver, a lawyer she had never met, stood at her side. Surrency wasn't there.

The prosecutor described Porter to the judge. "We believe she is much less involved in all of that than her mother and her brother and her uncles," he said, though he described her home briefly as "a place to buy drugs" and her mother as "the main one operating out of there." He then explained the offer of conditional discharge he was making to Porter. After, Judge Hulane George began a "colloquy" to explain to Porter her rights. She asked if Porter understood that she had the right to plead not guilty and demand a jury trial.

"Yes, ma'am," Porter said.

Did she understand that she was waiving her rights, including the presumption of innocence, the right to subpoena any witnesses, the right to a lawyer at trial?

"Yes, ma'am."

Despite Porter having told Surrency that she didn't want to take the conditional discharge gamble, the judge informed her that she was pleading under the conditional-discharge provision. "Do you understand that under this particular provision of the law, in five years, you will have no felony record? Do you understand that?"

"Yes, ma'am," Porter said.

"But if you get into trouble I could come back and sentence you to what is left of your five years. Do you understand that?"

"Yes, ma'am."

"All right, do you want to plead under conditional discharge?"

"Yes, ma'am."

"Do you freely and voluntarily enter your plea of guilty to the charge against you?"

"Yes, ma'am."

"You are represented here by Mr. Weaver, who is with you. Have you been talking to Mr. Surrency or Mr. Weaver?

"Mr. Surrency."

She then asked Porter if she had any problems with Mr. Weaver and if there was anything else she wanted Surrency or Weaver to do.

"No, ma'am," Porter said.

"Anything you want to say to me before I rule?"

"No, ma'am."

"All right. Mr. Weaver, is the sentence recommendation the State made the same one to which you and your client agreed?"

"It is, Your Honor."

"Have you had enough time to discuss this case with her?" Judge George asked Weaver.

"I would like about thirty seconds, if I could, just to make sure," Weaver said.

He and Porter conferred. And then he stepped forward: "I do not believe she is interested in the conditional discharge," Weaver said. "I don't think she fully understood."

Porter looked panicked. "I told Mr. Surrency that I didn't want to be under that," she said. "The first offender."

"But this isn't first offender," the judge said.

"But it operates exactly the same way, Your Honor," Weaver said.

The judge turned to the prosecutor. "It's my understanding, I could only sentence her to what's left on five years rather than the first offender up to ten," she said.

The prosecutor had to correct her. "I think you could sentence her up to the total amount she could have received."

The judge said, "Well, she said she doesn't want it."

"Well, it'll take us a minute to redraw the sentence."

Porter, nervous and disoriented before the judge, said later that she didn't understand what she was agreeing to. "I had never been up there before and everything was kind of moving together," she said of the panic.

The judge seemed confused and began to go on in a way that had little to do with Porter's case: "But this is not the time to impress me! It's the time to be honest. You know, if you don't think you can be successful on it, you're the one who'll have to go to prison! Not me!"

Maybe the judge was trying to be tough or thought Porter was intentionally playing games. Later, she explained that she had been especially irritable because she had a horrible cold, and because she had been forced to backtrack when she had a large number of cases to get through.

In court, Weaver tried to take control. "Your Honor, what I advised her is that if she is in a position where she is around drugs, whether they're hers or not, she can face a very real possibility of taking a hit for that."

But the judge was not listening. "Do you have children?" she asked Porter.

"No, ma'am."

"Do you work?"

"Yes," she said.

"Well, you need to get out of the environment or you're going to end up in prison . . . What color are the women's prison uniforms anymore?"

Porter stood there while a lawyer shouted out the answer.

"Brown? Are they brown? Not a pretty color!" said Judge George. "I don't think you want to go. But that is your decision."

In the end, Porter got what she wanted: She pleaded guilty and received five years of probation—not under conditional discharge.

Outside the courthouse, she bawled. She had no idea that her lawyer could have made the experience easier for her. A lawyer in a different position might have presented arguments to ameliorate the punishment or advance Porter's cause. She would have gotten considerably more than a five-minute conversation before court and would not have been exposed to a nuts-and-bolts consultation in court. But Porter wasn't angry at her lawyer; she seemed hurt by Judge George. "The judge told me to get out of the environment but I have no place to go," she said. "I don't want to leave my sister. I am the only one taking care of her." Another lawyer might have conveyed these concerns to a judge, as well as the plea Porter had wanted, not let her panic and nearly plead to something different.

In her hand, Porter had a pink slip that listed the costs she had agreed to as part of the plea: a $500 fine; $50 for the police officers and prosecutors training fund; $50 to the jail fund; $25 to the victims assistance program; $250 to the drug fund; $50 crime lab fee; $23 per month for the probation supervision fee; and one hundred hours of community service. Somehow, it amounted to $75 a month for the next year, which she could pay off if her boss at Wendy's, where she worked as a cook and cashier, gave her additional hours. "I got to find me another job," she said.

Back in the courtroom, another case was breaking down. This time a young woman in a leather blazer was talking in muffled sobs with the judge. While Weaver was looking for the file, Tasha McDonald stood before the judge alone. She was asking for her case to be continued.

"How many times has he talked to you?" Judge George asked about Surrency.

"Once," said the woman. The judge wearily announced that her case would be rescheduled to a different day.

In the hallway, McDonald was crying hard. When she calmed down she told her story. A single mother of three young girls, she freely admitted to having applied for a Sears credit card in the name of a colleague with whom she worked at a luxury vacation community. McDonald had the card sent to her own address, made herself a secondary user, and then bought $1,895.35 worth of merchandise: beds, sheets and pillowcases, a CD player, a microwave, a toaster oven—"everything for the house." She also bought a small trampoline for her eldest daughter, a ten-year old, who had just been diagnosed with scleroderma, a hardening of the skin that can weaken limbs. The trampoline, she said, was therapeutic, to help her daughter regain muscle control and mobility.

McDonald had been charged with financial identity fraud. She knew she had to be punished, but had only found out from Surrency in the hallway that the prosecutor wanted her to serve 90 to 120 days in a detention center or jail. If incarcerated, she feared she would lose her job, her mobile home and car, both of which she was still paying off, and become a burden to the state. "If I do four months in boot camp you know where my home is going," she said. She had already repaid Sears for the goods.

There were alternatives. Instead of jail, she could be sentenced to do community service or to attend one of various halfway houses or work release programs designed so people convicted of minor felonies can keep their jobs if they have them. She could also have been sent to a diversion center, which collaborates with minimum-wage employers like processing plants or fast-food restaurants. Inmates work during the day to pay for room and board, and then, if there is money left over, to pay fines, a mortgage, or to support family members.

Surrency contends that the results would have been the same, no matter how much investigation he did. However, if he had argued that McDonald shouldn't be taken away from her children, due to her circumstances, she might not have ended up facing any jail time at all. Certainly prosecutors and judges are likely to be more sympathetic to a defendant whose motive comes down to poverty or an ill child. Yet the odds that the judge or prosecutor knew about McDonald's particular situation were slim. You could hardly blame them.

On the other hand, maybe you could. Weren't there questions a decent prosecutor could ask if he suspected defense counsel was asleep on the job? Wasn't it apparent that Surrency was overloaded to the point of neglecting his clients? I started to get curious about the prosecutor and just how complicit he was when it came to pushing defendants through the system. It seemed like most everyone who appeared before the judge was confused and uninformed. What was the prosecutor's role in all this?

Wilson B. Mitcham Jr., had been the assistant district attorney in charge of Greene County since 1993 and had appeared in court with Surrency hundreds of times. They seemed on good terms with each other and with the judge. Often the courtroom felt like a private party, with the lawyers and judge huddled around the bench, preventing anyone else from hearing. It looked like they were teammates rather than opposing advocates duking it out before a neutral arbiter.

In an interview, Mitcham was surprised to learn of McDonald's situation. "I am shocked," he said, "because no one told me she has a disabled child." He was essentially admitting that he knew Surrency was doing a disservice to his clients by not discussing their cases with them. Still, he seemed defensive of their convivial rapport in court, noting that "even though we are cordial . . . we do have certain disagreements." But these were not enough to change the way Surrency conducted business. While Mitcham knew Surrency waited until the last minute to talk to his clients, he still maintained that cases were getting the attention they needed.

As for McDonald, Mitcham said he would look into it and possibly change his plea offer, which he eventually did. It turned out this was not her first crime of deception. A decade earlier she had received probation for using a bad check knowing it wouldn't be honored by the bank. For her identity theft she could have received a maximum of ten years in prison, but given his knowledge about her family, Mitcham asked the judge that she serve only the mandatory minimum of one year on probation and some time at a diversion center "until released by the center director." The center would allow her to leave on weekends to visit her daughters, who would be cared for by her mother.

For McDonald's subsequent court appearances, she fired Surrency and hired a private lawyer. Her case went before a new judge who seemed annoyed by how light Mitcham's negotiated plea was. Judge John Lee Parrott criticized McDonald for her premeditation—that she "went through too many steps" to commit the crime. "[I]'ve got some doubts about whether I ought to let her off even this light," said Parrott before agreeing to the plea. "To be honest with you, most of the time I put people straight in jail," he said. "I'm giving you a chance to get your ducks in a row with your kids." Since he understood McDonald's circumstances, he made an exception. McDonald apologized to the coworker whose identity she stole. "[I] was desperate. I knew that she had good credit," she said. "That's why I used her."

McDonald said she ended up serving only two months in the Macon Diversion Center. There, she worked in a factory pressing shirts, which helped her pay off her mortgage on her trailer. She left on weekends to see her family, and also took care of all the various penalties and of her one hundred hours of community service. Most important, she wasn't whisked away to jail. McDonald is still incredulous at the way Surrency told her that she was going to jail. She wanted to ask him, "How could you be for me when you have never talked to me?"

In the case of H, when Mitcham was informed about the boyfriend who might have intentionally given him HIV, he recognized that H's crime might have been done "in the heat of passion." "I wish I had known," he said; he would have thought about it differently. Still, H had gotten a good deal. When Surrency hadn't returned his calls, H pulled some strings: He called a prosecutor friend in a different county who vouched for H as a good citizen. As a result, Mitcham had changed his original offer from five years in prison to five months in a detention center plus ten years' probation.

It is not explicitly the prosecutor's job to ask for more information than the defense has provided, though nothing precludes him from doing so, either. The ethics are murky. Codes of professional responsibility require a prosecutor only to "do justice" but provide little guidance about what this means.[5] In theory, a prosecutor who realizes that a defense attorney isn't performing aggressively could ask him to improve his performance or else withdraw from the trial. If that doesn't work, he could tell the judge or make a motion to disqualify counsel, though this is unlikely as lawyers view "most reporting obligations with distaste."[6] In reality, many prosecutors consider defense attorneys a nuisance and don't think they need to know anything besides the crime and a defendant's prior record to assess sentencing recommendations.

But Mitcham was not a stereotypical, aggressive prosecutor who invoked protection of the community as his top priority. He sometimes helped defendants, as he saw it. Like Surrency, Mitcham had hundreds of cases piled up in his office; he seemed to think that by putting them off he was showing compassion to those charged and, in a complicated way, doing God's work. But he admitted that he couldn't keep up with his workload and had a problem with procrastination. "I am an administrative nightmare walking," he said. Mitcham had a rather unusual view of how and why he did things. "I was raised to be a good Christian," he said over lunch at Subway, as tears welled in his eyes and he stopped eating his turkey sandwich. He had begun his career as a defense lawyer then left to become a minister. But he found this path didn't suit him, either; the politics of the church bothered him. In the end, being a prosecutor was the best way he could find to show his forgiveness. "You can mete out a lot more mercy as a prosecutor than as a defense attorney," he said.

At the same time, he was cautious about appearing too compassionate on the job. "I have a bleeding heart, but I try to disguise it. I don't want anyone to think that I have a hair-trigger to dismiss a case." With good reason: If he showed his mercy openly, he could seem soft on crime and get fired. Prosecutors are supposed to be strict and aggressive. To solve his quandary, Mitcham found a silver lining in his procrastination problem. By delaying cases and letting things slide, he compensated for the defense attorney's failure to defend his clients—no one defends, no one prosecutes, and, as it turns out, no one benefits.[7]

Surrency and Mitcham had created a stable but dysfunctional relationship; and Judge George, who had presided over the two lawyers for years, seemed to compound it. A former schoolteacher, she wanted to keep things orderly. "I like to clean things up," she said. At the same time, under her authority, the lawyers had been permitted to treat the dizzying disarray of the courtroom as if it were the norm. She claimed that the day I visited had been one of the worst, insisting that in other trial weeks she took more care of the defendants. However, the other Greene County judges I observed during trial week seemed to have similarly bad days. They all blamed the problems on sheer volume, a lack of funding for public defense, and on the community's reluctance to spend money on the town's poorest and least law abiding. They also seemed resigned to an unwritten obligation to put the court on auto pilot—to make justice quick and easy and to dispense with the complications that accompany a true exploration of the facts. Judge George conceded to acting out of pressure. The jails were overflowing, so she needed to move cases forward. "Part of it is that you're standing up above everyone, in front of hundreds of people, all of whom want their cases to be number one," she said.

Besides its ease, auto pilot has certain advantages for the judge. If, for instance, a defense lawyer actually put forth arguments, the judge might have to make difficult calls about issues like admitting questionable evidence. Some decisions might be unpopular. Defendants considered guilty in the public's eye might have to go free. Doing justice would become much harder—both in and outside the courtroom—and messier. It was easier to take pride in maintaining the routine and the schedule. "[Too] many judges, consciously or subliminally, prefer the less aggressive advocate who cooperates in disposing of cases and helping to clear the judge's docket," writes Vanessa Merton, a professor at Pace Law School.[8]

In Greene County, there were additional incentives for judges to preserve the status quo. There, the opinion of the Board of Commissioners (the five citizens who control the county budget) carries a lot of clout. While judges are elected and often run uncontested, they are mindful of the influence of the commission and the sheriff, and of the possibility that these powerful bodies might support an opponent in the next election. Judges throughout the state are sensitive to the costs of a trial. Judges do not want to seem wasteful. "I'm a politician," said Judge James Cline, who also sat in Greene County. "Every four years I want fifty-one percent of the people to vote for me."

Like Surrency and Mitcham, Judge George denied rushing cases forward against the defendants' interests. When asked if being elected to her position every four years had anything to do with her need to please, she said no. She emphasized that what I saw was unusual. "It was just a god-awful day." She did, however, feel badly about the impression she had made. "The whole thing was hurry up and get it done. I fault myself for allowing myself to get pushed around and I am better about it."

With Surrency, Mitcham, and Judge George faulting the system, each other, and occasionally themselves, the court began to seem like a runaway train. It was hard to tell who was at the controls and if anyone there was awake.

■   ■   ■

Of course, Greene County is not unique. The real issue here is the poor quality of defense representation throughout the nation. There are three basic systems for providing attorneys. It is difficult to rank them comparatively by quality since all three are flawed and tend to come apart when underfunded, poorly staffed, or subject to the whimsy of judges and prosecutors.[9] Still, one can quantify the differences among them. The arguably best system is called the "public defender" structure, in which full-time defense lawyers, employed by the state, are provided with central offices, secretaries, computers, investigators, and legal research tools.* A public defender system aims to put the defense on equal, or near-equal, footing with the prosecution. In the more bountiful programs, public defenders are overseen by a statewide agency that sets uniform standards and expectations for counties or circuits. A variation on this program contracts with a non-profit program funded by public money and other sources.[10]

The second system is a panel program, in which private attorneys

---

* In this chapter, a public defender system refers to the ideal form where the public defender works full-time with equal or near-equal resources as the prosecutor. At other times in this book, people use the term "public defender" to refer to an attorney or an office that represents the poor part-time in addition to their private practices.

on a pre-approved list are appointed and paid to represent indigent defendants as needed. The idea, in theory, is for an independent agency or clerk to select lawyers from a list who want and are qualified to do the work. In many jurisdictions, however, a judge makes the assignments, which may affect the independence of the attorney, who depends on future assignments from the judge for his or her income. Lawyers who line up for assignments are paid by the case or by the hour (for which there is usually a fee cap) and can become accustomed to the quick disposal of cases. And in some places an attorney who is totally unqualified to do criminal work—an expert in real estate or matrimonial law—will be appointed unpaid as part of community service to the local bar association.

Further, private lawyers with paying clients may not want to make time for poorly funded cases. For years Virginia had the lowest fee caps in the nation for indigent representation.[11] In March of 2007, the legislature, under threat of a class-action lawsuit led by the Virginia Fair Trial Project, increased the fee cap for appointed attorneys and authorized judges to waive the caps, subject to a higher court's approval. However, the amounts are still meager and judges are unlikely to intervene. In 2007, the caps were as follows: $2,085 for clients charged with felonies that carry a sentence of twenty years to life, $600 for lesser felonies, and $240 for misdemeanors and juvenile felonies.[12] A lawyer who wants to prove his client's innocence could easily spend those amounts on the investigation alone. Prior to the fee hike, one Richmond attorney admitted that the fees were so low he reserved nearly all his time and labor for paying clients: Looking for witnesses, considering discovery, or using outside experts were impossible with so little funding. He tells court-appointed clients, who accounted for about 20 percent of his income, "to investigate the case themselves, look for witnesses and if they find them bring them to the office or to court."[13]

The third option for indigent defense is the contract system, in which one attorney or several contract with a county or circuit (group of counties) to represent a fixed or maximum number of cases for a fee, as with Robert Surrency in Georgia. Many counties prefer this method because it allows them to budget public defense for the entire year. It's also easier to administer than a panel program, which requires keeping track of many different lawyers and a complicated payroll.

There is much debate about which system is preferable, especially among county officials, who want to save money. Houston County in Georgia, for example, has employed full-time public defenders for decades. Three superior court judges, in a letter to their county commissioners, explained why the county shouldn't change to a less expensive contract system.

> Having a public defender system means having a group
> of lawyers who are obligated to handle the county's indi-
> gent defense work full time. . . . [P]rivate attorneys under
> a contract system . . . would simply be operating with a
> lot of competing interests which a public defender does
> not have. . . . It is naïve to think that any private attorney
> in this area would, or could, completely close their pri-
> vate practice and handle only the indigent contract cases.
> Expecting that attorney to neglect "paying" clients, or to
> make them a lower priority so that he or she may give
> first priority to indigent cases is equally implausible. . . .[14]

Another problem with the contract system is the implicit power it gives judges over lawyers. In a report by a commission convened by the Georgia State Bar to assess the state's indigent defense practice, the findings were that "[s]everal court-appointed and contract attorneys expressed concern that if they were viewed by some judges as zealous advocates—e.g., if they filed several motions in one case or demanded trials—they ran the risk of being removed from the *ad hoc* counsel appointment list or denied a future contract."[15]

So for the panel and contract systems, the problem is one of incentives. If these defense attorneys are going to be paid poorly and if, for what little effort they make, the consequence might be dismissal, they have little reason to work hard on an indigent client's behalf.

The better contract systems insist on quality controls, like limited caseloads and reviews of lawyers before awarding contracts. In San Mateo County, California, a contract attorney's fee will go up in a particular case that requires more work than is covered by a lump sum or flat fee. Also, lawyers have caps on numbers of cases based on a "weighted" study of how difficult they are; additional work is paid by the hour, with a higher rate for jury trials. For example, in a misdemeanor, a lawyer is paid a case fee of $190 plus $80 for a pretrial conference; if an attorney goes to trial he receives $125 per hour plus a per diem of $260 for preparation work. "By the time you add it up you're getting pretty much what retained lawyers get," said John S. Digiacinto, the county's chief defender. "We are able to keep our staff."

The worst contract systems, like Greene County's, feature a part-time lawyer who is hired based solely on how cheaply he is prepared to do the work. By 1985, even before Surrency took over the job, such "low bid" or "fixed fee" contracts had been condemned by the American Bar Association (ABA) House of Delegates, the policy-making body of the organization, for compromising the integrity of the justice system.[16] Unfortunately, local governments are often unaware of what the ABA says or consider its rulings advisory. In 2000, a report on the status of the country's contract defense practice by the Department of Justice's Bureau of Justice Statistics "noted a decline in the number of cases taken to jury trial, an increase in guilty pleas at first-appearance hearings, a decline in the filing of motions to suppress evidence, a decline in requests for expert assistance, and an increase in complaints received by the court from defendants"—virtually all of which described what was happening in Greene County.[17] Further, the county spent only $75.38 per case, the fifth lowest cost-per-case in the state.

Beginning in 1969, when adopting a plan for Georgia, the state legislature left it up to each county to determine which of the three systems to use. A decade later the legislature created the Georgia Indigent Defense Council (GIDC), which was based in Atlanta to oversee the different systems. The GIDC issued 11 percent of the total monies used to run 152 of 159 counties statewide. Of the 152 counties, only 20 decided on full-time public defenders, seventy-three employed a panel system, and 59 used contracts as their primary method.[18]

In exchange for the money, the GIDC asked counties to adhere to a detailed set of guidelines. These guidelines fixed standards for how to determine indigence and mandated appointment of counsel within seventy-two hours of arrest or detention, among other things. The GIDC also required that a tripartite committee of three volunteers be responsible for enforcing the standards. The tripartite committee, however, lacked a staff and often included nonlawyers or local businesspeople who had no interest in meaningfully supervising the indigent defense program, other than approving vouchers. The GIDC might admonish a county based on an anecdotal complaint, but a county could ignore a reprimand at will. A report in 2002 by the Spangenberg Group, a research and consulting firm in West Newton, Massachusetts, which specializes in improving justice programs, found that in recent years, the GIDC had not refused to provide funding for any county "in part because it fears political fallout or possible complaints from judges and other local people" to the state legislature. The GIDC "has no teeth," the report stated.[19]

■ ■ ■

Traditionally, the country's legal apparatus favors the office of the district attorney. The states instinctively supported the creation of prosecutors' offices because of a political will to solve crime and punish those who commit it. By contrast, the need to provide counsel for poor people accused of crimes is a burden that the U.S. Supreme Court thrust on the states in the sixties. Thus with a more popular mandate, prosecutors tend to receive more money and resources. For instance, Congress spent $26 million building the National Advocacy Center in Columbia, South Carolina, to train prosecutors. There is a similar school in Reno, Nevada, for training state and local judges. No federally funded counterpart exists for defense lawyers. Also, the Bureau of Justice Assistance gives federal aid to state and local law-enforcement agencies (e.g. $170,433,000 through the Edward Byrne Memorial Justice Assistance Grant Program in 2008) with no equivalent moneys for the defense.[20]

Nationwide, prosecutors also receive more funding because they have a higher caseload. District attorneys (sometimes called state's attorneys or county prosecutors or county attorneys) represent the state in virtually all prosecutions, so the state foots the entire bill. But when it comes to defendants, the state pays only when they are poor and only for minimum defense. In California, for example, reports show discrepant funding between prosecutors and public defenders—for every $100 the prosecution receives, indigent defense receives an average of $60.90, which is on the high end of what most states provide.[21] A report by the Spangenberg Group in 2002 estimated that states and counties nationwide spent $3.3 billion on indigent defense;[22] whereas in 2001, the ABA reported that $5 billion was spent in prosecuting criminal cases in state and local jurisdictions—a $1.7 billion gap.[23] (Both of these statistics are dated and experts say the discrepancy is probably greater, but an absence of nationwide statistics exists.)

With such a difference in resources, even the "best" public defender offices, which have full-time professional lawyers, cannot protect attorneys from problems like high caseloads. Instead, the overload has prompted new oversight measures in several states. Broward County, Florida, for instance, with a $15 million budget, has a prestigious public defender's office, but in 2005 the head of the office announced, to the dismay of some judges, that attorneys could not plead defendants guilty at arraignment without first having some "meaningful contact" with them. "We will make every effort to meet with clients prior to any court hearings," a memo to judges stated from public defender Howard Finkelstein, according to the *Broward Daily Business Review*. "However, if such a meeting has not taken place, we are legally and ethically constrained from recommending any plea to a client."[24] What should be a baseline standard has become so hard to reach that special requirements are needed to enforce it.

If the GIDC was failing to notice the problems in Greene County, others were not. Stephen B. Bright, the president and senior counsel of the Southern Center for Human Rights in Atlanta, had decided in the mid-1990s that Georgia's indigent defense system was so bad that his organization was going to keep challenging it until it was brought into line with the ideals of American justice. Bright, in his fifties, has made a career of championing unpopular causes. He became the director of the struggling Southern Center in 1982 and has often worked without pay in defense of people facing the death penalty and on litigation to improve prison and jail conditions throughout the South. The organization has eleven attorneys, an equal number of investigators, and a stream of student interns and volunteers.

The center is fueled by a profound sense of purpose and by Bright's inspiration. One staffer wondered when Bright ate, and then, one night at around three a.m., saw him downing an energy drink at his computer. For years, Bright had set his sights on creating a state-wide public defender system in Georgia with full-time lawyers. He toured clubs and community halls to arouse the public's interest, making speeches wherever possible. He told it like it is: People charged with crimes, no matter how small, whether they are guilty or not, are treated "like hamburgers in a fast-food restaurant." He discussed the defense attorney's need for independence from the prosecutor and judiciary "so that judges would not use lawyers for the poor as clerks to process their cases." He wanted to get rid of the hodgepodge system that contracted out defense for the poor and ended up with the likes of Surrency or worse. He sought more resources from the state and counties to train both new lawyers and existing public defenders.

Until the state made proper changes, Bright planned to expose and root out bad defense systems, one by one, by observing various courts in action and filing a series of lawsuits claiming violations of the state and federal Constitutions. I had learned about Greene County's problems from a series of phone calls with advocates in Atlanta, and when I told Bright it was one of the courts I was considering looking at, he said he had never been. I asked him to join me so I could get his perspective on how this court matched up to others he had seen. Even though he had appeared on *Nightline*, on the radio, and in various newspaper articles, legal professionals knew him by name but not always by face. In Greene County, Bright slipped into Judge Hulane George's courtroom unnoticed. He sat with a yellow legal pad in his lap, at the end of the first row, near a few other lawyers who had cases that day.

Bright believes that change begins on the ground, in the courtroom, and he doesn't hesitate to speak his mind, much to the annoyance of judges, who feel like he lectures them when it should be the other way around. As the day went on, the proceedings in Greene County became harder to hear. The less people could understand, the more frustrated, bored, and restless the audience became. Spectators shifted loudly in their seats. They whispered. I sat a few people away from Bright, attempting to take notes. The people couldn't hear a thing, and Bright sensed their frustration.

He leaned over and whispered, "Why don't you go and ask the judge to speak up?" I laughed. I considered myself an observer and wanted to be as inconspicuous as possible. I was also embarrassed to make a ruckus. This was court, after all.

I went back to straining to follow.

Suddenly Bright was on his feet. "Your Honor," he said in a deep, loud voice. "This is a public hearing and there are people here who want to listen to what is going on. So if you wouldn't mind speaking up that would be much appreciated."

Judge George looked like she had been slapped. Bright didn't seem like a commanding man, more like the lanky Kentucky farm boy he had been growing up. He had a wholesome face and full red hair parted to the side. His clothes didn't match his pedigree—he teaches at Harvard and Yale law schools in his free time but prides himself on buying eighty-dollar suits on the road. A deadening, somber silence followed his interruption.

"Excuse me, could you please come before me? I would like to talk to you," Judge George said.

"No, ma'am, that's fine. I don't need to appear before you. I will stay right here. I am just an observer. And I would just appreciate it if you would speak up. Thank you, ma'am."

Bright sat down, refusing to budge.

"Sir, I order you to come stand before me," Judge George said.

Bright climbed his way over the packed row. With gravitational force, whipping himself around to play to the audience, he took control of the courtroom.

"Your Honor, my name is Steve Bright and I am a lawyer visiting court today from Atlanta. I am here to listen to this public hearing. People have a right to hear what is going on. We're all here, missing work, having left our children in the care of others. And we want to hear what is going on in court today. You are denying us our right to listen to a public hearing. So if you wouldn't mind, please speak up."

The exhausted, twitchy crowd was now focused. Someone started to clap, and soon the entire courtroom was applauding with cries of "Amen" and "That's right," and "We can't hear anything," and "Thank you, sir."

"I have this viral junk in my throat," Judge George said. She did seem tired. Alarmed, too.

For the rest of the day the judge used a microphone and would tap it regularly asking, "Can everyone hear? I just want to make sure. There seems to be a lot of interest here today."

In a court where people had grown accustomed to being ignored, merely asking the judge to speak louder was blasphemously glorious. It shook things up so that someone in the audience shouted out, "We can't hear you," at Surrency, who was now also taking the heat. Surrency, tensely flipping through his notes, had to respond to the audience, most of whom were his clients. "Can you hear me now?" he said, facing the crowd.

"No!" people shouted.

Judge George clapped her hands together. She used to teach school, she told the crowd, and couldn't stand noise.

Bright had become a celebrity. In the breaks, people patted him on the shoulder and shook his hand in gratitude.

"I got something to tell you," said a man in denim overalls, and then he launched into the complexities of his case.

"Come talk to me next," said a woman hitting Bright on the arm.

■ ■ ■

Bright was not the only one trying to accomplish reform on the ground. There were courageous whistle-blowers in Greene County, but unlike Bright, they could not simply return to Atlanta unscathed; they had to stay put, where they didn't fare so well.

Cathy Crawford, who was in her forties, had started working for Surrency right after obtaining a degree in paralegal studies. She found his papers were "just thrown in a box. I remember looking at this system, or lack thereof, and wondering: Is this man a complete idiot or is he just so brilliant that he can get away with this and still do his job?"

Yet she liked Surrency. He had an easygoing manner. When they carpooled to court they sang, "We're off to see the wizard." She would laugh.

In court, when the line to see Surrency sometimes snaked down the hallway stairs, he would announce that clients could conference with either him or Crawford, as if they were both lawyers. Crawford began to listen to their stories. She advertised office hours when people could come talk about their cases. "I had a tremendous turnout three days a week," Crawford said. "I would pull reports and look at them. We had people sitting in the hallways to see me." When she tried to talk to Surrency about the cases, however, he often didn't return her calls. She didn't see him in person because she didn't work out of his office. "You could never find him," she said.

Crawford also noticed that Surrency rarely filed motions to ask the court for certain pre-trial hearings. These usually involve requesting that evidence, a statement, or identification be excluded. Judges don't grant them very often, but that's not the point. Motion practice is a way of discovering information about the prosecutor's case. For example, a police officer might testify at arraignment and then the defense is entitled to his reports and has the chance to cross-examine the officer about his practices. "Any investigative leads unearthed in this manner are most useful if they come sufficiently early so that the defense has ample time to follow them up thoroughly," reads a seminal treatise on how to defend a criminal case.[25]

Sometimes, when other lawyers' motions were being heard, Surrency would ask Crawford to come to court and sit in with him because the county commissioners might come by. "I said to him," Crawford recounted, "You're willing to sit there for a whole day just so someone will think you're working?" The answer was, apparently, yes. Crawford advised him to start filing some motions of his own and turned to the codebooks. She drafted up some documents based on sample forms she found and had Surrency sign them. Then she filed them with the court.

Crawford's next "assignment" was to begin visiting with the prosecutor alone. "Don't bother calling Surrency," she'd tell Mitcham, explaining, presumably on Surrency's behalf, that he would rather see ten than fifteen years on probation, or, for example, that he was considering a motion to suppress evidence.

Mitcham, who sat on the board of governors for the state bar, the governing body that recommends changes to ethical standards to the state supreme court, claimed that he "didn't feel comfortable negotiating with Cathy." The Georgia Code of Professional Responsibility prohibits a lawyer from assisting a non-lawyer in the unauthorized practice of law.[26] An advisory opinion by the state disciplinary board explains, "competent professional judgment is the product of a trained familiarity with law and legal processes, a disciplined, analytical approach to legal problems, and a firm ethical commitment." Among those duties that the board specified should not be delegated to paralegals are "negotiation with opposing parties or their counsel on substantive issues in expected or pending litigation."[27]

Yet Mitcham negotiated with Crawford anyway, risking sanction or disbarment. "She was very zealous on behalf of her clients," he said.

Mitcham claims Crawford was simply a messenger in a negotiation with Surrency, but it is unclear how often Surrency was involved. After some back-and-forth, a plea deal would emerge and Mitcham would write it down. Then, according to Crawford, she would put the terms in a folder, which Surrency would open in court. Surrency would stand in court with Crawford while she related the facts in a defendant's case.

"I was actually asking her to come close to the line in order to handle caseloads," Surrency said of an ethical boundary he knew existed. "There were only so many hours in a day. . . . I was working sixty hours a week. A lot of it was homework—I was talking to the families."

Surrency believed he was overworked. But it was hard to establish whether he actually had the time to spend on cases or not, whether he was overloaded, lazy, or something else. Mitcham felt that Surrency's competence was not an issue. "He is a bright young fellow and operates well on his feet, but his discipline and preparation may have been lacking." And in truth, Surrency's performance kept with the environment in which he worked, where just getting by, making do, pushing cases through was considered acceptable. Mitcham recalled that at one point Surrency didn't even bring files with him—relying on his memory for loads of cases, a hard if not impossible task for anyone, given the enormous number of dates and legal charges. Yet he was allowed to get away with it.

Cathy Crawford complained about Surrency's disservice to his clients to Marie Boswell, clerk of the court. Boswell had watched Surrency for hundreds of hours, and concluded that too many people were being railroaded into pleading guilty. "I can't get in touch with him! I can't get in touch with him!" she said, imitating the calls she received from his clients.

Boswell wrote to Michael Shapiro, then the executive director of the GIDC, and went to a county commission session as well as to the tripartite committee, which was supposed to ensure the competence of indigent defense attorneys. Boswell expressed her concern that Surrency was not meeting with his clients before court and rarely visited the jail. She said that judges expected little unless Cathy Crawford was in court.[28] According to a letter from Shapiro to Boswell, the tripartite committee agreed to "re-energize the current defender" or hire someone to replace him to improve services.[29] Despite this, no action was taken.

Walter "Bud" Sanders, vice-chair of the Greene County Board of Commissioners, also served on the tripartite committee. Sanders didn't recall a need to overhaul the office. "The only complaints I used to hear about were from the attorneys who said that the inmates were having trouble getting in touch with [Surrency]," he said, which he felt the committee had addressed by setting up a local phone at the jail. Sanders didn't hear of "real problems . . . Judges never complained. Many judges never complained," he said.

Crawford confirmed that no one complained. The only reason she was allowed to do the lawyer's work that she did is because "the system allowed it—the judge, the DA, the probation officer, nobody cared." So she took her complaints elsewhere, to the local indigent defense committee—"and they listened to me rant." Not that it made a difference, she noted. Crawford left her job soon after she complained; though the circumstances of her departure are unclear, there appear to have been financial issues. "It got to the point where I had to beg for my check," she said.

Boswell quit, too. She wanted no part of what was happening in Greene County's courts. "The commission thinks that if you don't talk about it, it is going to go away. But this is not going to go away. It's only going to get worse."

What was happening was routine injustice. Before she took a new job as a clerk for a judge, Boswell predicted that Greene County would "get hit with a lawsuit that is going to rock the world."

■ ■ ■

To its credit, the State Bar of Georgia did appear to recognize something of the problem that existed in Greene County and elsewhere. In 1988, the bar had established an Indigent Defense Committee, a group of volunteer attorneys who were supposed to coordinate lawyers and other agencies to help provide better representation and equal justice. Unfortunately, the committee had not done anything for years. But then in 1998, the president of the bar asked C. Wilson DuBose to take over.[30] DuBose worked in the picturesque town of Madison, Georgia, about a half hour from Greensboro, and didn't seem like the sort of man to champion the rights of the poor. He had almost no experience with criminal law. He did corporate work and civil litigation and had a conciliatory nature. However, DuBose wanted to be more involved with the state bar and agreed to become chair of the committee with no real idea of what he was getting himself into.

Over the next year, his committee interviewed various legal professionals and realized that the system was not what it should be. DuBose was extremely moved by what he heard. He discovered that people were being treated in a way that violated "common decency," and which put the integrity of the state bar at stake. Moreover, as he saw it, the current system of providing lawyers for the poor surely violated the U.S. Constitution. "I am a Republican and Republicans care about the Constitution," he said. "The Constitution clearly says you have a right [to a lawyer] which was becoming meaningless if you can't afford it."

In the fall of 1999, the committee passed a resolution to ask the state governor and the chief justice of the Georgia Supreme Court to appoint a commission to investigate Georgia's indigent defense and make recommendations for its improvement. "We believed that people of good will would listen and take action and respond," DuBose said. However, the Democratic governor at the time, Roy E. Barnes, didn't do anything with the resolution for twelve months. Ultimately, he deferred to then Georgia Supreme Court Chief Justice Robert Benham who by December 2000 had taken up the issue and decided to appoint his own commission.[31]

Meanwhile, the members of the state bar's committee had drafted what they hoped would be a simple resolution of twelve principles for the bar to endorse. Among the proposals were that the state rather than the individual counties absorb all indigent defense costs; that a single statewide body be established to administer a public defender system; that the contract system be abolished; that resources be meted out equally between prosecutors and defenders; and that defenders be independent from local governing and judicial authorities.[32]

The principles went through various upper-level committees and took two years to be endorsed, a "dreadfully laborious process," said Emmet Bondurant, a civil attorney who was also on the committee. Bondurant, named one of the top ten lawyers in the U.S. by the *National Law Journal* in 2001, had been working for over forty years to improve indigent defense systems in Georgia, but was still surprised by how much resistance the committee encountered. He blamed a group of "recalcitrant judges" who had input as members of the bar and felt unjustly accused of being more interested in moving cases along than in caring about poor people accused of crime. The general feeling among judges was, "we are doing things just fine down here and don't need Atlanta," Bondurant said.

Superior Court Judge Lawton E. Stephens of the Western Judicial Circuit in Athens, Georgia, wrote a letter summing up the judges' concerns. He said that more state funding would improve indigent defense but that eliminating judges from appointing defenders and deciding their compensation would not. The bar commitee proposals, Stephens wrote, "removes the judge from the process to the detriment of the indigent defendant and counsel."[33] Stephens wanted control of assigning which defender got which case, since he knew better than most which attorneys were competent to handle serious charges, like murder, for example; he feared that attorneys would be randomly assigned. He took issue with the insinuation that judges did not care about competent attorneys. "That was a myth," he said.

While the bar commitee did its work, Steve Bright of the Southern Center was pursuing reforms of his own. For him, being aggressive was the only way to amend the system, and it often seemed like public-interest litigation—e.g., the federal lawsuits of the 1950s, '60s and '70s that forced state schools to integrate—was the only way to make it happen. At a symposium on indigent defense in 2002, just as the state was considering essential reform, Governor Barnes noted in videotaped remarks that Georgia's indigent defense problems would not be solved overnight and called on conference participants to stay in the reform movement "for the long run."[34] Bright responded that while the governor took his time, new litigation would be "coming to a courthouse near you."[35] In fact, litigation was nothing new. The Southern Center had, since 1996, filed a number of lawsuits alleging that the state had defaulted on its responsibility to provide effective assistance of counsel to the poor.

Legal challenges, however, had to be precise and strategic to work. A 1986 federal lawsuit *Luckey v. Harris*, in which Bright was not involved, had tried to make changes too sweepingly. The class-action suit, which failed, claimed that Georgia's entire indigent defense system was "inherently incapable of providing constitutionally adequate services," and asked the federal court to implement standards and then monitor them throughout the state. But it was unlikely that any federal judge would find proof that all of Georgia's 159 counties had the same problem. Plus, the idea that federal courts would take over state courts entirely was unprecedented and improbable. *Luckey* was dismissed six years later.[36]

Bright's approach was to deal with each county's individual problems. He had put together a team of investigators, mostly recent college and law-school graduates who could build a civil class-action lawsuit against a specific county and the state. His employees sat in courts and watched, visited jails to interview defendants, and requested files from the clerks' offices. They were trying to see if a pattern existed—judges not assigning lawyers or defense attorneys not talking to their clients before court, or anything else that violated the law. It was tiresome work. The investigators thumbed through thousands of files to find individuals who had received excessive jail time, and they read reams of trial transcripts to uncover revealing moments. Bright often advised his team to go to court and "count the Constitutional violations," in part because he found that law school professors didn't inspire this kind of work. "They prefer to write about legal theory from the safety of their offices," he said, adding that, "unfortunately, as a general matter, no one wants to go into the courts and see what is happening." In fact, what people find so disturbing about Bright's lawsuits is that they name names of individual judges, prosecutors, and defense attorneys and specify what they do on a daily basis, thus taking people deep inside the actual courtrooms.

Some places were an easy mark, like Sumter County, Georgia, where former president Jimmy Carter had a home. There, a judge would immediately ask defendants to sign a form waiving their right to a lawyer without having informed them of that right or of the dangers and disadvantages of proceeding without representation. The judges "give the impression that . . . if you don't sign the form and return it to the clerk, your case won't be called," Bright explained. His suit against the county, filed in federal court, alleged systemic denial of constitutional rights and was settled in 1998 with the county's consent to implement improvements, including the distribution of a new form titled, "Constitutional and Legal Rights of People Accused of Crimes in the State Court of Sumter."

The Southern Center had similar success in Coweta County in a class-action suit it filed in state court. There, the center charged that over a two-and-a-half-year period, more than half of the poor people found guilty in felony cases had pleaded to crimes without a lawyer present. The complaint named two part-time defense attorneys who let their clients languish in jail without a visit for months, as well as a judge who had a habit of encouraging uncounseled defendants to speak to the prosecutor and then plead guilty without a lawyer. The suit was settled in 2003 after the county set up a public defender's office with three full-time attorneys.[37]

In Fulton County, Bright convinced a federal judge that poor representation had caused overcrowding in the jails, which had overwhelmed their health-care services. When Bright made clear that many inmates had spent more time in jail on misdemeanor charges than if they'd been convicted, a judge ordered the prisoners released. "Streaming out of the jail, the inmates clutched brown paper bags containing their few personal belongings, and the $1.75 bus tokens that jail officials had given them to get home," the *New York Times* reported.[38]

In Spring 2003, I caught up with Bright's team in Crisp County in the Cordele Circuit in south Georgia, where the Southern Center was researching a lawsuit. As the day was getting underway, loads of people were rustling nervously and crowding into court. Inside the courtroom, the prosecutor, Denise Fachini, a former president of the Georgia District Attorneys Association, stood on a chair and proclaimed that she was going to read out a list of names, and that defendants needed to stand up and announce whether they wanted to apply for a public defender—a tired-looking defense lawyer sitting at a table with his back to the crowd—or talk to someone from the prosecutor's office first. "When you stand up we want to know what your announcement is," she said smiling—as if it were equally acceptable for a defendant to talk to the prosecutor without a lawyer as with his or her own attorney. When asked why she did this, Fachini explained that "the last thing [she wants] is for someone to be treated unfairly" and that it was "not a constitutional violation for them to talk" to her so long as defendants understood that they had a right to talk to a lawyer. "People often know that they are guilty and want to hear what the offer is" from the source itself, she said, adding that "a lot of people know" her and her credible reputation. Also, at every juncture before someone pleaded guilty she would ask, "Are you sure this is what you are going to do?" Whether it was a credit to her or a rebuke to the public defender, almost half of the people picked the peppy, wide-eyed Fachini over the uninviting defense attorney. Many ended up pleading guilty without a lawyer.

One milky-skinned woman with small round glasses and jet black–dyed hair was sitting behind me, repeating to herself, "I'm just going to lose it, I am just going to lose it." This woman, twenty, had tried to contact her lawyer twice but had been told to talk to him in court. She wanted to meet with Fachini alone. "I did it," she said, as if her fate was sealed. "I am going to plead guilty."

She was charged with giving false statements to the police. Her husband, she said, a manic-depressive with a temper, had broken her baby's leg. On the state report she had lied and said that her husband had had nothing to do with it. "My husband threatened me that if I didn't write that, he would beat me."

At issue was her ability to get her baby back from the state. Marion Chartoff, a lawyer with the Southern Center, was observing court and sitting in my row. She leaned back to talk to this woman. Just because she lied on the report didn't mean that she was guilty of the crime. She could have a defense.

"What's a defense?" she asked.

"You acted under duress," Chartoff explained. "You could have been forced to do something."

"Well, that's me, that is me," the woman said. "I thought he was going to beat me up if I didn't sign the form like he said."

The woman stopped talking. Then she tapped Chartoff on the shoulder. "I need to plead not guilty right?"

"Yes, plead not guilty," Chartoff said. "You have a defense."

In Crisp County, the Southern Center found people without lawyers languishing in jail. Investigator Atteeyah Hollie came across Samuel Moore, who had been in jail for thirteen months on a loitering charge. He had never seen his court-appointed lawyer. He soon found out that he was being held in jail because there was an arrest warrant for him for selling drugs on a different occasion. The warrant was a year old.[39]

When Hollie was doing research she saw that Moore's drug charges had actually been dismissed four months earlier, but no one had told the people at the jail or him. When I spoke to Moore he produced letters he had written while in jail to five different organizations as well as to a lawyer appointed by the court, begging for help. But no one had answered him. "You feel like a castaway," he said. "Nobody knows you exist."

After the Southern Center looked into Moore's case, the jail let him out immediately. As Moore emerged into the bright sunshine in the same shoes he had worn more than a year earlier, he felt distrustful. "I am constantly looking back to see if they are going to lock me up again," he said as he walked the eight miles back to the town. His family, with whom he now lives, would never have intervened. "They think if they say the wrong things they are going to be locked up."

People like Moore made perfect examples for Bright. He would tell reporters about them, use them in his speeches, and feature them in his lawsuits.

■ ■ ■

Bright's efforts to ensure that every defendant be provided a lawyer should have been redundant. The U.S. Supreme Court has ruled that every person in state court charged with a crime who is subject to imprisonment has a right to a lawyer. Even if the person is put on probation and has his or her jail time suspended, this individual has a right to a lawyer; he cannot go to jail, otherwise.

The court based its rulings on the Sixth Amendment, which says: "In all criminal prosecutions, the accused shall enjoy the right . . . to have Assistance of Counsel for his defense."[40] It may seem obvious today that this amendment means everyone, rich or poor. After all, the adversarial system is based on a concept of symmetry: two somewhat equal sides going head to head to produce the truth. If one side can't properly challenge the accusations because of poverty, something has to be done to rectify the imbalance. The history behind the amendment, however, explains why the states enforce it so unsuccessfully.

To begin with, the colonial courts of eighteenth-century America did not permit the accused even the presence of a lawyer. Like the English courts, they permitted counsel for "petty offenses" but not for important cases like felonies and treason.[41] As Yale Law School professor John H. Langbein writes, the rationalization for having no lawyers in the big cases was that "if falsely charged, the accused would clear himself through the 'Simplicity and Innocence' of his responses, whereas the responses of guilty defendants would 'help to disclose the Truth, which probably would not so well be discovered from the artificial Defense of others speaking for them.' "[42] In general, though, the British system was not palatable to the American settlers; judges appointed by the Crown oversaw venomous prosecutions that resulted in the conviction and execution of innocent people,[43] and so, inevitably, the Americans sought to protect themselves against this kind of injustice.[44]

By 1791 when the framers adopted the Bill of Rights (containing the first ten amendments of the Constitution), virtually all of the colonies had written into their own state constitutions that defendants could use lawyers.[45] In his book *The Bill of Rights*, Akhil Reed Amar notes that the new Americans wanted "notions of basic fairness and symmetry" to exist in a criminal court. "If the prosecuting government could have a lawyer, why not the defendant?"[46] The Sixth Amendment, which provided a right to counsel in federal court, merely kept the federal government in step with what the states had already sanctioned.

Still, the Sixth Amendment was originally thought to mean that the defendant couldn't be *barred* from having a lawyer in federal court, where a minority of criminal cases were tried in revolutionary times. The framers could not have imagined that criminal procedure would become so complicated that a defendant would need a lawyer just to understand what was happening, much less that the U.S. Supreme Court would impose a burden on the states to provide lawyers. States had the authority, as they still do, to decide the rights of men and women put on trial; so long as the treatment was fair and decent, the U.S. Supreme Court or the federal government wouldn't intrude. The lack of federal involvement in state matters began to change after the Civil War with the ratification of the Fourteenth Amendment in 1868 to protect the newly freed slaves in the South from oppression by local governments. The amendment, which declared that no state would deny any person due process and equal protection of the laws, would have an enormous impact in the century to come; but few gains occurred immediately in terms of the rights of poor people accused of crime.

The status quo prevailed until 1931 when the much-publicized trial of the so-called Scottsboro Boys became a symbol of American racism and Southern injustice. Nine young black men, ages thirteen to twenty, were charged with raping two white women on a train traveling through Alabama. At the time, local citizens were incensed and threatening a lynch mob. All nine were tried in Scottsboro, the county seat. When the judge inquired whether the parties were ready for trial, the prosecutor answered yes, but no one answered for the defense. Originally, each of the members of the Scottsboro bar had been appointed as defense counsel, but each had found a reason to get out of it—except for one lawyer, Milo Moody, described as a "doddering, extremely unreliable, senile individual who is losing whatever ability he once had,"[47] and Stephen R. Roddy, from Chattanooga, Tennessee, who was unsure if he had agreed to take on the case or not. Roddy had not been employed by the boys but had come to court as an observer at the request of a black doctor, P. A. Stephens, who presided over a Tennessee church. Roddy, apparently drunk, would not clarify whether he had agreed to represent the defendants.[48] "If I was paid and employed it would be a different thing," he told the judge, "but I have not prepared this case for trial . . ," He also said he wasn't familiar with Alabama law. If he had to take the case alone, "the boys would be better off if I step entirely out of the case," he told the court.[49]

Nevertheless, the nine black youths went on trial with these two attorneys who had spent barely half an hour talking to them, had not investigated the crime or prepared a defense, and who did not seek a continuance to do so or file a motion for a change of venue despite the enormous pre-trial publicity. The trials began immediately in three separate groups; each trial took one day. Three all-white juries found eight of the nine defendants guilty and imposed the death penalty (the exception was a mistrial for the thirteen-year-old, Roy Wright).[50]

The case was appealed to the U.S. Supreme Court, which reversed the lower court's decision on grounds that the lawyers did not have a chance to work on their clients' behalf. The majority opinion in *Powell v. Alabama* said that, "during perhaps the most critical period of the proceedings against these defendants, that is to say, from the time of their arraignment until the beginning of their trial, when consultation, thorough-going investigation and preparation were vitally important, the defendants did not have the aid of counsel in any real sense, although they were as much entitled to such aid during that period as at the trial itself."[51] The court referred to the Fourteenth Amendment's due process clause, citing a defendant's right to "the guiding hand of counsel at every step in the proceedings" and the "fundamental nature of that right." However, the court limited the right to "a capital case" and to a situation where the defendant is indigent and "incapable adequately of making his own defense because of ignorance, feeble-mindedness, illiteracy, or the like."[52] (After the decision, the case became a cause célèbre for the Communist Party and many appeals and re-trials followed. Eventually, one of the women later admitted that she had invented the story of the rape.[53])

Powell was groundbreaking. It recognized a right to counsel for the poor and that the representation had to be meaningful. Equally important was the court's decision to apply the Fourteenth Amendment's due process clause to the states on an issue of fundamental fairness: the trial court's failure to make an effective appointment of counsel. As Justice Pierce Butler wrote in dissent, it was "a field hitherto occupied exclusively by the several States," adding that "Nothing before the Court calls for a consideration of the point. It was not suggested below [by the lower court judges] and petitioners do not ask for its decision here."[54] So why did the Supreme Court choose to intervene when it had not been called upon even to consider the issue of effective counsel under the Fourteenth Amendment?

Perhaps the justices read the papers and wanted to step in to correct this notorious case.[55] Or maybe they felt a need to acknowledge the new unchecked power of the prosecutor. In the nineteenth century, a major power shift in courts across the country favored full-time prosecutors who were marshaled in to deal with increasing levels of crime presented by industrialization and migration to cities.[56] Before this, the public prosecutor had been a minor actor in the criminal process, more of an adjunct to the judge, presenting cases to grand juries or trial juries, or simply expediting prosecution on behalf of victims or their families, who at times hired private lawyers to act as prosecutors.[57] As a bureaucracy of police arose to manage an increasing number of arrests, prosecutors began, somewhat by necessity, to take on the role of deciding which cases made it to court.[58] By the early twentieth century, writers were expressing outrage at the steep increase in prosecutorial power: prosecutors were dismissing cases, pleading a high portion of them guilty, and holding fewer jury trials.[59]

No matter what the cause, the court found the Scottsboro case so disturbing that it decided to federalize the issue of representation for indigent defendants. But it did so with half-measures, leaving the states to decide whether to appoint counsel except when the defendant was poor, uneducated to the point of illiteracy, and charged with a capital case. Only under these circumstances was denial of counsel considered a violation of due process. The states still had the right, within this limit, to decide the rest.

In the years that followed, the U.S. Supreme Court struggled to find the perimeters of the right to counsel within the context of a fair trial. First, the Supreme Court expanded the right, finding that a lawyer must be provided when the defendant could not afford one, regardless of his education or the nature of the crime—but still only in criminal cases in federal court. In *Johnson v. Zerbst*, the court quoted *Powell* to recognize that "without the assistance of counsel even the intelligent layman usually lacks both the skill and knowledge adequately to prepare his defense, even though he has a perfect one."[60] The right applied unless an accused affirmatively waived it.[61] But four years later, the court, while still recognizing the validity of *Johnson v. Zerbst*, explicitly refused to apply the full right to counsel to the states. In *Betts v. Brady*, it ruled that due process required the appointment of a lawyer in state court only when the issues were difficult and the defendant inexperienced—basically broadening the due process protection of *Powell* to other complex criminal cases where the accused could not defend himself, case-by-case, but still maintaining a distinction between what was mandated in federal and state court.[62] As a result, under *Zerbst*, a defendant who was poor could always get a lawyer in federal court; but in state courts, under *Betts*, a defendant could only get one if the trial would be "fundamentally unfair" otherwise (depending on the circumstances) and violated due process.

All that was needed, then, to apply the rule across the United States, was a Supreme Court majority that regarded the right to counsel as fundamental under any circumstance. Why did the court take such incremental steps toward establishing this right? In general, our Constitution does not frame rights in affirmative terms. It says what the government cannot do—e.g., it cannot prohibit publication of offensive statements, or prevent a religious group from practicing its faith.[63] The idea of forcing the states to give the indigent lawyers was not only unprecedented but unique in terms of the Constitution's reach.

In 1953, President Dwight D. Eisenhower appointed Earl Warren as the chief justice of the U.S. Supreme Court. Warren, the former governor of California, had spent many years as a prosecutor in Alameda County, where he had a reputation for fair-mindedness. "It was said that the DA's office in Alameda County in the years Earl Warren ran it never extracted an involuntary confession from a defendant," writes historian Richard Kluger in the classic work *Simple Justice*. "Anyone who wanted to see his lawyer before submitting to police interrogation was permitted to do so. No conviction ever won by Warren's office was thrown out on appeal by a higher court."[64] Warren and several of his associate justices, such as Hugo Black and William J. Brennan, Jr., were the driving forces in developing a body of case law that has been called a mini code of criminal procedure to prevent coerced confessions, warrantless wiretapping, and interrogation conducted in the absence of a lawyer.[65]

In 1956 in *Griffin v. Illinois*, the Supreme Court tackled the issue of poverty and inequality in the state courts. Judson Griffin, an indigent man, argued he was denied his right to appeal his conviction of armed robbery because he couldn't afford a trial transcript. The court found Griffin had been denied his right to equal protection under the Fourteenth Amendment. In a famous opinion, Justice Hugo Black wrote: "There can be no equal justice where the kind of trial a man gets depends on the amount of money he has."[66] In dissent, Justice John Harlan compared the right to counsel to a college education, commenting that it was tantamount to demanding that states provide fee waivers to students who couldn't afford a state university. "[I] think it is beyond the province of this Court to tell Illinois that it must provide such procedures," he wrote in conclusion.[67] Nevertheless, the ruling furthered protection for poor people accused of crimes.

In 1962, the Court received a letter in scrawled pencil from a prisoner named Clarence Earl Gideon who claimed he had been tried without a lawyer in Florida for breaking and entering and petty larceny. He had seemed fairly intelligent in conducting his own defense, going so far as to call a character witness and attack the credibility of the main witness against him. Still, he had been found guilty and sentenced to five years in prison.[68]

Gideon filed his hand-written petition for habeas corpus to the U.S. Supreme Court, arguing that he had a right to counsel under the Sixth Amendment. The court appointed Abe Fortas, then a partner at Arnold, Fortas & Porter and a distinguished member of the bar, to represent him. (Fortas later became a U.S. Supreme Court justice and his name was dropped from the firm, which became Arnold & Porter.) Fortas argued that the right to counsel was indispensable for a fair hearing. In 1963, the Court found in *Gideon v. Wainwright* that what had been an "obvious truth" for federal criminal trials now applied to the states as well: "Reason and reflection require that in our adversary system of criminal justice, any person hauled into court, who is too poor to hire a lawyer, cannot be assured a fair trial unless counsel is provided for him."[69] *Gideon* overruled *Betts v. Brady* and put the burden on the states to provide the indigent with lawyers in felony cases.

Ultimately, Gideon was retried with a lawyer at his side and acquitted. But the battle to enforce the Court's ruling continues to this day, in part because *Gideon* did not prescribe standards for what passed for an effective lawyer, and many states do not want to pay for lawyers to defend the poor—a resistance that has given way to token representation.

In the decades which followed *Gideon*, the U.S. Supreme Court went to great lengths to limit the right to counsel.[70] *Strickland v. Washington* set a very low bar for what constituted effective counsel in 1984. The *Strickland* court held that "[n]o particular set of detailed rules for counsel's conduct can satisfactorily take account of the variety of circumstances faced by defense counsel or the range of legitimate decisions regarding how best to represent a criminal defendant."[71] The Court said only that a lawyer's representation must meet an "objective standard of reasonableness."[72] However, it granted counsel tremendous leeway by presuming a lawyer is competent unless a defendant can prove there was "a reasonable probability that, but for counsel's unprofessional errors, the result of the proceeding would have been different." The Court defined "reasonable probability" as "a probability sufficient to undermine confidence in the outcome."[73] Justice Thurgood Marshall dissented. He found the standard adopted by the Court so malleable as to be meaningless. He wrote, "To tell lawyers and the lower courts that counsel for a criminal defendant must behave 'reasonably' and must act like a reasonably competent attorney, is to tell them almost nothing."[74]

The benchmark for what constitutes adequate assistance is so low that in 2001 in the infamous Calvin Burdine trial, the Fifth Circuit Court of Appeals openly debated whether to affirm a death-penalty decision where the lawyer, Joe Frank Cannon, had slept through significant parts of his client's case (a three-judge panel of the Fifth Circuit had initially upheld the conviction and death sentence, 2–1). Nine judges of the Fifth Circuit Court agreed to overturn the death penalty decision and grant Burdine a new trial, but not without five dissenters, two of whom took issue with how much of the trial it was permissible to sleep through and still be adversarial: "[O]f utmost importance . . . there is no state-finding that Cannon was 'repeatedly unconscious' during 'substantial' portions of the trial." The dissenters said information was missing about:

> When Cannon "dozed" as opposed to "slept"; How long he slept, individually and collectively; How many times he slept; How deeply he slept; What happened while he slept, including which witness(es) was (were) testifying or other evidence was being presented; and When the sleeping occurred—which day(s), or whether during the morning or afternoon.[75]

To this day it remains debatable whether a lawyer can sleep during his client's death-penalty trial.[76] So we can only imagine what is tolerated in ordinary cases that fail to attract scrutiny from the public or appellate courts.

According to an ABA report published in 2004 apropos *Gideon*'s fortieth anniversary, "Indigent defense in the United States remains in a state of crisis, resulting in a system that lacks fundamental fairness and places poor persons at constant risk of wrongful conviction."[77] And while this is true at the state level, the federal system is much improved, beginning with the Criminal Justice Act of 1964 that compensated counsel at an hourly rate on a case-by-case basis; several years later Congress authorized the federal courts to establish federal defender organizations (FDOs), which today represent approximately 64 percent of the federal indigent cases and have a very good reputation. The organizations have resources similar to those of prosecutors— reasonable salaries for its staff, funds for expert services, investigators and paralegals—and they also provide regular training and supervision to full-time staff so that they develop the expertise that results from practicing federal criminal law full-time.

If it is true that the federal system is considerably better than what is in place state by state, it is still difficult actually to assess whether an indigent defense system is effective because there is no single barometer of success. The *ABA Standards for Criminal Justice* outlines how a lawyer should defend a criminal case so that an office can assess whether it has the personnel, time, and resources to do the basics to meet with clients and investigate. The guidelines are better than other attempts to set out principles, but still lack an ongoing methodology to ascertain how well an office is serving the nation's poorest defendants.[78]

When North Carolina's Indigent Defense Services (IDS) sought in 2001 to develop a set of indicators that would measure the quality and cost effectiveness of the system, it could not find a model to emulate. "There is so little objective measurement in this business, it is astonishing," said Malcolm Ray Hunter Jr., IDS executive director until December 2008. Instead, Margaret A. Gressens, IDS research director, had to begin from scratch to establish indicators of system performance. The plan was for North Carolina's one hundred counties to report data: if a county shows below average performance on one of many indicators, IDS will be able to get involved. The percentage of defendants who are released from jail pretrial, for example, or who promptly see their attorney, say within forty-eight hours of arrest, are both indicators of what Gressens called the "cornerstone" of good criminal defense. "It costs a state a lot of money to have people in jail who don't need to be," she said. While in jail, people can lose their jobs and homes, become welfare recipients, and have their lives ruined—considerations of vital importance to an individual, which, from a policy perspective, also entail significant costs for the state.

IDS hopes eventually to take the indicators a step further and do what no state has come close to doing: to look at the impact of indigent defense services on the criminal justice system and the community. Gressens says that governments quantify hard-to-measure things all the time, like quality of life. But the health of our courts has been left virtually unchecked. According to Gressens, part of the problem is that each entity in the adversarial system works independently, and rarely, if ever, sits down with the others to solve problems or inefficiencies. "No one steps back and says we are really one system, how is this system working." The project is still in its initial stages but IDS hopes to have an evaluation tool in place by 2010.

■ ■ ■

As had happened in North Carolina, the Georgia Supreme Court Chief Justice's Commission on Indigent Defense had to figure out a basis for evaluating the system when it finally convened. Chief Justice Robert Benham, the first African-American to lead the court, appointed twenty-four professionals to the commission. Many were impressive members of the legal and business establishment but knew almost nothing about indigent defense except that it was an embarrassment. Some, like legislators, judges, prosecutors, and county commission members, had interests in funding priorities for their own programs and other concerns that came ahead of representation for indigents.

The commission eventually hired the Spangenberg Group to produce a report involving data collection analysis and on-site assessments and to give a macro sense of how the state's system matched up against others nationally. Robert Spangenberg has been assessing indigent defense systems for decades in more than forty states across the country. His work focuses more on comparing the ways different states fund and provide representation (e.g., whether funding is at the state or local level, if a contract or public defender system is in place, and how the cost per case compares in different locales). The analysis puts the state's representation into a broader context than Bright's reports or North Carolina's IDS assessment tools.

Notably, the commission did not invite Bright and the Southern Center to join its members, even though his was one of the few organizations involved in monitoring Georgia's services for the indigent. Bright was too combative, too outspoken and blunt. He openly criticized prosecutors and judges and got into arguments with them. His absence from the commission has been called a politically savvy move on the part of Chief Justice Benham.[79] It allowed the members to come to a consensus and Bright to push his agenda without compromise. He went to almost every commission meeting and told stories about the people his researchers had found; he even brought video tape of defendants and their families. When the commission considered testimony, Bright made sure they did so under the watch of former defendants or family members of those still in jail, whom he asked to fill the audience.[80] Bright also pushed the commission to drop in unannounced on a court, watch proceedings, and see the process in its raw form, but this never happened. "The only visits to courts were carefully controlled ones, where the judge was called in advance, gave a tour, and let the commissioners sit in on one or two minor hearings, after which the DA and defense lawyer waxed eloquent about how fair the judge was," said Bright.

The court visits may not have been necessary. The commission held seventeen public sessions over two years, in which sixty-five individuals testified about how the various different public defense systems worked in Georgia and elsewhere. Many of those who testified came from Bright's research, and virtually all parts of the criminal justice system and civil rights community in Georgia were represented, including judges, sheriffs, prosecutors, defendants, and their families.

The commission's chair, Charles R. Morgan, then executive vice president and general counsel to BellSouth, said that after a while the testimony became so repetitive that members wanted to stop the hearings because they had heard enough. A recurring theme seemed to be defense lawyers who felt themselves to be victims of the system, whether because of excessive caseloads or the nature of their clients. They didn't seem to think from their clients' point of view, nor did they notice their own deficiencies. "A small lie" that lawyers had told themselves became "a big lie and the next thing you know you believe it," Morgan said of the process by which the attorneys had lost sight of their purpose.

Take Mark Straughan. A lawyer at a private family firm, Straughan had won the contract to do indigent defense work in the Oconee Circuit for less money than anyone in the state of Georgia: fifty dollars per case. He had represented defendants for the five-county area for twenty years. "I have absolutely no complaints from the people that I work with," he claimed. His testimony was astounding in its disregard for his clients. "I remind many of you that guilt is what it's all about," he said on one occasion. "If he's guilty and he admits it why jerk everybody around with a trial?" He admitted that he didn't keep records about his cases, saying that "too many records just give things for people to come back at you, anyway." And then, as if he knew how shocking his words were, he warned, "don't take me wrong and rewrite my words to saying that I don't represent my client totally."[81]

And yet listeners were left with the impression that he did not. Indeed, he seemed not to understand counsel's role, which is, quite obviously, to test the prosecution's case and mount a defense. Instead, he mused that the true role of the defense lawyer was to assume his client's guilt. The panelists could not believe their ears. When one member pressed Straughan about whether the defense attorney or the judge should decide a defendant's guilt, Straughan said, "It's an error to go in there and assume your client is innocent," adding that, "the vast majority of the time if you're going to go to trial, the client has been lying to you the whole time."

Straughan's testimony clinched the issue for most members of the commission. "Jaws dropped while he was talking," said Marion Chartoff, who was watching. Straughan sounded more like a lawyer from a totalitarian country.[82] In the American court system, innocent until proven guilty is a precept; if this was not clear to a defense attorney then the entire system needed help. "Everybody on the commission would remember that day," said Charles Morgan. "I don't care how liberal or how conservative you are. This is America. Not Bolivia."

Bill Rankin, a reporter for the *Atlanta Journal-Constitution* who wrote a startling set of articles putting indigent defense on the front page, picked up on the story.[83] Straughan was fired by the county soon after Rankin's article was published.[84]

Robert Surrency was also asked to testify. He spoke against instituting a statewide public defender's office and warned that by recommending improvements, the commission would be insulting the very best of lawyers. "If you think that I am incompetent just because I handle . . . more than the Supreme Court says [I should], then you had better be willing to take that statement and apply it to some of the best lawyers in the state of Georgia who routinely do the same thing," he said.[85]

Surrency had a point. Exceptional lawyers could handle a substantial number of cases, especially if they had the right investigation and support staff. No one element ensured that a lawyer was effective. A well-funded system could be corrupted by shoddy lawyers, while a poorly funded one could succeed now and then because of outstanding efforts by some dedicated yet overworked people. Nonetheless, Surrency's caseload would likely prove impossible for even the greatest lawyer in the world. No amount of leadership can make a hopelessly underfunded system work. Surrency wanted to suggest that any effort to improve matters would be futile. "I hasten to add there is no one villain you can go after," he said.[86]

He asked the commission to protect those who currently worked in the system. "I hope [you] will have some consideration for the people . . . who are willing to do this job in the first place."[87]

After Surrency's statement, Rankin interviewed him for the *Atlanta Journal-Constitution*. The paper ran a short profile that included the following scene from an afternoon with Surrency in court:

> "Mr. Chester?" Surrency asks one of the prisoners, thinking he's Eric Chester, who is charged with receiving stolen property.
>
> "Mr. Surrency, that's Mr. Smith," Superior Court Judge James Cline says impatiently, referring to Chester's co-defendant, Marcus Smith. "Get your client."
>
> Minutes later, Surrency solves the mystery, but then two co-defendants facing armed robbery and aggravated assault charges approach the bench, the old courtroom's wooden floors squeaking beneath them.
>
> "Are you Waddell?" asks Surrency, looking over his wire-rimmed glasses at a short, unshaven man.
>
> "No, that's Eric Penn," the judge barks, this time rolling his eyes in exasperation. The judge points out Surrency's client, Darren Waddell, a tall, gangly man standing off to the side.

In the profile, Surrency speaks of himself in the third person, which he had a tendency to do, as if his conduct belonged to someone else. "It doesn't matter how Robert does it. If the system doesn't can him, he must be doing it right," he said, for the entire state of Georgia to read.[88]

■ ■ ■

In its seventy-page report, the commission severely criticized the system that allowed lawyers like Surrency to handle such crushing caseloads. Their solution was twofold. First, Georgia needed to put up some money. The state and federal constitutions mandated that all citizens get effective assistance of counsel, but Georgia hadn't been providing the funds to meet the order. The state funding added up to a little more than one-tenth of the total expenditures, which pales next to what other states provide; twenty-four states in the United States provide total state funding.[89] Spangenberg concluded that none of the nineteen counties he visited (representing approximately 45 percent of the state population) provided sufficient funds to assure quality representation to all indigent defendants.[90]

Second, the commission recommended that the extant structure be replaced by a uniform public defender system in which lawyers would be accountable to a higher authority. The commission suggested bumping the responsibility for indigent defense to the circuit level, rather than the county, so that forty-nine circuit public defenders would serve 159 counties. Overseeing the entire system would be a new organization, which would have the power to hire and fire the circuit public defenders. They would work full-time under specific guidelines and performance standards, and if additional panel or contract lawyers needed to be hired, these too would be supervised by the board. Further, the commission acknowledged the need for "a comprehensive data collection system designed to provide an accurate picture of the provision of indigent criminal defense services in Georgia."[91] Finally, the commission instructed the legislature to make the changes within two years, noting, ominously, that if the state of Georgia didn't take over and face this problem openly, "Further litigation is being contemplated and likely will occur."[92]

The commission released its report weeks before the 2003 legislature convened in January. Costly legislation intended to help unpopular people who commit crimes might have seemed like a futile effort, but the timing was right. The bill had the support of the new Republican governor, George E. "Sonny" Perdue III.[93] "The governor is kind of open-minded about those kinds of issues," said Terry Coleman, the Democratic house speaker from Eastman, Georgia. "It was an easy deal." Chief Justice Norman Fletcher, who had replaced Benham as new head of the state's Supreme Court, also played a crucial role in lobbying legislators and encouraging the court to endorse unanimously the commission's report.[94]

But the real incentive for legislators to get the bill passed was the ongoing and prospective litigation against the state. In the midst of the commission's study, the Southern Center had filed its suit against Coweta County, which brought press attention to the issue of defendants pleading guilty without the protection of a lawyer. And as the debate rose over the bill in the state senate, the Southern Center filed a lawsuit in Cordele Circuit alleging that defendants often went months without seeing a lawyer, met their lawyers for the first time in court, and were urged to plead guilty after only a brief conversation. The complaint was filed against individual judges, prosecutors, County Commissioners, and other local officials, as well as the governor of Georgia, and the Georgia Indigent Defense Council.[95]

Few politicians, however, gave Bright any credit. "I don't think the [lawsuits] were the major impetus on getting things done," said Charles C. Clay, a Republican senator who served on the commission and introduced the bill. He credited the bill's passing to "a quiet bipartisan groundswell to do something," which had been informed by articles and editorials in the *Atlanta Journal-Constitution* and other newspapers.

On the final day of the 2003 session, the legislature unanimously passed the Georgia Indigent Defense Act. Shortly thereafter, the *Fulton County Daily Report*, the local legal periodical, named Bright "Newsmaker of the Year: Angry Man of Indigent Defense," and featured a cover image of him looking grave. "Sometimes with lectures, other times with pleas, threats or impassioned speeches, Bright was the most implacable and visible crusader for better legal defense for the poor," the article read.[96]

Under the new legislation, the circuits would still contribute funds toward public defense (about $67 million), but obtain state supplements ($38.5 million up from $8.3 million). This new money would be used to create the Georgia Public Defender Standards Council, based in Atlanta, to monitor the quality of legal services, formally lobby legislators, and advocate for individual lawyers when they needed support. The Standards Council would oversee forty-nine judicial circuits, staffed by full-time lawyers, investigators, and a networked statewide computer system to track cases. It would also have the sole power to remove defenders who failed to meet the formal standards set by the Standards Council, thus protecting them from prosecutors, judges, and county commission members.

The only counties allowed to opt out of the new system were fourteen "single-county" judicial circuits that could prove to the council that they exceeded the new performance standards.

■ ■ ■

Robert Surrency was not around to see the new system installed in Greene County. Shortly after Bill Rankin's interview with him ran in the *Atlanta Journal-Constitution*, a large firm in Washington, D.C., began to prepare a suit with the Southern Center against Greene County, alleging systemic violations of the Sixth Amendment. By accident, the firm sent the county a draft of the lawsuit it planned to file, which focused the county commissioners' attention on Surrency. The county then asked Surrency for the number of cases he was working on and responded that the caseload seemed inflated. In answer, Surrency said he wanted his budget more than doubled from $40,000 to almost $90,000, and to prove that he needed the funding, he handed over his numerous case files. He wanted to hire a lawyer to help him, "and not pretend anymore," he said. "So I presented them with a real bill. And the commission didn't like that."

He quit shortly thereafter, and as a result, the firm did not bring the suit.

After seventeen years working as the contract defender in Greene County, Surrency suddenly had time to reflect on his experience: How had he managed to process thousands of cases to the approval of judges and prosecutors and yet still become a notoriously disreputable lawyer? He seemed angry that Bright had singled him out, that the commission had chosen him to testify, and that the press had covered him extensively. "Not a lot of people get tested like that," he said. He thought Bright's expectations were excessive. "He wants a private investigator! He wants witnesses talked to! He wants the defendant talked to multiple times and the police taken through every single legal loophole they are going through in every single case. And if they [the lawyers] don't do that, you are not doing your job!"

In contrast, he appeared proud of his ability to forgo investigating his cases. "That is the fun part," he said, "when you finally have enough experience to be able to make a long drawn-out practice into something pretty straightforward. That is when it really gets fun. Instead of having to spend sixteen hours investigating something or looking up some piece of the law. Just to be able to get right down to it. Just to be able to talk to these people—whoever these people are—and answer [them]." He could weigh what a case was "worth" based on a combination of experience and intuition.

"Surrency could give results," he said. "If I bought a Ouija board and every case is done by Ouija board, my decision as a lawyer is to do that. And you can test me by my results." He seemed to be saying that every case is not distinct but that there is an ineffable formula to determine how best to proceed with each one. At the same time, he could trot out some reasonable platitudes: "The main thing is don't judge the book by its cover! Look into the case before you make your decisions of who is doing what to whom!" Paradoxically, he also argued that he was doing his clients a service by ignoring them. As he put it, had he taken the time to research their cases, they would have languished in jail. "I think my clients are much happier because I didn't do that."

■ ■ ■

In 2006, a year and a half into the state's new public defender system, Michael Mears, a longtime advocate for the poor, was appointed director of the Standards Council. Before that, he was the director of the Georgia Multi-County Public Defender's Office, which represented defendants in death penalty cases. Robert Spangenberg seemed excited about Mears, exclaiming that "Georgia in three years is going to have the best system in the south."

When Mears was appointed, the Standards Council was still in the initial stages of trying to figure out how to monitor its new lawyers. For example, the council wanted them to record how their time was spent so that cases could be "weighted" according to effort. A murder trial should count for more than a simple drug possession plea because it would take more work. Public defenders, however, were not especially willing to comply. They had enjoyed their freedom from authority and, because they took less money than private lawyers, didn't see a reason to account for their time. Consequently, the data accrued by the Standards Council "just sucks," said Gerald P. Word, who chaired a committee that dealt with the information and is also a circuit defender in Coweta. "Over two thirds of it had to be thrown out."

Next, the council borrowed a new computer system from California that enabled lawyers to log data about their cases. For Greene County, Mears could see how well lawyers were complying with the rule that they meet their clients within seventy-two hours of arrest. The new circuit public defender there had an 88 percent compliance rate. "I don't get a lot of complaints," about Greene County, Mears said.

Was there really a solid turnaround? According to Ben Mitcham, the county's assistant district attorney, the system was improved because now the public defender didn't have a private practice competing for his attention. "It's a lot easier to get a hold of him," he said. Still, Mitcham refused to say that the new public defender was actually doing a better job than Surrency. "I wouldn't say anybody has approached it more conscientiously," he said. He had a great deal of sympathy for Surrency. "He's a good guy, I like him. We are possessed by the same demons, disorganization and what not."

Mitcham admitted that he himself was performing at an all-time low. He was really behind, with a stack of cases on his desk as high as two hundred to three hundred felonies and two hundred to four hundred misdemeanors. When asked why the pile had accumulated his answer was lamentable and human: "Because I put things off." His boss, Fredric D. Bright, the district attorney who oversees all eight counties in the circuit, thought the numbers might be higher but wasn't sure by how much. Greene County has the "worst backlog," he said. He was trying to get the county to hire an assistant district attorney to help Mitcham, which he eventually did.[97]

I checked in at the courtroom to see if the new system really was an improvement. That day, a twenty-six-year-old man had been charged with "criminal damage to property second degree" and "family violence battery." He told me he wanted to move to Kansas to start a new life, and, after a few whispered exchanges with the public defender, pleaded guilty to a lesser crime and agreed to one thousand dollars in fines. ("You mean I could say I couldn't pay?" he asked, when I inquired why he had agreed to that.) Darel C. Mitchell, the assistant public defender, said his exchange with his client had made him feel "dirty." He used the word a lot to describe compromises he felt he was making in his new position. "I'm not being all that I can be," he said over a beer at the Yesterday Café across from the courthouse.

Mitchell had been on the job for a year and a half. In his fifties, he had taken the work in Greene County after twelve years as a private lawyer in Gwinnett County, a suburban area near Atlanta. In Gwinnett, he had taken on so many court-appointed cases that he "had evolved into a de facto public defender," though he still had a base of paying clients as well.

Even with such good experience, he was sorely unprepared for what his new job entailed. As it turned out, Mitchell had an equal if not greater caseload than Surrency. He and another attorney shared the responsibility for 436 cases, but he still had 1,034 others left over from previous years. Mitchell was also the public defender in nearby Morgan County, which had 249 new cases and 543 pending from years before. With this enormous load, he was constantly making the forty-five-minute drive between the two places to make sure he interviewed defendants within seventy-two hours of their arrest. He seemed to feel that the function of the initial meeting with clients amounted to checking a box when his time could have been better spent doing legal work. "I should not have to go to jail to do seventy-two-hour interviews," he said, even though a paid lawyer would probably want to have this initial meeting when a client's story and argument were most fresh.

As Mitchell spoke, he became increasingly angry. He sputtered with frustration about his struggle to get furniture for his office, much less a printer and stamps. "I will bust a gut before I walk three blocks to buy postage stamps in this ninety-eight degree heat!" he said when asked if he communicated with his clients by mail. Mitchell had originally taken the job because he wanted benefits and a steady income. "I thought it would be like semiretirement, but no one told me it would be five hundred to six hundred cases," he said.

The lack of resources was making the basics unmanageable. Mitchell was supposed to have access to investigators, but the circuit had only one whom he never used because the investigator was too busy.

Though Mitchell met his clients within seventy-two hours, he rarely saw them after that. "Our office isn't staffed, we don't know when people are coming," he said, though he recently received an office assistant three times a week. With little knowledge of the cases, "you shoot from the hip" in court, he said, drawing his fingers into a gun position. His card, he joked, should be a handshake with the words "meet 'em and plead 'em" underneath.

For the first time in his career, Mitchell said, he had been the subject of a rash of grievances sent to the state bar, which suggests that Mears and the Standards Council were not as in touch with what was happening in Greene County as they thought. Eleven defendants had complained. The content of the accusations aren't public, but in essence, Mitchell said, they came down to, "My lawyer won't see me, he's not doing anything on my case." In short, more of same. Mitchell didn't appreciate the complaints. "I just get ticked off. A guy with no education, and no job skills . . . It's like being called ugly by a possum."

One complaint, he said, involved a defendant charged with felony obstruction for kicking an officer. Mitchell took the case to trial but lost.

Then he did not file an appeal or seek a new trial within the thirty-day deadline, which he is obliged to do by law if his client wishes. But Mitchell didn't have time to talk to him before the state swept him away and a visit to prison was impossible given his hectic schedule. He could have drawn up the necessary pleadings, little more than a fill-in-the-blanks sheet of paper, and sent it in, but he "had no computer and no desk," he said. "Looking back I should have filed something to protect his right to appeal," he conceded. His client lost his chance. He would have to seek new relief by himself, without a lawyer, from a distant prison.[98]

Mitchell's failure to appeal his client's conviction is odd. It wasn't as if he had so many trials to finish up; he had taken only three cases to trial in Greene County (and one more in Morgan County, a robbery case that he won) in a year and a half. Surrency in some years actually took more. Mitchell also didn't put motions (aside from standard discovery motions) on the calendar. Instead, he would go to the prosecutor with the threat of a motion, which was usually enough to get him or her to reduce the charges. "My DAs are lazy," he said. Finally, Mitchell often was not prepared in court. He'd ask for continuances on a lot of old cases, which prosecutor Mitcham accepted, rarely opposing the continuances or announcing ready for trial, probably because he, too, was behind on all his cases. In a year and a half, Mitchell had only filed one demand for a speedy trial, which requires that a case be tried within two terms of court from indictment or be dismissed.

While it might have been too soon to assess the effect of the Georgia Indigent Defense Act on the ground, Mitchell seemed to be having as hard a time as Surrency. But why? Unlike Surrency, he did not have a private practice to attend to, and in theory, he had a larger operating budget. But his caseload was still monstrous. And the courtroom culture that grandfathered in bad habits year after year persisted. Every court has a set of values and attitudes that standardize expectations. Groups as well as individuals can sense it. For example, Mitchell said of his old job in Gwinnett County that the prosecutors there made him a better lawyer. "The harder they worked, we got better," he said. "It's a back-and-forth volley." By contrast, in Greene County he felt certain forces had made him soft. He wasn't expected to nail cases so he didn't. He could have announced that he was ready for trial or have filed a speedy-trial demand in several cases, but he didn't. "Life is too short to go around getting people mad at you," he offered as an explanation. "My dad"—who had been a judge and lawyer—"said there are two ways to practice law. An easy way and a hard way. There's no need to file a demand for a trial if you get everybody mad at you. My daddy said, 'You don't kick a horse in the ass when you got your hand in his mouth.'" When asked what he meant, he said, "It's like animals in the wild that travel in packs. You have a pecking order of superiority and ranking." Defense lawyers, however, are not supposed to be part of the pack. Their job is to fight for the lone man against the state—not join the state. Mitchell clearly knew this and felt exhausted by his compromises. "Sometimes I just think, 'why am I doing this?' When I run out of ammunition I am going to throw down my gun."

At the end of the day, Mitchell seemed well on his way to surrender.

■ ■ ■

To see how a system could work successfully in Georgia, I decided to look at what is widely considered one of the best, if not the best, in the state. The public defender's office in Houston County, just a few hundred miles away from Greene, was exempt from having to participate in the Standard Council's new system because its performance surpassed the minimum required. I wanted to know whether the chief public defender there, Terry Everett, deserved all the credit. She had won numerous awards for excellence and was the first public defender to head the Georgia Association of Criminal Defense Lawyers.

The Houston County office was widely hailed as "the model," though as I found out later, the designation drove Everett crazy. She maintained that her office was only "better than average," and that they had a long way to go and a very big job to handle. She saw her role as a protector of the underdog. "A public defender is really . . . biblical, David out there with Goliath. I don't have much but I am taking what I've got and using it. I have these little rocks. I've got to make them work and hopefully the giant is going to tumble." The "giant" was her caseload, which was too high, and her schedule, which was over-booked. She often didn't have enough time to prepare for a trial. "Sometimes I have to say I am just not ready." The office only had one investigator, who couldn't do everything, so Everett has been known to get up at two in the morning to wait for a witness to change work shifts so that she might talk to him.

Her office's caseload averaged 228 cases per attorney for felonies, she said, which is well over the 150 that the ABA recommends as the absolute maximum an attorney can perform competently. But her staff, paid by the county, received equal pay as the district attorney.[99] Plus, they were committed. "We have a whole lot of people who are really concerned about people charged with crimes who are not guilty," she said, referring to her eleven lawyers, four secretaries, and one full-time investigator. Since she took over the office in 1989, Everett had been aided by the same assistant, Angie Coggins, a fellow "true believer," she said, who is also known for her aggressive advocacy in court and who wins more cases than she loses.

Not that Everett kept a win-loss record. What her lawyers have to do to be successful is to meet clients soon after arrest, advocate for a reasonable bail amount, and investigate. In almost every drug case, she said, her assistant public defenders request a motion to suppress the evidence so that her client can have a hearing to test whether the evidence was rightfully seized; doing so also preserves the right to appeal the issue at a later time. Her lawyers routinely ask prosecutors to knock a few hundred dollars off of fines, and Coggins offhandedly mentioned sparring with the prosecutor to "expunge" an unprosecuted arrest so that the defendant wouldn't have to worry about having a record when he sought a job. This could help a client get back on his feet. "A public defender is more than a lawyer," said Everett.

She herself maintained a full caseload, which she said kept her in the courtroom so she could see how her assistant public defenders were performing. She also required her lawyers to go out and check the crime scenes at the time of the incident. "You have to know what the lighting is like," she said.

Everett came to the public defender's office with experience as a county attorney, a private lawyer, and a city-court judge in Alabama before she moved to Houston County. She worked as a legal aid lawyer doing civil cases before taking the position of public defender. When she came in, the office was filled with lawyers who did the job for a few months until another one came along. Everett aimed for long-term hires. "I did this because it was something I wanted to do," she said, "and I convinced everyone else it was something they wanted to do, too." Because of her prior experience in county government, she knew how to fight for resources. She requested an investigator for ten years before she received funding for one from the county commission; she fought for networked computers and the office space she resides in today, complaining that the design of the new courthouse wasn't sufficient until it included a workable place for her lawyers.

In court, Everett wants to make all her points for the record for her client's appeal. "Just one more thing," she would continue even after a judge had decided against her and wanted to move on. Judges would threaten her with being in contempt of court but she just kept on talking. "I have never had a fear of going to jail," she said.

One court reporter, who travels all over the state to make legal records, claimed that Everett's office was by far the best. "I had never heard a lawyer talk to a judge like that," she said, having witnessed Everett's refusal to back down. Once, a judge tried to fire Everett. "He wouldn't give me a reason why," Everett said. So she went to the county commission and said she was going to sue for age and sex discrimination. "I am over forty and I am a woman," Everett said, "which was not at all the reason that he was doing it, but tell that to the federal courts." She seemed to find the entire incident amusing. Judge L. A. "Buster" McConnell Jr. said when Everett first came in he tried to fire her several times a week adding that, "she wouldn't shut up sometimes," as she fought even the smallest objection or adverse objection unrelentingly. Since then he has come to admire her. "She is probably as good a trial lawyer that you can find. If you pay one hundred fifty thousand dollars you can't do better. She is quick-witted and does her homework."

Hard-charging District Attorney Kelly Burke complained for years that Everett received too much funding, certain that she was manipulating her costs per case. "She has more cases per year than I have. How is that possible?"

In a widely chronicled tempest-in-a-teapot, Burke advised a special grand jury, which meets regularly to study the budget, that the county could replace Everett with contract defenders to save money. The grand jury issued a report stating that "the county is spending almost one million dollars for indigent defense, which seems excessive. . . . In this day of privatization of government services, this seems to be one area that the county should study to determine if the county is getting the best use of its dollars."[100]

Everett, at the time, was taking leave to be with her son who was ill with cancer. She was sitting with him in his room where he was strapped to an IV when she received a call that the county commission was considering abolishing her office. At first, she told the commissioners to take their job and shove it. "Put my things in a box," she said. Then she fought back. She called judges for help. "I said, 'Are you going to let them tell you how to run the court?' " Three judges wrote letters supporting her. One private attorney remarked in the local newspaper, "If [the district attorney] was whipping Terry more in court, he wouldn't be trying to abolish her job."[101] Burke, in an interview, claimed no such animosity. "I don't want to give the impression that it's war down here. It's not," he said, adding, "there's not a private attorney who does a better job than the public defenders." Maybe too good a job. Everett said the key to her survival is to keep making alliances, even with former enemies like judges.[102]

The irony is that the county commissioners who were asked to abolish Everett's position were the same people who then later opted her office out of the Standards Council precisely because of the good job it was doing. However, this was a mixed blessing. The Standards Council offices offered better pay, and Everett's senior lawyers, who had been with her for years, would receive a twenty-thousand-dollar raise if they went to work for the state under the new public defender system. Some did, which left Everett with five rather inadequately compensated openings. "We couldn't fill them initially," she said. So the new legislation, designed to improve the system, had inadvertently weakened one of the better representatives of that system.

As a result, Everett was forced to look for castoffs. "I am sort of a rehab place," she said. She hired a former judge who had left the bench after being charged with shoplifting, and eventually welcomed back one former employee, Carolyn Hall, who had left for a new job with the Standards Council. According to a formal grievance Hall filed to the council in May 2005, she was terminated by the head public defender in the Dublin Circuit after conducting a meeting to discuss the staff's failure to meet the seventy-two-hour interview obligations.[103] Hall said lawyers in her office weren't doing the basics and they hated her for insisting on them. "The worst thing was feeling I was there alone," she said. In fact, the chief of that office stepped down after an official audit found that public defenders were not seeing jailed indigent defendants in a timely fashion and cases had been left unassigned.[104]

One of the job applications Everett received was from Robert Surrency, whom she had known previously from state defense-lawyer meetings. He had plenty of experience and, by his own admission, nowhere to go. Given his bad reputation, the Standards Council itself had been unwilling to hire him. But Everett didn't care: "Sometimes people like that need some structure." So she hired him and watched him carefully. "We started him out slow," she said. "And he has done very well." He used an investigator more than most lawyers, she said, and seemed to have a good courtroom presence.

By all accounts, Surrency was a man transformed. "I love to watch him in court," said Angie Coggins, Everett's assistant. "He knows the law. He's a very good trial attorney." She didn't accept Surrency's former reputation. "I have no doubt he did the best he could for his clients," she said. "He is motivated. He volunteers to go on jail visits."

I went to visit Surrency several months into his new job. We met in his immaculate office, where his degrees hung on the wall and his color-coded files were lined up on his shiny modern desk. He looked more at ease than during his days in Greene County, less burdened, almost vibrant. Everett had created the type of office Surrency wished he had run at his old job. He could order an investigator and not have to worry about running up a bill that would bother the county commissioners. Everett's lawyers had trained judges to expect a healthy fight. "Terry is good at making it clear that if [the judge] is going to ignore [the law], it's going to hurt," Surrency said. Judges in Greene County would never think of granting a motion to suppress evidence—they behaved as if such a thing were unthinkable. In Houston County, Everett filed them regularly, even though she usually lost. In Greene County, Surrency had stopped trying to push cases to trial when he thought judges would consider them unimportant; in Houston County, "they empanel juries constantly."

Real change, it seemed, had been best effected by good, tenacious lawyers who, over a period of time, had created high expectations for themselves and each other. Clearly, the people who work in the system have to take a stand. If Surrency had any regrets about Greene County, it was that he didn't realize he "had a good negotiating position to get better resources." In his mind, he had been doing the best he could. The court reporter, who had seen Surrency at work in both jobs, noted how much he had changed. The old Surrency had gone downhill as his caseload had increased; he simply couldn't keep up. "It wasn't Surrency that got worse—the system got worse because of the overload of cases." Now, she was impressed. "If I hadn't seen him, I would have thought . . . he couldn't do it."

Miraculously, the conditions in Everett's office suited Surrency's temperament: once slipshod and ineffective, he'd become competent and successful. Plenty of social science evidence proves that systems often shape the individual. In what psychologists call a "strong" situation of controlling structures and norms, an individual has almost no chance of changing a system. J. Richard Hackman, an organizational psychologist at Harvard University, has given much thought to the individual's capacity to oppose the cultural current of a group or organization. "The power of the situation is like the current," he said. "To try and swim against it is a losing proposition." Extraordinary individuals are "extremely rare," Hackman says.

Terry Everett may have been that atypical, major force, but there are two caveats here. While she is somewhat of a missionary who has fought hard for her office, Everett started out, seventeen years earlier, in a better place than Surrency. She operated from the sound structure of a public defender's office, which gave her a foothold in the courthouse (Surrency never even had an office in Greene County), a full-time job, and the basic platform from which to push for more resources. She had worked numerous jobs as an attorney and didn't seem to mind the possibility of getting fired—she would land another job.

Second, she had a partner in Angie Coggins. At different times, when one of the women threatened to quit, the other convinced her to stay. They were a team. In Houston County, "every single lawyer would help every other lawyer if they had to," said Surrency. "My compatriots have achieved wonders." In Greene County, Surrency had no colleagues. He was a solo practitioner, which made him potentially more skittish about going up against judges—he had an incentive to perform for his paying clients. Plus, he had no one at his back to oppose the prosecutor, or the judge, if necessary. To keep his job, he behaved in ways that undermined his role in the adversarial system. Over the years, he adjusted to the demands of the very colleagues he was supposed to keep in check.

Surrency really only had two good alternatives: find a way to alter the situation or get out. To alert the system of its failings was not something he would do; he never saw himself as a problem in the first place. He was also helpless to change it. Further, someone would have to feel pretty self-confident to say publicly that his job was unmanageable. For instance, in 2006 an ABA ethics committee said that attorneys who represent the indigent and are overburdened must, if no other alternatives are available, file motions to withdraw from a case or to ask a judge to stop new appointments when they have too many.[105] In the two years since the rule passed, only five public defender's offices have stepped up to admit they couldn't do their jobs properly.[106] Given how rampant the caseload problem is, this is a modest response at best.

On the other hand, maybe a lawyer can never really know how battered he is. After leaving Greene County and joining Terry Everett's office, Surrency behaved in keeping with his character and perhaps human nature. He melded into the system. Without a conversion experience or sudden condemnation of his past performance, Surrency changed—or the system changed his behavior—for the better. He wasn't redeemed. His workplace simply created new expectations that he was capable enough to fulfill. The last time we spoke, I told Surrency that the public defenders of Houston County seemed to be passionate about their work. He agreed and added, "I fit right in."

CHAPTER TWO

A TROY CHAMPION

Henry R. Bauer is one of the most popular men in Troy, New York. In the fall of 2005, he won a landslide election for city council president. To walk the streets with Bauer was to accompany a celebrity. People leaned out of their car windows to shout his name. On the day we met, a female cop apologized for not contributing to his election campaign and pressed a check into his hand. A courthouse secretary begged him to use her copy machine, an offer that is technically prohibited. "Just don't tell anyone," she said. An old man selling candy at a kiosk wanted to know if Hank (who's on a first-name basis with everyone, it seemed) was going to his favorite bar after work. Like everyone else, he wanted to hang out with Hank Bauer.

And yet less than a year before, Bauer had ended a career as a city court judge that was pegged as one of the most disastrous in Troy's judicial history. After working on the bench for eleven years, he'd been removed from office by the New York State Commission on Judicial

Conduct, a punishment from which most judges do not recover. Unless you're Hank Bauer.

By nearly all accounts, Bauer is a congenial and decent man, full of smiles and laughs, with time and tolerance for everybody. As a judge, his reputation was stellar. Independent court watchdogs, local prosecutors and councilmen, defense attorneys and even a few defendants who had appeared in Bauer's court all attested to the judge's fairness and decency. In fact, most people in the city were stunned when the commission alleged frequent violations of the law during a two-year period. These included:

- Failure to inform defendants of their right to a lawyer nineteen times.
- Twenty-six situations in which he set excessive bail or failed to regard the statutory factors that must be considered.
- Ten instances of coerced guilty pleas.
- Four excessive sentences that were illegal.
- Two convictions of a defendant without a plea or a trial.

The allegations were serious and Bauer's failure to uphold the law egregious, so the obvious question here became: What was happening in Troy that so many were willing to turn a blind eye to such gross injustice? Why was the judge so beloved? As it turned out, the people of Troy thought Bauer's brand of practical justice better served the community than a strict and tedious upholding of the law. The lawyers didn't mind because the judge did most of their work for them, and the community didn't mind because when injustice in the lower courts is ostensibly aimed at keeping the streets safe and the system moving, the only people who suffer are the poor and neglected—in short, the lower class.

■ ■ ■

Hank Bauer came to power at a time when Troy was demanding tough justice for the vagrants and drug dealers who had seemed to take over downtown. It was an especially dire time for the city. Troy had fallen into disrepair. Indeed, in 1996, the city nearly went bankrupt. A once-thriving town renowned for its architecture and industry had turned into a cesspool of crime and poverty. The city's fall from prominence was dramatic. In the nineteenth century, Troy was second only to Pittsburgh in the production of iron and steel. Here, the Arrow collar was born, and strides were made in valve manufacturing and tempering. Here, Herman Melville, author of *Moby-Dick*, spent his early manhood and published his first piece of fiction. Here, the myth of Uncle Sam took flight. But it's the architecture that really makes the city. Magnificent churches and white marble buildings dot the skyline. Charming blocks of Victorian-era brick and stone brownstones with Tiffany stained-glass windows, fancy iron work, vast ceilings, and marble carvings line Second, Third, and Fifth Streets. The most extravagant housing surrounds a private enclosure called Washington Park. The area so perfectly projects an image of nineteenth-century wealth and stability that it has been used in movies like *The Bostonians* and Martin Scorsese's *The Age of Innocence*.[1]

By the early twentieth century, however, the image was just that. Many textile manufacturers had moved away with an eye toward being closer to the source of raw materials. Industries wanted cheaper, more flexible labor markets. As industry left, so did the people. Troy's population began to dwindle. It peaked with almost 77,000 in 1910 and dipped to 48,310 in 2005. By the late 1980s, unemployment rates had skyrocketed with a national recession. Troy was devastated. Two historically important companies, Cluett-Peabody, in the collar district, and Portec, in the iron-working heart of Troy, moved their bases elsewhere. Others closed their doors completely. The city experienced staggering budget shortages. After six straight years of deficits, the city's financial rating dropped below junk-bond status. Facing insolvency, Troy opted for a complicated scheme of financing that included mortgaging City Hall to pay operating expenses. Eventually, the New York State Legislature bailed the city out.[2]

But this did not solve the majority of Troy's problems. The police drug unit, like everything else, was underfunded, and crack had hit the streets. By 1995 and 1996 crime had reached an all time high—especially robberies, burglaries, and larcenies.[3]

Chief of Police Nicholas F. Kaiser had worked in the department for thirty-four years and had seen brownstones turn into crack houses maintained by absentee landlords. As he put it, "Along with crack came a more violent type of criminal," in large part because many a "smart" drug dealer had migrated from New York City to Troy. The market, he said, had soaring possibilities. "What you can buy down there in New York City for five to ten dollars, you could come up here and sell for twenty to twenty-five."

On the other hand, New York City seemed to have its crime problem under control. In 1998, under Mayor Rudolph Giuliani, the city boasted the lowest murder rate in three decades. Though crime was dropping throughout the country, New York's drop seemed more "marked" than in other cities, the *New York Times* reported.[4] So the obvious question for Chief Kaiser was: What was New York City doing that worked so well?

He and two deputies decided to take a trip to One Police Plaza in Manhattan to find out. There they learned of the city's zero-tolerance arrest policy, justified by the "broken-windows theory," which holds that a seemingly minor matter like a broken window results in more crime because the failure to uphold general civil order signals that greater levels of crime are acceptable. The theory was made famous in a 1982 article by James Q. Wilson and George L. Kelling. Accordingly:

> . . . serious street crime flourishes in areas in which disorderly behavior goes unchecked. The unchecked panhandler is, in effect, the first broken window. Muggers and robbers, whether opportunistic or professional, believe they reduce their chances of being caught or even identified if they operate on streets where potential victims are already intimidated by prevailing conditions. If the neighborhood cannot keep a bothersome panhandler from annoying passersby, the thief may reason, it is even

less likely to call the police to identify a potential mugger
or to interfere if the mugging actually takes place.[5]

Troy decided to implement New York City's system. No longer would
jaywalkers be allowed to proceed unticketed. People who urinated in
public or cursed or yelled loudly or engaged in other disorderly conduct would be held accountable. Many attorneys, also citizens, welcomed the decision.

Enter Judge Hank Bauer, whose passion for the law began early.
The middle child of seven, he was born in Suffern, New York, to parents who were both teachers. Bauer, however, had a different career in
mind. He admired a family acquaintance who was an attorney and
seemed to be a godsend to those in need. "I always knew I wanted to be
a lawyer," he said. When he attended Siena College in Loudonville he
took a business law class with a local attorney who told stories of his
experiences in criminal law. "It made me see the importance of counsel
and what you could do for somebody accused," he said. Being a criminal defense lawyer seemed to him the epitome of helping the underdog.
He never wanted to be a prosecutor. "It wasn't my idea of what lawyers
did," he said. "Lawyers defend people in trouble."

After graduation, Bauer became a night student at Western New
England College School of Law in Springfield, Massachusetts. During
the day he taught English, reading, and history as a special-education
teacher for troubled boys at the La Salle School in Albany. Many were juvenile delinquents recommended by the court system or another state
agency, who, decades later, would come before him in his capacity as
judge and still address him as "Mr. Bauer." "You couldn't believe their
plight," he said of his students, whom he recalled as having "bad luck
beyond imagination," with fathers in prison and mothers who were
prostitutes. "[The experience] supported the idea that these are the real
people who need help and support and a defense."

He married his girlfriend, Laura Wells, who was studying at the University of Albany to become a probation officer. The two settled in Troy,
where one of Bauer's professors from college, attorney Peter Kehoe,

offered him a job at his firm. Bauer "is just affable," said Kehoe of what made him hire his former student. "He's always interested. He listens. He is not always spouting out about his own view of things. He has opinions," but he "express[es] himself at the appropriate time."

Kehoe's firm gave Bauer some work, but he had to solicit his own business as well. When he found out the Rensselaer County Public Defender's office needed a part-time lawyer, he jumped at the chance. In Troy, the public defenders all worked part-time; they had private practices with paying clients who also needed their attention. When asked about Bauer as a public defender, his fellow attorneys mentioned nothing noteworthy except one case that had made headlines. Bauer's client, the "hillside burglar," was charged with several break-ins, and the judge refused to set bail or release him for fear he might recommit the crime. Bauer appealed the decision—and won. *Bauer v. McGreevey* stands for the proposition that a court cannot deny a bail application "solely for the reason that it wishes to protect the community from any possible future criminal conduct of a defendant."[6]

Bauer thought he had found his calling as a part-time attorney for the indigent until Jack Casey phoned him. Casey, a lawyer, also headed the local Republican Party. The current city court judge had been elected to county court and a position had opened. Did Bauer want to become a city judge? He had a good image—a family man with two daughters. He was also dapper and handsome with greenish eyes that always seemed amused by whatever you had to say. Plus, very few Republicans were interested in the job. Troy is a historically Democratic town, and a win in the next election for a judgeship would be unlikely. This meant Bauer's appointment might last only until the election, just twelve months away.

Bauer decided to give it a go. "Being naïve is somewhat helpful," he said. "I had never given a moment's thought to becoming a judge and this opportunity came up." He took the job as an interim position, and a year later ran for election.

The institution of elected judges is a particularly American phenomenon.[7] It developed in response to colonial judges who were beholden to the Crown, so much so that the founders noted the problem in the ninth specification of the Declaration of Independence: The King of England "has made Judges dependent on his Will alone, for the tenure of their offices, and the amount and payment of their salaries." After the revolution, the new Americans remained hostile toward a judiciary filled with privileged aristocrats. Some state governments required that judges be elected by the people. Vermont, for example, provided for the election of lower court judges in its state constitution in 1777. A few other states, including Georgia, followed, but only for some of its judges.[8]

Over the course of the nineteenth century, many more states, especially those entering the union in the west in the Jacksonian period, favored the election of public officials in a trend toward populism. Among the reasons cited were a need to check corruption, opposition to English common law, and a reaction to the appointment of federal judges who were nominated by the U.S. president and approved by the Senate, but had the power to invalidate laws made by popularly elected representatives. Federal judges are also appointed for life—a system designed to encourage the judiciary to preserve fundamental Constitutional values without worrying about being thrown out of office. The state system stands in contrast: all in all, citizens wanted to be able to remove a judge from the bench who made unpopular decisions.[9]

However, having judges chosen by popular election soon proved problematic and by the early twentieth century, reformers were calling for change. "Putting courts into politics and compelling judges to become politicians . . . has almost destroyed the traditional respect for the bench," said jurist and educator Roscoe Pound in a speech before the American Bar Association in 1906.[10] Albert Kales, a faculty member at Northwestern University School of Law, devised a plan for selecting judges that preserved some influence by the people, yet insulated judges from political influence. "Merit selection," or the "Missouri Plan" (named after the first state to adopt it) provided that the executive branch or governor appoint judges from a list of nominees chosen by a nonpartisan nominating commission. Once appointed, the judge is subject to retention elections or panels that make sure judges are in compliance with ethics standards.

Merit selection also limits the influence that big money can have in campaign contributions to judges running for election. As of now, it is common for elected judges to hear cases involving lawyers and parties who have spent money to support their campaigns.[11]

Thirty-nine states currently employ some form of judicial elections for their appellate courts, trial courts, or both. In New York, approximately one-fourth of judges are chosen through merit selection and the rest in partisan elections, which is how Bauer came to the bench. Scholars are split or ambivalent about which system is preferable. After all, who's to say appointed judges aren't simply beholden to a different community of people? The debate can be reduced to a tension between whether judges represent the majority or exist independently of the political controversy and community pressures that could prevent an elected official from protecting the minority. A court is obliged to abide by state law as well as the federal Constitution, which lays out a series of rights. While these rights often protect the individual, they can conflict with the ethos of a democracy, in which the majority rules. In a courtroom, the prosecution—that is, the people and the state—represent the "majority;" and one of the challenges of a sound legal system is to balance how much power to cede the "majority" while still safeguarding the rights of the individual.

In Bauer's race to become judge, the campaign got dirty when his Democratic opponent, Patrick Morphy, accused him of misleading the public by advertising himself as a crime fighter. "Bauer Warrant Nails New York City Drug Dealers," one flier said, when in fact the police were the ones interrupting criminal activity, not the judge. Morphy also attacked Bauer for claiming he set high bails to keep predators off the street, a policy that contravened the purpose of bail, as Bauer himself had ironically proven with his "hillside burglar" appeal.[12] It was an ugly battle, which eventually came down to a formal count and an appeal to the state's highest court because Bauer won by only one ballot. But Bauer, it turned out, had a way of glossing over the difficult events in his life. "It was a fun election," he said of the cut-throat, down-to-the-wire vote.

Bauer found that he loved his new job. And it certainly seemed like he was committed to helping the little guy. He attended a series of educational programs and decided to help start a "drug court" that diverted drug users to a special system of frequent drug tests, treatment regimens, and sanctions, including prison for those who didn't comply. After this court was established, he visited a Brooklyn courthouse where he learned about a new "domestic violence court" that empowered a single judge to handle inter-related cases in family, criminal, and matrimonial matters. He then helped set one up in Troy, which gave special attention to victims' needs. Through the process, he picked a day he would deal only with domestic-violence issues—"This is not her order, but mine," he would say as he put pressure on men charged with battering their significant others. "It wasn't that he was perfect," said Mary A. Lynch, a clinical professor of law and co-director of the Albany Law Clinic and Justice Center, who helped Bauer start the court. "But I think he learned, which is amazing because by the time most people are judges they think the learning is done."

"It was fascinating," Bauer said of his early experience.

In the meantime, as the city police began cracking down and adopting the "broken-windows" approach to law enforcement, more and more cases started to appear in Bauer's court.[13] City court handles misdemeanors or crimes punishable by up to one year in jail, as well as smaller violations and traffic offenses. The outcome of these cases can have long-reaching and significant collateral effects on a person's future. For instance, a guilty plea or conviction for a misdemeanor can sway the outcome of a child-custody case. For an immigrant, a conviction can deny him or her a green card. Local public-housing agencies can refuse lodging to anyone with a criminal record. Federal student loans and grant assistance can be denied to anyone charged with a drug-related offense, including a marijuana violation. Judges also consider a defendant's history of misdemeanors when determining punishment or bail. For a defendant who has immigration issues a conviction in city court can lead to deportation. And anyone who fails to pay fines and fees levied on a conviction may be rearrested or jailed. In short, pleading to a misdemeanor, which might be as minor as jaywalking, can wreak havoc on a defendant's life.[14] The fallout is a series of "invisible punishments" for the forty-seven million people who have criminal records—approximately 25 percent of the nation's adults.[15]

Understandably then, the judge's role, even in the lower courts, is extremely important. Ideally, everyone attempts to protect the rights of the defendant. In practice, it's the lawyers who do most of the legwork, but the judge who runs the courtroom sets bail, accepts guilty pleas, conducts trials, decides what evidence to admit and what sentence to impose, all of which greatly shape a case's outcome. In addition, during plea deals, a judge's role can vary from staying out of negotiations completely to allowing parties into chambers to encourage plea bargaining, or even to encouraging plea bargaining "off the record" at the time cases are called.[16]

So Bauer's job was not to be taken lightly. The stakes were high and he approached his work with zeal. However, at some point he began to display a little too much zeal: he stopped assigning lawyers to people who needed them, and began setting extraordinarily high bails for some minor crimes. He did this for years and yet no one in Troy complained—officially or otherwise. So there was little reason to think he was remiss, let alone conducting his court illegally. If not for a lifelong criminal who wrote from jail to complain about Bauer, the judge might well have escaped censure indefinitely.

The whistle-blower, Eric Frazier, didn't seem likely to launch a judicial investigation. One look at his rap sheet suggests he broke the law for a living. He had spent a large part of his thirty-eight years behind bars. As he saw it, his life could be laid out as a series of legal disputes. Sitting in the maximum security Clinton County Correctional Facility in Dannemora, New York, he was serving seven years for attempted robbery, which "started out as attempted murder," he explained. At first he'd refused to plea to the lesser crime of attempted robbery because the charge was not borne out by the facts, he said. "My lawyer thought I was crazy." Eventually, though, he took the plea.

Frazier was suing several people civilly, among them his wife (for custody of their child), Rikers Island prison (for abuse by a guard), and the state (for improper medical care of a knifed hand). He may have been sitting in a prison, but he still had his rights "because I am a human being," he said loudly. Then he grinned and kept grinning—he might have been imprisoned but he had the smile of a free man. Or maybe he was saying, *Take me or leave me.*

The incident with Judge Bauer began during Frazier's early thirties. Frazier had been in jail in Troy for "a couple of more petty crimes" when he heard stories about how Bauer set extremely high bails, like twenty five thousand dollars for loitering. Other judges might set bail at a few hundred dollars, if anything. Even with a bondsman, most inmates couldn't afford Bauer's sums. If they had that kind of money to spend, they'd hire a lawyer. The upshot was that people who could not pay the high bails often pled guilty just to get out of jail. "If he ever do that to me, he ain't going to be getting away with it," Frazier said he'd promised himself. Shortly thereafter in May 2000, he got his chance. He'd been working at an Ames department store packing boxes when his boss caught him with a stolen ninety-nine-cent pack of Big Red chewing gum. Here court records depart from Frazier's account, noting that he was arrested for stealing not just the gum, but also a Sony PlayStation game and ChapStick lip balm—a total of $27.77—all of which still constituted petty theft. Either way, the police gave him an appearance ticket to come to court.

On his appointed day, Frazier sat among the crowded benches and waited for his name to be called, with hopes of paying a fine and putting the matter behind him. But Bauer was having none of it. He threw Frazier in jail on fifty thousand dollars bail.

Frazier felt he had been trying to do the right thing by coming to court on his own and obeying the law, but he had gotten sucked back into the system, a recurrence that incensed him. "By their constantly pulling us in, that's what makes us bitter and all you want to do is rebel," Frazier said. "And then that person comes out a hardened criminal."

Behind bars, Frazier knew exactly what to do. He typed a page-and-a-half letter with his name in the left-hand corner, along with his residence, the county jail, and addressed it to the New York State Commission on Judicial Conduct, an Albany-based agency that prosecutes abuses by judges. The grammar and spelling aren't perfect, but he made his point:

> Dear Sir/Madam,
>
> I write this informal complaint with the hopes of igniting an investigation into the unprofessional actions rendered by the Judge of Troy Police Court, Henry Bauer.
>
> First and foremost, the hierarchy of the Judicial System have set rules and guidelines to be followed by its constituents when rendering judgment in a court of law.
>
> The subject of bail is the major issue being question at this time: Is it a privilege? Or, is it a law being neglected by the same system set up to help those in need of rehabilitation and teaches us to believe, "In God We Trust," and "Justice for All!" . . .
>
> I make this request for those chosen to vanguard people such as Judges, District attorneys, etc. . . . to compell such a Judge as, Hank Bauer to remain within the realm of proffessionalism and not abuse his authority and/or continue to commit Malicious Acts by imposing excessive bail upon those he finds personal contempt for.

Frazier then mentioned the names of two other inmates with misdemeanor charges and bails set at fifty thousand dollars and cited the pertinent New York statute. He continued:

> I find this and actions similar to this to be a blatant disrespect to Taxpayers as well due to the fact that the problem of overcrowdedness is sustained from instances like this. Also, in light of information given excessive bail is also a violation of Constitutional Rights, Amend. 8.

Please look into this matters and render justice to
those due and penalize those at fault.

Respectfully Submitted,

Eric S. Frazier

#1001312

The letter landed on the desk of Stephen Downs, chief attorney at the Commission on Judicial Conduct in Albany. Downs had worked for the commission for more than two decades, investigating "bad" judges who had shown favoritism, tipped off suspects about arrest warrants, used racial slurs, had sexual relations with employees, or simply abused power, like one judge who ordered a snacks vendor arrested for being the worst coffee maker ever (the judge was removed from the bench).[17]

Downs was shocked by fifty thousand dollars bail for a crime as small as Frazier's. Under the Eighth Amendment, which Frazier had cited correctly, "Excessive bail shall not be required, nor excessive fines imposed."[18] The notion came from the English, who had allowed detainees to be released or "bailed" out by third parties who took on the responsibility for the accused's reappearance in court. The concept of using money to guarantee the defendant's presence became the substance of bail, and thus the English prohibited "excessive" bail in the English Bill of Rights in 1689.[19] Exactly why the American founders intended to adopt the amendment in 1789 in the Bill of Rights rather than put it in the original Constitution is not clear. Overall, they recognized "the nightmare image" of King George III, who had attempted to hold defendants indefinitely without specifying charges.[20]

Bail solves the problem of not imprisoning untried defendants while still ensuring their appearance at trial. According to the seminal U.S. Supreme Court case on bail, *Stack v. Boyle* in 1951, bail can't be set higher than an amount reasonably calculated to ensure the defendant's presence at trial.[21] What makes a bail excessive is determined by a number of factors, including "the nature of circumstances of the offense charged, the weight of the evidence against [the defendant], the financial ability of the defendant to give bail and the character of the defendant."[22] This was the issue in *Stack*, where twelve defendants were indicted with conspiracy to overthrow the government. The trial court set bail at fifty thousand dollars for each defendant solely because others charged with the same crime had previously jumped bail. The U.S. Supreme Court found that "to infer from the fact of indictment alone a need for bail in an unusually high amount is an arbitrary act," which would "inject into our own system the very principles of totalitarianism which Congress was seeking to guard against."[23] In other words, the individual's situation or circumstance must be taken into greater consideration than precedent.[24]

In New York, judges who set bail must look to statutory "factors," which include the defendant's reputation, mental condition, risk of flight, work history, criminal record as an adult or juvenile, and strength of a person's family or ties to the community. The judge may weigh these as he sees fit so long as his decisions aren't "excessive" and "arbitrary," and so long as they are based on the defendant's circumstances. What's more, neither poverty nor the mildness of the crime alone prove that the bail is excessive. Peter Preiser, an Albany Law School professor, is not the first to note: "The lack of nexus between the financial resources of the defendant and the amount of bail reflects a certain absence of logic to the whole procedure . . ."[25]

Once bail is set, defendants can either pay the entire amount to the court and recoup it later when the case is concluded, or hire a bondsman. The bondsman guarantees to the court that the defendant will pay the bond forfeiture if the defendant fails to appear. In some instances, defendants are released without bail on an ROR—Released on Personal (Own) Recognizance—where the judge decides or accepts a recommendation from law enforcement to let the defendant out without any surety.

Bauer should have been well versed in the Eighth Amendment and in particular in the protocols of how to set bail. He had worked as a part-time defense attorney for the indigent for eight years and had been celebrated for his role in *Bauer v. McGreevey*. He also had been to a new judges training program held at the New York State Judicial Institute in White Plains that offers classes on a gamut of topics—from ethics to controlling your courtroom to arraignment to bail.

So why, given what Bauer knew, had he set Frazier's bail at fifty thousand dollars?

According to court papers, the prosecutor had requested that amount because Frazier was a danger to his community. He had violated two previous paroles. Had a record of not appearing in court at the appointed time, and had built up a history that included convictions for robbery, petty larceny, sale of controlled substances, and assault while in a correctional facility. In addition, Frazier could receive up to a year in jail for his current crime, had strong ties to New York City, and therefore was "a substantial flight risk."

As per *Bauer v. McGreevey*, "the only matter of legitimate concern in determining a bail application is whether any bail or the amount fixed is necessary to insure defendant's future court appearances."[26] Stephen Downs felt that however treacherous Frazier's character seemed, he had come to court on his own—a good indication that he wouldn't flee. Moreover, a man who committed petty theft could probably not afford fifty thousand dollars bail. It didn't seem reasonable to Downs, and as a result, he began to get interested in Judge Bauer. Since Frazier's letter had mentioned a couple of similar incidents in Bauer's court, Downs started to dig into his record. Ten years of bail rulings was too much to sort through, so Downs requested a print-out from the jail log. What he found was very odd. The bails seemed outrageous, from ten to fifty thousand dollars for crimes of almost no significance like loitering, trespassing, drinking alcohol from an open container on the street, even bicycling on a sidewalk.

The commission investigators decided to hold an exploratory hearing in its Albany office and invited Judge Bauer to respond to its concerns. "Please bring with you at the time of your appearance court dockets and files pertaining to the cases mentioned," Downs's initial letter said.

When Bauer showed up, he volunteered transcripts of every case that had appeared before him. He had nothing to hide. As soon as the commission's investigators reviewed the transcripts, they'd see he was a good judge and dismiss the charges. He appeared each day, upbeat in his crisp shirts and handsome blazers, ready to aid the investigation in any way, from carrying a prosecutor's heavy file case to sharing information. He had a comforting, caring tone to his voice, and he had a tendency to talk at length. He couldn't resist explaining himself.

In Frazier's case, Bauer said the bail was valid because of his criminal history. In the past, Frazier had appeared in Bauer's court twice—once on a domestic-violence charge and the other on a probation violation—and Bauer had arraigned and released him without setting bail. "I took all sorts of heck, so to speak, from probation because they were frantic and furious when I had released him on a probation matter," Bauer said. Now, it seemed, he was being criticized for setting bail too high. Why were the investigators not interested in his having let Frazier go without bail before? "[I]f I can abuse my discretion on the high end," Bauer said, "I suppose I can do it on the low end too."

Of course, a single instance of high bail was not the issue. The commission was generally more interested in issues of questionable conduct: bias, favoritism, or using judicial influence to benefit others in private. As they investigated Bauer, the commission tried to establish whether his court sanctioned a pattern of errors that denied people rights fundamental to the founding principles of the Constitution. The question came down to how much power a judge should have to do his job.

Before the birth of defense lawyers in the eighteenth century, judges in England played a stronger role than they do today in the United States, examining witnesses and actively representing the claims of litigants. But by the early nineteenth century, a visiting French observer to England reported that the counsel for the defense and the prosecution had taken over to such an extent that the judge "remains almost a stranger to what is going on."[27] In America, judges may have started out equally removed, but today our legal procedures have changed,[28] and so has the role of the judge. Due to an increasing number of procedural safeguards to protect the defendant from unfair conviction, the American jury trial has become "one of the most cumbersome and expensive fact-finding mechanisms that humankind has devised," writes Albert W. Alschuler, a professor at Northwestern University School of Law. Among the features that have made trials increasingly baroque are "our prolonged, insulting, privacy-invading jury selection process; our wrangling over evidentiary issues; our frequently repetitive (as well as pointless and degrading) cross-examination by lawyers; and our formulation and delivery of jury instructions that, all the empirical studies tell us, jurors frequently fail to understand."[29]

These complex procedures have also made justice more expensive. A defendant has to spend more money for legal advice. And trials take longer. A felony trial that averaged an hour at most during the eighteenth century averaged 7.2 days in the late 1960s.[30] Today, the system simply cannot afford everyone a full-blown trial. As Alschuler says, "procedural safeguards backfire when those whom the safeguards are intended to benefit find them too burdensome to use."[31] Particularly in city court, where cases are smaller and defendants generally poor, they rarely benefit from the adversarial system because it tends to work best for those who can afford to exercise their right to a fair trial. According to Thomas Weigend, a German comparative legal scholar, "By affording the whole collection of procedural rights to a small minority of defendants, the system deprives the great majority of [people] rights available to the accused in most civilized countries,"[32] particularly the right to a meaningful day in court.

In this context, the adversarial system has been subjected to limits. Many judges, burdened with a backlog of cases, are not just arbiters but case managers whose job it is to keep things moving. They have become responsible not just for the legality of the proceedings but their speed. This means at times having to pressure defendants to plead guilty so that cases can close and calendars thin out. Judges often so dominate court proceedings now that "judicial case management has brought many American trial courts closer to the 'inquisitorial' or 'continental' model of the civil law," found in Europe and South America, in which "judges actively participate in the proceedings, affirmatively directing the assembling of evidence and moving the case along toward disposition" and "lawyers play a correspondingly lesser role."[33]

Certainly in Judge Bauer's court, legal professionals set the stage for the judge to take over. At times, many of the attorneys seemed semiconscious while matters conveniently moved forward without the vehemence or irritating interruptions that can make a day in court really hard. Things ran smoothly. Court ended early. People went home or moved on to more pressing work. Most notably, in Bauer's court, the right to counsel had become discretionary, even though this right is probably the most important one the Constitution accords a defendant; without counsel, it is nearly impossible to assert all the other rights granted under the due process clause.

LaShawna Bobo, a nurse's assistant, swears she did not have a lawyer at her court proceeding, even though the transcript of it says that she did. "I don't remember talking to him at all," she said. Bobo's charge stemmed from a stroll she took one early spring day. On a street down by the river, she saw two people she knew, Smash and Shaka, sitting on a brownstone stoop. The two had missed an appointment at the hair salon where Bobo worked on weekends. After a short negotiation, she began braiding their hair.

Suddenly a police car stopped. Apparently, a sign against trespassing was posted in the brownstone's window. Similar signs were posted all over downtown Troy, and property owners had requested that the police arrest anyone who wasn't on a preapproved list of residents or visitors.[34] But Bobo figured they could sit on the stoop because Shaka had a relative who lived in the building.

The police handcuffed Bobo and took her to the police station. No record exists of the arraignment but Bauer set her bail at twenty thousand dollars and charged her with trespass. Bobo immediately called her father, who couldn't understand why her bail was so high. "You must have done something else," she remembered him saying.

A lawyer for Bobo might have filed a speedy-trial motion that demanded trial within five days. If the prosecutor wasn't ready by then, she would have had to be released on the sixth day.

Instead, she stayed in jail for eight days. She missed work at the hospital. Her mother moved in with her four children, and her coworkers dropped by the jail to bring socks and underwear.

When she returned to court, Bauer asked whether she lived at the residence, to which she replied, "No." He advised her that if she wanted to plead guilty she would have a fine imposed, be sentenced for the eight days she had already served in jail (more than enough punishment for what she had done), and be released.

Then she pleaded guilty to a trespass violation. Judge Bauer gave her a ninety-five dollar fine and released her. By pleading guilty she had agreed to pay the amount, but in her heart she knew she would never give the court any money. "Screw them," she said to herself as she walked out the door. That night when she got home, she threw a party. Shaka and Smash came, also having pleaded guilty to trespass.

Bobo thought the entire incident an unfortunate, demeaning mistake, which it would have been had the conviction not taken her from her hometown and family. Several months after the incident, when she interviewed with the Troy Housing Authority, the city rejected her as a housing candidate. At that point, Bobo had a fifth child on the way. She couldn't afford a non-subsidized home. Daniel P. Ryan, a senior housing officer who managed the lease enforcement department, said the agency runs a criminal background check on every applicant and errs on the side of refusal because applicants can always appeal the decision at a hearing. "It depends on the circumstances of the crime," he said, adding that even small crimes can be enough to reject an applicant at first.

But Bobo packed up her children and moved to Virginia, which was far away from her family, but less expensive to live. A year later, when she discovered that she could receive city housing in Albany, near Troy, she moved back, but only after shelling out the fine she swore she never would pay.

The commission investigating Bauer found in Bobo's case an instance of "excessive bail." In response, he argued that Bobo had been trespassing on what he "believed to be" a crack house or a building about which he had "some recollection of prior drug activity." "It wasn't somebody wandering through somebody's backyard in search of their dog or cat," he said.[35] As for having a lawyer, Bauer insisted Bobo had a public defender on the day she pleaded guilty. One had indeed been in court that day. "[I]t was a Tuesday, that's an Art Glass public defender day," he said, referring to the lawyer on call. Glass was in fact listed on the transcript, though he found the eight days Bobo had spent in jail "inexplicable." He didn't believe that he would have represented her so poorly. At the same time, he seemed unwilling to blame the judge. Along with nearly everyone else, he liked Bauer. The commission had subpoenaed Glass to testify against Bauer, but, he said, "I tried to minimize it as much as I could. I certainly was uncomfortable. . . . We are still really friendly." Like Glass, so many lawyers seemed to feel an allegiance to Bauer. They had seen each other frequently and managed to make the job of deciding men's and women's fates somewhat agreeable. A reservoir of good will had developed.

Glass and I were sitting in a Troy restaurant one night after he had returned from night court. He looked tired, his large eyeglasses sliding down his nose. In addition to city court on Tuesdays, he worked in two other courts. He seemed to be constantly running around. He had been working for the public defender for more than thirty years and his caseload, he said, had increased threefold. "When I go to court Tuesday there are one hundred and fifty cases on the calendar and I represent 75 percent of them. There is something fundamentally wrong with that." Like so many public defenders, Glass was swamped and simply did not have the time or wherewithal to confront what was happening in Judge Bauer's court.

What's more, Glass's boss, public defender Jerry Frost worked part time as chief, maintaining a private practice as well, which gave him a disincentive to spend time on public defender cases. Also, Frost was a trial lawyer at heart, not an administrator who wanted to develop the office. He wasn't like Terry Everett, who had created a "model" public defender's office in Houston County, Georgia, by keeping a tight watch on the adversarial balance in court. Solving systemic problems just wasn't on his To Do list. "We are not a court monitoring system," he said. "We represent individual defendants." However, the numbers made it impossible to represent individual defendants, so not everyone got equal treatment. Frost took a special interest in the high-profile cases. For them, he was prepared to gear up his office and make considerable personal sacrifices at the expense of other defendants, the city court regulars. He had, for example, put aside his private practice for months to appeal Christine Wilhelm's case, a diagnosed paranoid schizophrenic convicted of the murder of one son and attempted murder of the other. During her four-month trial, he "didn't put three days into [his] practice," he said. He was doing her appeal for free, though his contract with the public defender's office didn't oblige him to do so. To Frost's credit, Christine Wilhelm was eventually placed in a secure psychiatric center.

Frost seemed to have come to a sort of truce with the prosecution with regard to the less "important" cases. As Robert Axelrod writes in *The Evolution of Cooperation*, precedent for this kind of deal making can be found in the way troops in World War I conducted themselves. Soldiers on opposing sides sometimes implicitly agreed to fight only at certain times, adopting a "live-and-let-live system." The troops would attack each other when ordered, to maintain the appearance of being at war. "Such practices of tacit cooperation were quite illegal—but they were also endemic."[36] It behooved both parties to limit conflict in order to survive. Frost's public defender's office bore evidence of Axelrod's theory at work. It was littered with volumes of transcripts and manila folders from the *Wilhelm* case, and little else. Frost would work hard at cases that pushed the bounds of the law or drew public attention; but for the load of ordinary cases, the attorneys seemed to have decided that almost nothing could or should be done. They all had private practices to attend to, and so this "détente" gave them the chance to return to their paying clients, whose cases mattered more to them. As a result, it was easy for Bauer to pass people through.

Frost was, however, an admired attorney. Surely he could see the procedural problems at work in Bauer's court? And yet he defended him. "I think that the Judge Bauer case was a gross injustice," he said. "I think they nitpicked him."

I assumed that Frost must not have known what Judge Bauer had actually done, so I pressed him further. His response? "If you're relying upon the findings of the commission, I think you're off the beam."

Steve Downs could not understand Frost's response, either. "I have never been able to figure [him] out," said Downs. "He has a good reputation . . . But he has the same blind spot as Bauer." And as everyone else.

Again and again, lawyers and court officials claimed that Bauer had gotten "a raw deal." Ken Bruno, who was district attorney during Bauer's tenure, had watched him in court several times and never saw anything wrong. "I thought he bent over backwards to be fair to defendants, protecting their rights." In fact, he added, "the only complaint to the DA's office was that he would allow defendants too much lenience." Before a preliminary hearing "he would allow access to our whole file—all the victims' statements, stuff [the defense] normally wouldn't have access to at the beginning of a case."

Everyone was surprised when the charges came out. Most thought he'd been faulted for technicalities. "I didn't think that his sentences were by any means harsh," said local attorney Alexander Perry. "He gave all kinds of people breaks," he said, recalling instances where Bauer arranged for treatment for defendants with drug problems, or when he spared Perry's client jail time because he was a single parent and Bauer didn't want the children put in foster care; and even once acknowledged that the police were harassing a client. "There were so many of these that it's hard to pick one." If anything, he and his fellow prosecutors had been convinced that Bauer was too lenient. "He actually pressed the DAs to make reasonable deals."

Defense lawyers echoed this endorsement, saying that in spite of what the commission found, Bauer was very much a defendant's judge. "He was fair, consistent, and pretty reasonable," said assistant public defender John Turi.

"It is so funny," said Brian Donohue, a defense attorney who appeared before Bauer hundreds of times. "You take these fifty incidents or whatever you want to call them. That would make you think he was the embodiment of everything you don't like about a judge. The . . . thing is that he is unlike that." Donohue remembered the judge's generosity to a toothless prostitute who kept getting arrested. Donohue would argue repeatedly that she was trying to get better. "Most judges wouldn't even have listened. They wouldn't have had any sympathy at all. She was more or less a harmless person, a poor soul, and that is the way the judge treated her. He would release her on her own recognizance. He felt sorry for her." Bauer hadn't acted consistently badly. "He did not suffer from what they refer to as black-robe disease," said Donohue, adding that many worse judges existed—the type who "yell at a lawyer for being five minutes late," he said.

How to square Donohue's account with what the transcripts proved, that Bauer routinely stripped people of what should have been inalienable rights? One theory holds that when attorneys like Donohue cared about a client—even a toothless prostitute—Bauer was fair, helpful even; but when they were disinterested, Bauer could do as he wished and lawyers either looked the other way or literally didn't observe what went wrong.

One defendant, Adam Russell, in his early twenties, today a program analyst for the Department of Labor in Albany, was home on break from college in August 2000 when he got caught up in a fight at a convenience store. His head was wounded, and he was arrested for loitering after the police had told him to leave the area. In an interview Russell said that he had no idea what his crime was, except that he had been present during a sweep. In court, Bauer didn't read him his rights or ask whether he needed an attorney; then he threw him in jail with a ten thousand dollar bail even though Russell had significant family ties to the community and no arrest record. Russell looked every bit the prep school graduate, with his sandy hair and checkered shirt messily tucked into his khakis. He teared up when talking about the four hours he had spent in jail. "You don't know what's going to happen to you," he said. A friend paid his bail almost immediately and his father hired a private attorney to represent him. The case was dismissed a week later.

Compare this treatment to that of John Casey, a rail thin man who can be found sitting on park benches drinking fifty-cent beers. Casey often described himself as homeless even though he lived with his father, who owned a flooring business. He had a thick file of small crimes and in April 2000 was arrested for trespass, loitering, and an open-container violation, among other charges. Bauer didn't assign him a lawyer and set bail at twenty-five thousand dollars, he said, because of Casey's criminal history. But seven days later, without Casey even in the room, Bauer called the case and pleaded him guilty, declaring, "The matter of People against John Casey was a plea and time served." Casey was discharged from jail without ever having to come to court. In other words, the judge had simply pleaded Casey guilty for him.

Two months later, Casey was arrested for an open-container violation while drinking a beer on a sidewalk and Bauer did it again. This time Bauer set bail for five hundred dollars, which was strange given the high bail he'd set last time, and sent Casey to jail without an attorney. Casey, if he had the money, could have simply given fifty dollars to a bondsman, but he remained in jail for twelve days. On the day he was supposed to have a hearing, Bauer again pleaded him guilty without his knowledge, reading into the record, "The matter of the People against John Casey" was "a plea and time served," and he ordered Casey's release. This time, Casey wandered back into court.

"What happened to my case?" he asked.

"Your case was resolved," Bauer said.

For the commission, Judge Bauer had an explanation for every instance of misconduct it cited. The first time Casey was arrested, city court was under construction, which made transporting prisoners cumbersome. When he and Phil Landry, the assistant public defender on duty, "closed out" other pending cases, they mistakenly did this one as well. (Landry claimed that didn't make sense because he didn't remember doing the paperwork to plead someone guilty without his presence.) In the second instance, Judge Bauer admitted a mistake. He "erroneously" thought that Casey had counsel. "It wasn't because I was trying to screw him," Bauer said.

Casey himself wasn't that offended that his rights had been abrogated. "I knew they had to release me sooner or later," he said. Yet he was the type of person who needed a lawyer most. With no one to speak up for him, he would have submitted to almost anything. There was nothing standing between him and the power of the majority.

Again it was striking that Bauer's behavior went unnoticed. Most likely, incidents like Casey's happened so fast that an outsider sitting in court would not be able to tell what was happening. It was probably easier to notice how well Bauer acted when he actually did what he was supposed to do, because this slows the process down. Tellingly, a court-monitoring group, the Fund for Modern Courts, a nonprofit organization based out of New York City, randomly monitored his courtroom in 1998, years before the charges were brought. Citizen monitors were there over thirty-two different days, sixty-four times, and had only one criticism: sometimes it was difficult to hear him in a crowded courtroom. Judge Bauer "explains clearly and fully all matters and options" to defendants and "goes out of his way to ensure defendants understand their rights and receive adequate defense." Furthermore, his manner pleased the citizen watch group. "He was roundly lauded for his 'courtesy' and 'compassion,'" the report read. "Politeness" and "respect" for defendants characterized Judge Bauer's demeanor. Monitors reported that the judge greeted "every defendant with 'good morning' or 'good afternoon'" and addressed them as Mr. or Miss. "To each defendant who is placed in a program, [the judge] wishes 'good luck.'"[37]

■ ■ ■

The problem for Bauer was that he had come to regard himself as the only one responsible for what transpired in his court: he did not expect defense counsel to show up, or if they did show up, to do anything of value. "[S]ometimes they step up and say a lot of things, other times they don't step up at all or don't say anything either, because it's a done deal and everything has been worked out," he told investigators. He did not seem to mind one way or the other. Still, if you believe Bauer, he never denied people's rights intentionally. He did it because he seemed to imagine that the attorneys were there, as if he had internalized their arguments and heard them in his head, making the lawyers themselves unnecessary.

Chris Cruz, thirty-three years old, appeared before Bauer in April 2000. Six years later, Cruz remembered nearly every word he said in his court hearing, maintaining that he'd been railroaded. "I'm not stupid," he said in an interview in his home in Troy. "I am just short." Cruz stood four foot five. He called himself a dwarf. Sitting on a shiny blue bedspread in a back room of his aunt's apartment on River Street, he explained that he always needed to sit. He suffered from lumbar stenosis, among other ailments, which is a degeneration of the spine that caused him to fall over. To get places he drove a green truck whose pedals he had doctored with blocks of metal so that his legs could reach the gas and brake. Or else he rode a bike.

Cruz had once been a professional wrestler traveling all over the world. Photos of his buff, naked torso were pasted on the wall. But to his disappointment, the job ended when organizers scaled back after protestors argued that the events had turned "little people" into a spectacle. "To me, it was the foremost time in my life," he said.

What followed, he explained, was something he is not nearly as proud of. He sold drugs. "I am not making excuses," he said, but he held up his arms. They were lumpy and didn't stretch above his head. "You can't stack shelves or nothing." Even McDonald's wouldn't hire him. He tried Project HIRE, which provides employment services to individuals on public assistance, like welfare. But no job seemed to work out. "And that's when I went to the dark side. I've been to prison twice."

His run-in with Judge Bauer occurred at the end of one prison term, when he was out on work release for good behavior. Under this program, Cruz would return home for five days to look for a job, then he would go back to prison for two days. This cycle would continue until he found a way to support himself. In April 2000, on one of his days out of prison, the afternoon he was arrested, Cruz had pedaled his bike half a block from home. He stopped to talk with a man he knew, who was sitting on a stoop. Cruz continued on to the corner store to

buy a sandwich, which was where the cops arrested him. The police report alleged that he had lingered "for the purpose of possessing 'crack'
cocaine." Cruz was charged with loitering and a pair of lesser violations: riding a bike on a sidewalk and riding it without a bell.

"Now how can I be loitering if I'm riding on the sidewalk with a
bike?" Cruz asked in court.

Bauer appointed a local lawyer, James Brearton, to defend Cruz.
Brearton and Cruz were willing to go to trial on the charge and turned
down several plea offers from the prosecutor. On five different occasions
Bauer repeated the DA's plea offer to Cruz: ninety days in jail (of which
he would probably serve only sixty), a fine of two hundred dollars, and
forfeiture of one hundred and twenty dollars Cruz had in his pocket.

"But I am not guilty," Cruz insisted to Bauer. Subsequently he
awaited trial in a jail cell for six months on the charges of loitering and
biking on the sidewalk and without a bell.

On his seventh court date, neither Brearton nor the prosecutor
showed up. Cruz stood alone before Judge Bauer, who set a trial date
for two months later.

"Oh, man, why are you delaying this?" Cruz cried from behind the
defendant's table.

"I have the shortest trial calendar in America," Bauer said. "So you
are confusing me with another court if you think I'm delaying you. If
you want to resolve it today, we will. If you want to try it on December
fourteenth, we will. I have no preference . . ."

In another two months, Cruz would have spent more than double
the time in jail than if he took the plea and agreed to time served. "I
already served the max time you can give me on this sentence," Cruz
argued.

"Do you want to go until December fourteen, then?"

"Yeah," Cruz said.

"December fourteenth, it is," Judge Bauer declared.

"No, I got a motion," Cruz interjected, meaning a legal motion.

"Provide it to your attorney and we will see you on the fourteenth.
We are all set."

"Forget it, I will take the plea," Cruz said.

Spending two more months in jail seemed ridiculous, much worse than the punishment of time served and the one-hundred-fifty-dollar fine Bauer had offered. Bauer was, essentially, blackmailing Cruz into taking the plea. Also, Cruz felt he was not going to get a fair trial in front of Bauer. Naturally, he gave up in the end, pleading guilty without his lawyer present. The plea revoked his work release, so although he was freed from city jail, he was sent back to state prison.

Shortly after Cruz pleaded, his attorney, Brearton, arrived in court. A lawyer's absence at the time his client pleads violates the Sixth Amendment, which requires a lawyer to be present at every critical stage of the proceedings. The moment Cruz decided to waive his right to a trial and receive punishment was when he needed help the most. So Brearton filed a notice of appeal. However, as a court-appointed lawyer, he would not have been paid for taking the case to the next stage, so he never followed through with the appeal. "I assume that some other attorney handled that," Brearton said.

Back in prison, Cruz learned from a fellow inmate that his plea violated the Constitution. With the help of a jailhouse lawyer, an inmate who had schooled himself in the law, Cruz said he petitioned the county court on grounds that his Sixth Amendment rights had been violated. A judge vacated the case and sent it back to city court. Three years later, with Bauer no longer in office, the case was finally dismissed.[38]

To explain why he pleaded a man without his lawyer present, Bauer said simply, "I did that in absolute error." He assumed that the public defender, who was present, was Cruz's attorney.[39] A public defender was probably sitting in court, not doing or saying anything, but since this was the norm, Bauer mistook the silent attorney for Cruz's lawyer. Brearton said he "didn't appreciate at all the way [Bauer] handled things in that court," but didn't want to slam him because "he's a very smooth individual," with lots of clout in the community. In addition, he said, "I am a little sensitive to the fact that I don't want to give a guy a black eye. He already suffered through enough." Lawyers identified with Bauer, perhaps more than with their clients, who in most cases had in fact done something wrong, or else lived on the borders of the social order—out-of-towners, drunks, drug dealers, and thieves who were not likely to make a fuss about unfair treatment. Except, of course, Eric Frazier, whose letter to the commission instigated the mess in which Judge Bauer one day found himself.

■ ■ ■

If Bauer was denying defendants their right to counsel, the crucial question is specifically why a judge, whose job is to enforce rights, would fail to do so time and time again. One reason speaks to a broader national problem, which is that "customary American trial procedures" are, as legal scholar Alschuler says, "plainly unworkable in small-stakes cases" in which the Sixth Amendment means little, if anything.[40] In courts nationwide, judges have to manage a conflict between due process and expediency, between the letter of the law and the reality of the cases he presides over. Bauer, himself, seemed aware of the problem, since he often urged me to go sit in other local courts with Gilbert's, a commercial study guide for law students, and check off everything they were doing wrong. "If you see them doing things the way they are supposed to be done," he said, "I will eat my shirt."

Still, in New York state, a judge must let a defendant know of his right to counsel at arraignment or at a first appearance hearing. In most states, within a day or two of arrest, a person is taken before a judge who determines whether "probable cause" exists that a crime has occurred. At this time, a judge advises the defendant of the charges as well as the right to counsel in a much-repeated mantra: "You have the right to counsel; if you can't afford one, one will be appointed for you." Then the judge must take "affirmative steps" toward ensuring that right. A judge may ask, "Can you afford counsel?" as part of a "colloquy" or conversation that potentially leads the judge to inquire into financial circumstances, like how much the defendant makes. In Troy, Judge Bauer had a form he asked people to fill out requesting information about their income and property.[41]

And yet despite the form, defendants in Bauer's court often had to ask for their rights, and even then, Bauer would only consider the request. He rarely took the rote steps in the cases the commission investigated. He almost never said the mantra, engaged in a colloquy, or talked to people about their finances. At the commission hearings he explained that, "Everyone, virtually everyone, says they can't afford an attorney . . ." and asserted that "it doesn't take much employment to retain one's own attorney . . . as opposed to saddling the county with the expense . . ." So he was "inclined to give people an appropriate opportunity to retain their own counsel, if they have an ability to do that." Even if the defendant was obviously destitute or mentally incompetent.

Here is how one transcript with defendant Kenneth Brooks read:

Bauer: "Are you on probation or parole?"

Brooks: "I don't know."

Bauer: "Do you work or go to school?"

Brooks: "I don't know."

Bauer: "Ever been arrested before?"

Brooks: "No."

Judge Bauer had a sheet that said Brooks had been arrested at least twenty-one times, and had been convicted several times on charges of criminal trespass, resisting arrest, and criminal mischief (intentional damage to property). Brooks had also violated his parole and orders by judges to show up in court on previous occasions.

Bauer then explained the new charges to Brooks. In the wee hours of the night before, Brooks had been riding a bicycle in a popular part of town where college students eat pizza and drink beer—Fourth and River, to be exact. A cop had stopped him. Brooks's twenty-one-speed bike, the cop said, didn't have a bell. The bike needed a "warning signal" as well as a light. In addition, Brooks had been riding it on the sidewalk—all state and local law violations.

In neighborhoods across Troy, little kids rode their bell-less bikes without notice. But Brooks was not your average cyclist. At the top of his arrest sheet was the word *homeless*. His social security number was *unknown*. An asterisk at the bottom of the arrest sheet drew attention to the words, *Subject is unkempt in appearance. Body odor is offensive.*

Bauer: "Are you getting a lawyer?"

Brooks: "I don't know, I never had one before."

Bauer: "How old are you, please?"

Brooks: "I don't know how old I am."

He was, in fact, twenty-eight.

At this point, Bauer might have advised Brooks of his rights (to adjourn the case so he could obtain a lawyer, call a friend or a relative to get one, or, most important, to have a lawyer appointed if he couldn't afford one). But Bauer moved on:

"I will set bail at twenty-five thousand dollars. I will adjourn the case until next Friday and somehow we will figure out how old you are."

To make bail, Brooks would have had to raise twenty-five thousand dollars in cash or give twenty-five hundred to a bondsman. Unsurprisingly, he went to jail. Can someone really go to jail for not having a bicycle bell? States and localities have all sorts of arcane laws that most citizens would not support if ever enforced—sex outside of marriage is a crime in some states, for example. But sometimes those laws do get implemented. In New York, a first bike violation allows for not more than fifteen days of jail or a fine of $150. Brooks had three violations (riding on sidewalk, no bell, no light) so he faced forty-five days and a $450 fine.[42]

After a week in jail, Brooks appeared back before the judge, alone. This time, Brooks gave better answers.

"Are you on probation or parole?" Judge Bauer asked.

"Yeah," he said.

"Excuse me?"

"Yeah," Brooks said.

"Which of the two?"

"Probation."

"Three or five years?"

"I don't know. I think it's three."

Bauer then explained that if Brooks pleaded guilty he could walk out with a fine of $180. He also had to stay off Fourth Street as part of an "order of protection" against the street. Orders of protection are usually used against violent people (ordering a wife beater to stay away from his victim, for example), but Bauer made a practice of banishing people from Fourth Street. When a lawyer working with the American Civil Liberties Union challenged Bauer on whether "exile" was a valid form of punishment, Bauer wrote that "hundreds" of cases stem from the area: "The court is also aware, for evidence of it is seen in this court almost daily, of efforts by the police and the city to clean up the area, for the benefit of merchants who work there and residents who live there. Those people are the victims of the defendants' crimes. Those citizens are entitled to quality of life." Bauer's attitude kept with the broken-window theory of crime. And even small crimes could be infuriating. Who wanted to come home to an entrance where someone had urinated? What about the windshield that got smashed? Kenneth Brooks was contributing to the problem.

The judge asked Brooks whether in exchange for a guilty plea, the fine and street restriction amounted to an acceptable resolution.

"Acceptable," Brooks said.

"Excuse me?" Bauer said. "How do you plead to the charges?"

"Guilty."

Bauer gave Brooks a fine slip and released him. "Thank you, sir," Bauer said, and that was that.

And yet the proceedings could not have been more inappropriate. Brooks pleaded guilty without a lawyer. Had he wanted to proceed alone in court he would have needed to "knowingly and intelligently" waive his right to a lawyer and make an unequivocal request to do so. Before a judge permits anyone to do this he has to hold a hearing to be sure that the defendant understands the seriousness of the charges and the consequences of a conviction, none of which occurred here.[43]

Moreover, since Bauer set a very high bail and let Brooks know that he would be released if he entered a guilty plea, Bauer arguably coerced the plea. In legal cases, coercion is often hard to define; it can be quite subtle. A good plea occurs, as the saying goes, "in a shadow of trial." This means that a defendant and his lawyer assess the strengths or weaknesses of the government's case, anticipate an outcome, and choose to take a plea that is to everyone's advantage. The bargain reflects the guilty outcome that would have occurred anyway but allows for some "fixed discount" by not making the state expend time and money on a full trial.[44] Ideally, before agreeing to a plea, a defense attorney provides the same modicum of adversarial testing that occurs in a trial. Robert Kagan writes in his book *Adversarial Legalism* that "many guilty pleas *do* reflect the extraordinary legal complexity and stressfulness of adversary jury trials, which cast fear into the heart of the unpracticed defense lawyer and vastly increase the difficulty of a prosecutor's and trial judge's job."[45]

In city court, however, no one really operated under the "shadow" or threat of trial since the threat itself was negligible. From 2000 to 2002, Bauer conducted only four trials, all of which were nonjury, the commission found. "Everybody knows a trial would never happen in city court," said Alexander Perry, an attorney who practiced there as both an assistant public defender and a prosecutor over the course of eight years. "Cases always pled out." The bottom line was that trials were too expensive, too exhausting, and too complicated. (In Troy, jury trials are only available for misdemeanors and not petty offenses like violations and traffic infractions, though a defendant could always ask for a trial conducted by a judge for both.)

If cases were being pleaded out in Troy, it was in the shadow of jail time and bails that were unaffordable. Put simply, until the accused pleads, he can be detained if bail is not met. In his award-winning book, *The Process Is the Punishment: Handling Cases in a Lower Criminal Court*, Malcolm Feeley, professor of law at the University of California-Berkeley, found that in a lower criminal court in New Haven, Connecticut, defendants suffered merely by being engaged with the system, and that challenging a charge often cost more than submitting and pleading guilty:

> For every defendant sentenced to a jail term of any length, there are likely to be several others who were released from jail only after and because they pleaded guilty. For each dollar paid out in fines, a defendant is likely to have spent four or five dollars for a bondsman

and an attorney. For each dollar they lose in fines, working defendants likely lose several more from docked wages. For every defendant who has lost his job because of a conviction, there are probably five more who have lost their jobs as a result of simply having missed work in order to appear in court . . . When we view criminal sanctioning from this broader, functional perspective, the locus of court-imposed sanctioning shifts dramatically away from adjudication, plea bargaining, and sentencing to the earlier pretrial stages. In essence, the process itself is the punishment.[46]

It sounds amiss, but a defendant waiting to be punished might have a far harsher experience than the punishment itself, and this is legal. Thus the incentive to plead guilty to a small crime is huge.

A judge who forces a plea by threatening to detain someone longer than what the actual punishment for a crime entails flexes a great deal of power, which raises questions of fairness. Generally, the U.S. Supreme Court's rulings have been supportive of plea bargaining, maintaining that a guilty plea is not compelled and invalid when "motivated by the defendant's desire to accept the certainty or probability of a lesser penalty rather than face a wider range of possibilities extending from acquittal to conviction and a higher penalty authorized by law for the crime charges."[47] That said, a plea has to have certain protections so that whether coercion is apparent or not, a plea becomes involuntary if counsel has been denied.

Had Brooks not pleaded guilty in his second appearance before Judge Bauer, he might have gone back to jail for who knows how long. He had already spent seven days there. He had no lawyer and could not afford bail. Brooks had little choice but to plead guilty.

Brooks's inability to answer questions about himself should have also raised the flag of mental illness. In the case of mental illness, arrest is going to mean nothing to a homeless man traversing the city streets. He's just going to get rearrested.

Brooks did in fact get rearrested, for spending a night in a motel with no money to pay for it. This time, an Albany court judge ordered a mental-health evaluation and Brooks was diagnosed as schizophrenic. A network of professionals was deployed to help him find housing and handle his own money. Since then, Brooks has had no brushes with the law, according to his social worker.

At the commission hearings, Bauer said it hadn't occurred to him that Brooks might be mentally ill, even after re-reading the transcript.

"I didn't have any indication that he was not competent," Bauer said.

"I see. The transcript didn't indicate that . . . ?" Downs asked.

"No, it did not."

Investigator Downs didn't get it. How could Bauer, who by all appearances seemed sympathetic to defendants, assign high bail and no lawyer to a homeless, schizophrenic man?

"I don't know that he was homeless," Bauer said. Sometimes, he claimed, with a wanted person, "the last thing they want to give anybody—whether it be a court or the police department—is an address because . . . then there is a way to track these people."

But what of Brooks's fundamental rights?

"He had a right to counsel, didn't he?" Downs asked.

"Yes. Well, I don't know that, based on his answers."

"You don't know?" Downs asked incredulously.

Bauer turned the question on his inquisitor: "Well, on what basis would he have a right to an assigned counsel?"

"If he couldn't afford a lawyer," Downs responded.

"Based on what?"

"I'm sorry, what?" Downs replied, not understanding where Bauer could possibly be going.

"On what do you base that he couldn't afford a lawyer?"

"On the fact that he was *homeless*," Downs replied.

"That was on the arrest report," Bauer countered. "He didn't know if he worked or went to school. He could have—we just don't know that . . . He could have had a job that paid him two hundred thousand dollars a year."

It defied reason that a homeless man, who the police said reeked of body odor, could have had that kind of job. "I see," Downs said.

"And it was his choice to say that he didn't know," Bauer continued. "So I didn't know if he was indigent or not and, based on my inquiry, he wasn't that helpful."

Summing up, Downs asked Bauer: "Does it trouble you or are you concerned about the fact that [Brooks] spent half the maximum possible time in jail, on bail, without counsel, without being advised of his right to counsel, and then was given an opportunity to plead guilty? Just looking at that picture, does that trouble you at all?"

"I don't know that I am troubled or not troubled by it," Judge Bauer said.

Downs couldn't understand how a judge could fail to see any problems with this. He asked again: "You don't see anything unjust here?"

"No. I mean, in looking at what is unjust or not, again, risk of flight, danger to the community. . . ."

For Judge Bauer, what seemed wrong on principle was fair in context. When it comes to setting high bail, a judge has to take into account the defendant's criminal history and responses to court appearances. Bauer noted that Brooks had a rap sheet filled with petty larcenies, criminal mischief, and resisting arrest charges, as well as twenty-two arrests. Additionally, Bauer argued, Brooks would not answer any questions. If, for example, Bauer had known that he had ties to the community he could have released Brooks. "He didn't know if he worked or went to school, so it was hard to get any sense of whether he was going to show up or not. . . ."

With regard to the arraignment, if Bauer had committed a wrong, he had done no harm, he felt. Omitting the mantra was "a matter of efficiency or perhaps sloppiness." *A matter of efficiency* is the key phrase here: Bauer contended that defendants benefited from his style. He might break the rules with high bails, no lawyers, and no colloquy, but what he doled out were reasonable fines and no jail terms. If he followed the rules, bad things might happen. Defendants would incriminate themselves if given the chance, "He started the fight!" and so on. Better for them to avoid any conversation that might prompt self-incrimination. This was Judge Bauer's reasoning.

What's more, at times defendants didn't really want their rights, anyway, he claimed. "'I'm not going to get [an attorney],'" he said, imitating them. "'I don't want one assigned. I'm guilty.'" As for the mantra, judges tended to jumble it all together, in the rote, day-to-day manner of having to repeat it every few minutes: *youhavetherighttoanattorneyandonewillbeprovidedforyou*. Bauer felt most defendants didn't really understand what he was saying when he advised them of their rights. "If I had used the clear language in and of itself, does it have much value? I suggest it does not." Furthermore, he argued, many of the defendants were repeat offenders who knew or who should have known what their rights were already.

Besides, what would a defendant rather have? The clunky, drawn-out, judicially correct procedure or the trouble-free best outcome? As Bauer saw it, a trial that delivered a severe sentence was the real danger, not his lenient sentences. Responding to the claim that he had coerced defendants, Bauer compared his brand of coercion to what he witnessed when he worked in the public defenders' office. "Coercion was always a part of the process," he maintained. "'If you exercise your right to a trial, if you lose, we're going to max you out.' That's coercion." His version, which was "Plead today and go home," didn't seem all that coercive in comparison. In fact, it was the "the opposite of coercion," he said.

Nonetheless, the commission investigators found that Bauer had violated Brooks's right to counsel and coerced a guilty plea. Moreover, they were deeply troubled by what they had heard from the judge, especially since his behavior could not have been maintained without some help. As Downs noted, Bauer's "misconduct was so huge" and had gone on for "so long that it could have only been sustained if the entire community was behind it." After the initial investigation, Downs delved into the transcripts, which many city courts don't even keep. These turned out to be a prosecutorial goldmine. Subsequently on October 4, 2002, the commission served Bauer with formal written charges.

▪ ▪ ▪

Even the commission, however, did not have the time or resources to delve into every transcript. Instead, it looked for red flags, like excessive bail or no lawyer assigned. Beyond reading the proceedings in every one of Bauer's cases, there is no way to reconstruct a full pattern of what happened. This difficulty is one reason why Bauer's peers could watch court and, if they saw something wrong, deny that it amounted to substantial injustice. Assistant public defender Phil Landry remembered watching the accused pleading guilty without lawyers. He didn't object because he thought other people in the office had already done so—although one would think that high bails and use of release from jail to coerce guilty pleas would have been the talk of the staff. He also couldn't be sure that the defendant was being harmed. Most were getting out of jail. "I don't know what the original charge was, I don't know if he's getting a break or not," he said.

The idea of "getting a break" is the essence of what is known as "substantive justice," and what Bauer obliquely referred to when defending himself—that the accused gets what is fair in the end, even if the process accorded him is not exactly what is required. In state felony courts as well as lower courts like Troy's, the doling out of substantive justice is rampant. As Malcolm Feeley puts it: "The process takes for granted that the defendant was involved in the trouble and immediately tries to determine the magnitude of the trouble and the nature of his responsibility as a prerequisite for disposing of the case."[48] Often, as Feeley notes and Bauer claimed, the outcome works in a defendant's favor. For instance, in a domestic-violence case the prosecutor may decide that one night in the slammer is enough for a man who assaulted his wife since she refuses to testify and clearly wants to reconcile.[49] Perhaps the accused is required to see a social worker and the system leaves it at that. Investigating the facts, applying the law, and enforcing punishment would in this case do more damage than good. That's the idea of substantive justice.

In Bauer's situation, the question is whether asserting a right to counsel and to a trial would have helped defendants in his court.

Would these gestures have protected the individual or made things worse for him? When people in the system believe the latter, there is little incentive to test rights in lower courts. According to Feeley, it is possible that asserting rights may produce more rules that give "an *appearance* of increasingly principled decision making while in fact doing little more than providing the props and lies for a ritualistic drama devoid of meaningful content."[50] In other words, to enforce rights might dress up and perhaps obscure a simple process of thumping down on those who "deserve" it, while giving a break to those who don't. "[T]o one familiar with the court, there is a logic—even if it is unwritten and unarticulated—to the process," Feeley writes.[51]

In Bauer's and other lower courts, plea bargaining is the main vehicle for facilitating substantive justice. Plea bargaining is justified on grounds of expediency. It also tends to make judges, prosecutors, and defense attorneys look good. Unlike a trial, pleas, by and large, cannot be appealed: the defendant has in effect bargained away his rights. Pleas also keep the conviction rates high because a prosecutor doesn't run the risk of losing in a trial. And it keeps a defense attorney's workload more manageable.

Professor Alschuler has made a comprehensive study of the problem of plea bargaining and coercion. "Once you get used to it," he said, "you don't even notice the injustice." The cost is a metamorphosis of the system, in which power comes to reside in the one person who has the authority to approve a plea. "I think you ought to use the word *fascism*," he said when asked about the conditions in American courts. "Most people don't understand what rights and procedures are for. They look to the bottom line: did we do rough justice in most cases?" They don't realize that "the answer is usually going to be yes. If you asked about justice in the former Soviet Union or the People's Republic of China or Saddam Hussein's Iraq the answer would also be *yes*. If you make me a czar and you say I can do whatever I want . . . well, I am going to do rough justice in most cases. But that is intolerable." According to Alschuler, one solution is to get rid of plea bargaining altogether. In its place, the system should reduce the "over-proceduralization" of full-blown jury trials with simpler trials which may, for example, be conducted by a judge alone.[52]

Another leading scholar, John H. Langbein, a professor at Yale Law School, has decried plea bargaining as a form of a tortured, forced confession.[53] In an interview, Langbein argued that adversarial criminal procedure is unworkable as a system of mass justice. In practice it comes down to "coercion," he said. "And it is truth disserving."

Langbein blames the U.S. Supreme Court. In what he described as several "sad plea bargaining opinions of the 1970s," the court sanctioned the sacrifice of fundamental values.[54] For example, *North Carolina v. Alford* holds that it is constitutionally permissible to accept a guilty plea from a defendant even if he or she claims to be innocent, so long as there is a "strong factual basis for the plea." The defendant for that case, Henry C. Alford, had been indicted for first degree murder, which carried the death penalty. Strong evidence of guilt existed and no support for the claim of innocence. So Alford's attorney recommended that he accept a guilty plea offer that didn't carry a death sentence. After the prosecution presented a summary of the state's case, Alford took the stand and gave his version of events; he testified that, "I ain't shot no man," but was pleading guilty "because they said if I didn't they would gas me for it. . . ." Normally a defendant when asked "Are you in fact guilty?" must answer "yes" or "no." But in what is called an "Alford plea," the judge may ask, "Do you now consider it to be in your best interest to plead guilty?" and "Do you understand that upon your Alford plea you will be treated as being guilty whether or not you admit that you are in fact guilty?" Then, the defendant, saying he is not really guilty, can plead guilty.

What is good about an Alford plea is that an innocent person doesn't have to lie. Someone can plead guilty while still maintaining that he is innocent, in the process avoiding the death penalty and saving his life. But a defendant might plead guilty for the sake of expedience or to prevent a larger sentence at trial, when he has waived his rights and has not been able to tell his side of the story. The reason why this happens is that the system can't handle too many trials. As the U.S. Supreme Court noted in 1971 in *Santobello v. New York*: "[I]f every criminal charge were subjected to a full-scale trial, the States and the Federal Government would need to multiply by many times the number of judges and court facilities."[56] Bauer's rationales and those of his community were entirely in keeping with those of the nation's highest court.

■ ■ ■

No one believed in Bauer's innocence more than his own lawyer, Robert P. Roche. When he speaks of Bauer, Roche's eyes water and his voice shakes. "I think he is one of the finest men God ever put robes on," he said. Having hired Roche to defend him, Bauer's confidence in his position was such that he decided, in the meantime, to tell no one about the investigation, not even his wife.

Eventually though, a legal newspaper went public with the investigation, putting an end to Laura Bauer's ignorance. She worked as a part-time county legislator. She "is one of the most beloved politicians," said Jack Casey, head of Troy's Republican party.

One afternoon in her office, a colleague said, "I heard about the investigation."

"What investigation?"

After that, she ran home. How could Hank not have told her that he was being investigated for misconduct? Or that he had hired a pricey lawyer from Albany?

Why wouldn't he have told his wife?

Bauer explained that he was waiting to find out whether he would be officially charged. He hoped he could take care of it and explain later. But from then on, his wife, like Roche, never left his side.

Not that it helped his case. At the hearings, Bauer's explanations were discursive and inadequate, probably because he was certain he'd be cleared of all wrongdoing. About the allegations, he said to his lawyer, "Where is the serious stuff?"

When the commission served Bauer its formal complaint, alleging fifty-one charges of judicial misconduct (which included multiple violations in each charge), Roche did not know "whether to laugh or to cry . . . it was so absurd."

Bauer felt betrayed. The commission must not have been listening. "Why did we put all this information on the table if it doesn't make a difference?" he said. Given the outcome, Roche thought that the next stage of the proceedings, the formal hearing, should be open to the public. "Knowing the type of person you are, you don't want this done behind closed doors," Roche told his client.

"Arrange it," Bauer said.

In the past thirty years, only about ten judges had ever requested an open hearing.[57] The press had a field day. With such unusual access to the proceedings, they gave Bauer's case loads of attention and praised him for opening up a closed process. "Whatever the outcome of the charges against Troy City Court Judge Henry Bauer, he deserved credit for wanting to face his accusers in public," began an *Albany Times Union* editorial.[58]

At the formal hearings in Albany, in front of the press, Bauer, via Roche, tried to expose the commission for what he called, in his opening statement, a "woeful lack of understanding" of Bauer's sense of justice. Roche also condemned the commission for the "vagueness, the shallowness, and the misunderstanding of these charges," which tainted a scrupulous judge. Roche intended to show that in almost each and every instance, Judge Bauer had obeyed the law. "I know you, Your Honor, will be impressed with the fact that this man crossed all his Ts," Roche said to Referee Richard D. Simons, selected by the commission to conduct the hearing and report on it.

Roche accused the commission of having been corrupted by civil-rights activists. The first culprit, he charged, was Rosalind Becton, a commission investigator who had been "incomplete and incompetent" in her work, according to the brief. Becton, an African-American woman, had received her training in advocacy organizations working as an investigator for Prisoners' Legal Services and the New York City Commission on Human Rights. She had "an 'us–them' background," the brief charged, which made her stop short in her investigation of Bauer. For example, she had never bothered to corroborate testimony from defendants who claimed they had been arraigned in their cells rather than in open court. Becton conceded the point, and these particular charges were eventually dropped.

Bauer's brief also noted a connection between Steve Downs and the ACLU. Since beginning the investigation, Downs had become a celebrity of sorts for an entirely unrelated episode. He had been wearing a T-shirt with peace and antiwar slogans in a shopping mall in Guilderland, New York, and was asked to leave. He refused and was arrested for trespassing.[59] Charges were dropped but the story won international attention, while the New York Civil Liberties Union, a chapter of the ACLU, unveiled an ad that said, "Welcome to the mall. You have the right to remain silent."[60] Meanwhile, in relation to Bauer, a lawyer from the ACLU had investigated the judge's banishment practices in which he had issued orders of protection for Fourth Street in Troy. Roche tried to argue that a conflict of interest was at work.

The third part of Bauer and Roche's strategy involved a series of witnesses who attested to the judge's character and reputation. One by one, the legal community's most powerful testified on his behalf. "Judge Bauer has an excellent reputation as Troy city court judge," said Jerry Frost, the public defender, who, as an advocate for the rights of defendants, should have been an unlikely ally. He had heard no complaints from his staff and knew of no incidents in which his assistants had found problems with bails and appealed them. Of course not: Bauer pushed people through the system and made everyone's job a little bit easier. Why would anyone complain?

Administrative judge Thomas Keegan had also never had a complaint from an inmate, former inmate, judge, or citizen. He said Bauer "was an energetic judge, innovative, trying new programs relating to alcohol, domestic violence, drugs, that sort of thing. Generally, he was well received." Judge Patrick McGrath, a county court judge who used to work in city court, added that he reviewed maybe a dozen appeals over eight years. "Other than an application to reduce bail, I have heard no complaint," he said.

Perhaps the most surprising testimony came from Ray Kelly, a well-known defense attorney and longtime advocate for the poor in

Albany. Kelly knew Judge Bauer from appearing in his court "fifteen to twenty times," he estimated. "From the defense bar and the community of the defense bar . . . I've never heard anybody say anything bad about Judge Bauer . . . he is known as a man of integrity, a man of honesty." Kelly said that Bauer was one of the few on the bench who actually deserved the designation, *Your Honor*.

In December 2003, Referee Richard D. Simons, selected by the commission to conduct the hearing and report on it, found forty-nine of the original fifty-one charges against Bauer had been proved: the judge had failed to inform people of their rights, given excessive bails, and coerced guilty pleas.

Now that a referee had made its findings, all the commission had to do was decide whether to admonish, censure, or remove Bauer. For this, the full eleven members of the commission meet for a final hearing, which was public in this case, at the Association of the Bar of the City of New York. Each side had to give a single fifteen-minute argument as to what the punishment should be. The commission placed a premium on remorse and willingness to reform, yet Bauer and his lawyer still maintained his innocence on nearly all counts. In fact, Bauer remained surprisingly upbeat and relaxed.

At one point during the hearing, Raoul Felder, a prominent New York City divorce lawyer and member of the commission, asked the judge, ". . . have you changed your practices regarding bail, the amount of bail?"

"I still consider the same factors," Bauer said.

"But, I mean, are you still holding people on twenty-five-thousand and fifty-thousand-dollar bail for these kind of relatively minor things?"

"If—depending on the extenuating circumstances, yes."

Bauer did offer that he now made a point of providing the accused with a public defender "whether [defendants] want it or not," implying that there might be something onerous or ridiculous about doing so.

He also admitted wrongdoing in a couple of cases and acknowledged that he had sometimes failed to give attention to the right to counsel. In a final five-page statement, he pointed out that he had started the first drug court and domestic-violence court in Troy. "Courts are created by good judges," he said. "Can a person be both a good judge and a bad judge at the same time? I respectfully suggest that one cannot. I am a good and competent judge. I am not a judge who ought to be removed." Second, Bauer claimed that he had found at least eleven factual errors in the charges, which showed that anybody could make silly mistakes under pressure. "It would be absurd for me to suggest to this commission that these errors and omissions are some type of proof that my adversaries are incompetent or evil," he wrote. "They are not. Are they busy or perhaps overworked? Yes. Are they less than perfect? Who isn't?! Are they doing the best that they can and are they well intentioned? I, for one, believe that they are."

Last, he pointed to one case that he had dismissed, ordering the prosecutor to assist the defendant. He "did not have any specific legal authority to issue such a directive to the District Attorney, [but] it was the right thing to do and it was done," he said, justifying unorthodox involvement. "In conclusion, the late great United States Supreme Court justice Louis Brandeis once said, 'When making your case, don't appear to be fanatical.' I like the quote and I have always attempted to heed his advice. As you might imagine, when one is arguing his or her own case, it is more difficult and hence more important to adhere to this rule. My hope is that I have done so. Finally, I respectfully suggest that Justice Brandeis's advice should apply to the entirety of the matter. Thank you."

The commission was unmoved. In its final decision in March 2004, it found that "over a two-year period, respondent engaged in a pattern of serious misconduct that repeatedly deprived defendants of their liberty without according them fundamental rights." Still, the commission dismissed twelve of the original fifty-one charges and members seemed to disagree with each other on most of the remaining thirty-nine. For thirty-seven charges, individual members had differing, nonunanimous votes. "Nothing in this record suggests that he was 'vindictive, biased, abusive, or venal,'" wrote Karen K. Peters, a New

York supreme court judge in the Third Department, which covers Troy. She was concurring in part and dissenting in part.[61]

Three of the eleven members dissented entirely and argued for censure instead of removal. One dissenter, Lawrence S. Goldman, chair of the commission, was persuaded by Bauer's legal and factual reasons for his bail decisions. While he found that Bauer had offered defendants a "Hobson's choice"—plead guilty and get released or refuse to plead and stay in jail—he didn't find evidence that Bauer had the "intent" to coerce guilty pleas. He also dissented in those cases where Bauer asserted he had "made some effort" to assign lawyers as well as those where defendants said they didn't want counsel. Last, he disagreed with the majority's view that Bauer's failure to acknowledge his conduct should be a factor in determining sanction. A judge who believed he had acted correctly shouldn't be penalized for defending himself. "The commission should be careful not to send a message that discourages judges from offering a vigorous defense of their actions," Goldman wrote.

But Goldman was in the minority, since the determining factor of the commission's decision appeared to be Judge Bauer's failure to recognize the inappropriateness of his actions or attitudes.[62] His lack of self-indictment compounded the impropriety and concluded his downfall. The commission found:

> At no stage of this proceeding did respondent give any persuasive indication that he recognized the impropriety of his conduct. Even at the oral argument, after the referee had sustained most of the charges, respondent adhered to his position that on undisputed facts (i.e., his failure to advise defendants of their right to counsel and assigned counsel and his responsibility to effectuate the right to counsel), his conduct was appropriate. In responding to the Commission's questions, he had the opportunity to demonstrate that he understood the importance of strict adherence to the statutory mandates and recognized

that his procedures were inadequate, but he appeared unwilling or unable to do so. The conclusion is inescapable
that respondent's future retention on the bench would
continue to place the rights of defendants in serious jeopardy. Accordingly, we conclude that the appropriate disposition is removal from office.[63]

Roche appealed the decision to the state's highest court, the court
of appeals, but failed to get a reversal. Although Roche and his client
now appeared far more contrite, the judges upheld Bauer's removal
from the bench. They faulted him for not advising defendants of their
rights and for "concealing from them that the statute requires the court
to assign counsel when warranted . . ." The court then found that Bauer
had punished people by setting exorbitant bail, which, "where the offense does not carry a jail sentence, demonstrates a callousness both to
the law and to the rights of criminal defendants." Moreover, the court
found that when coupled with a failure to advise people of their right
to a lawyer, Bauer's "imposition of punitive bail all but guaranteed that
defendants would be coerced into pleading guilty: it was the only way
to get out of jail." The court also noted that Bauer's defense, which
asked the court to examine the commission members' credentials, was
off base. For all the harsh language of the majority opinion, however,
the decision was a close one. Only four judges voted to affirm his removal, while three dissented. "If I had gotten one more of those four I
would have won," Roche said angrily.[64]

Bauer had been punished as severely as any judge could, yet he
continued to believe that he had done nothing to warrant his dismissal.
"I'm not above saying I am sorry," he said. "But I thought a lot of things
had context." His mistakes were "sloppiness." "I know this sounds defensive," he said, but the commission, he believed, didn't understand
"the realities of the local court."

The city's leaders agreed. "Judge Bauer did his job well and only
had the interests of the people of this great city on mind," Troy Mayor
Harry Tutunjian told the local paper. "Judge Bauer was not the only

one who lost today. The people of Troy did as well."[65] County Legislator Bob Mirch told the *Troy Record* that Hank Bauer "is a good judge, a good person, a good family man and he did what was best for our city by being tough on the New York City drug dealers and because of that, today he paid the price."[66]

Messages flooded the newspaper's "sound-off" column. "I think the citizens of Troy should back Judge Bauer completely," one said. "He's trying to straighten out the streets, he's trying to get rid of crime. It's the lowlifes that should be put in jail or lose their jobs, if they have jobs."[67] This point essentially rephrased what "substantive justice" is all about: in the basement of the criminal court system, who cares what rights are denied the lower class so long as these people are punished?

Another writer, Joyce McAlister, said she used to work for the corporation counsel for Troy and appeared before Bauer on several issues. "I found him to be an exemplary judge, fair, courteous, and respectful of the rights of all who appeared before him. I sincerely hope that he is not permanently removed from the bench."[68]

Even one defendant, Frank Grasso, who admitted Judge Bauer had given him five thousand dollars bail "for taking three packages of cigarettes from Price Chopper Hoosick Street store," wrote Bauer a letter of support saying, "Although I do agree that your way of running your court is a little <u>unorthodox</u>, you are a just and fair man."[69]

Only a few felt otherwise, but the consensus, as the *Troy Record* wrote in a hedging editorial, was that "Despite Conduct, Judge Bauer Still a Troy Champion." After calling him "one of the finest judges the city of Troy has had on the bench of City Court," the paper illogically concluded that "we must live by rules, and judges are held to the highest standard. We lament the loss of such a popular champion, but understand why he had to go."[70]

Bauer's supporters had a myriad of explanations for the outcome of the investigation, from the personal to the political. Attorney Alex Perry echoed a widely held view that Bauer's ouster became inevitable once he challenged the commission by requesting open hearings. "By making it public, he put a chip on their shoulders," he said.

To Roche, the commission's Rules Governing Judicial Conduct gave too much discretion to the referees, with their vague guidelines, and thus too much power to arbitrarily interfere. "A judge has to uphold the integrity and independence of the judiciary," the rules state, which is so vague that the commission could file almost any alleged violation under it, Roche complained.[71] His point speaks to the commission's main function, which is to discipline judges to ensure compliance with established standards of ethical judicial behavior and maintain public confidence in the judiciary. All fifty states have adopted a commission to meet goals such as these—to review not errors of law but errors of ethics, though the difference is often hard to establish.

In Bauer's case, Roche felt like the commission had misrepresented the facts and concocted ethical violations. Since none of the alleged improper bail decisions had been appealed by lawyers in the community, no legal problem seemed evident. As for not assigning lawyers, Bauer had actually reached out to defendants and addressed them as individuals whereas the commission wanted him to use a meaningless formula. Said Roche: "In one sentence I can sum up my angst with the commission. We have once again focused on form over substance because it is more important that a mantra protects idiots rather than the judge engage in a dialog with a frightened defendant." Roche also believed that the investigators were out to get Bauer because he didn't share their pristine view of bail law, which, according to papers that he filed, "is consistent with the policy that the American Civil Liberties Union has publicly taken on bail since 1996." Bauer "became the victim of some people who quite simply didn't know what the hell they were doing," Roche said.

Attorney Ray Kelly broadened his defense of Bauer, saying "The overall problem was the lack of commitment to the criminal justice system by the state of New York." It was a standard defense of injustice in the lower courts: the system is ill-equipped. "There aren't courthouses with sufficient judges and defense counsel to man the justice system so that it operates and it is attuned to handling the daily grinds," he said. The system took everyone down with it. "We are all human beings. The system is supposed to be a system of checks and balances, and when you leave someone out there alone you're asking a person to be perfect. And nobody is perfect. Somebody is going to lose their cool and do something that is out of character."

■ ■ ■

Given the upswell of support for Bauer and the chaos that presides in city courts all over the country, I began to think that perhaps the commission's decision really was harsh. Maybe Bauer had been hung out to dry. Maybe he truly was the fall guy for a dysfunctional system. Maybe the citizens of Troy had gained more than they had lost from Judge Bauer, and it was okay to ignore a few rules so long as the job got done.

I decided to look at one more transcript, this one from a 1999 trial that never made it into the commission's hands. It recorded Bauer arraigning a seventeen-year-old girl in eleventh grade named Dena Wagar. She was charged with harassing another girl at Troy High School—"an enemy," the girl told the court, whom she despised because of "something that happened in sixth grade."

If convicted, Wagar faced fifteen days in jail (as a juvenile she would be held in a designated section for people eighteen or under), one thousand dollars in restitution, and ninety-five dollars for an order of protection. In the transcript, Bauer says, "You can get a lawyer on these matters if you wish to, but don't have to." Then he added, "On the other hand, if you were to admit to harassing her, which I'm not suggesting you do at this stage and you are not obligated to do at any stage, but if you pled guilty, I would impose a fine"—meaning only a fine and no jail time.

The girl, who had as much legal knowledge as most seventeen year olds, said, "What do you mean, guilty or not guilty?"

When Bauer asked if she had a copy of her own file, she said, "I think I lost it."

The rest of the trial transcript reads like a Kafkaesque nightmare. At times, the girl posed irrelevant, self-incriminating questions to the other girl in court whom she had supposedly assaulted. "If *we* jumped you, why are you blaming it all on *me*?"

Bauer found Wagar guilty in a trial he conducted himself, but postponed sentencing. As for Wagar's getting a lawyer, he said, "You mentioned when we began this process that your mother was contemplating getting a lawyer. I was not in a position to put this matter off, because it has been put off a number of times. You may want to bring a lawyer for the sentencing stage of this matter. I put people in jail every day, for better or worse, but I generally do it when they have a lawyer standing by their side to protect their interests."

Facing jail time, the girl decided to look into getting a lawyer. She called the New York State Defenders Association, Inc., the largest criminal-defense bar association in New York. Executive director Jonathan Gradess wrote a letter asking Bauer to give her a lawyer because she couldn't afford one and expressing concern that, "she has proceeded this far without the appointment of counsel." He estimated a lawyer would have charged two thousand five hundred dollars to three thousand dollars to represent her at trial.

At the next hearing, Bauer sparred with her.

"Can I have an application for an appointed lawyer?" the girl asked.

"Maybe, yes, but you are gainfully employed, right?" he asked.

"I don't make that much at Price Chopper," said Wagar of her supermarket job.

"But you were working. Right?"

"Yeah, part-time."

"How long have you worked there?" he asked.

"About six months."

"How many hours do you work a week?"

"It depends. This week I only have fourteen hours."

"Let's see," Bauer said. "How far back does this case go? Have you saved anything since May eleven?"

"I have been paying bills," she said.

"Have you been saving anything for a lawyer bill, though?"

"No."

"Do you live on your own or with others?" he asked. "My recollection is you handled this *pro se*, without a lawyer, by your own choosing; isn't that accurate?"

"Yeah. I didn't think I needed one in the beginning."

"Fair enough," Bauer said before telling her that she could have had a lawyer if she wanted one but that her mother had said she had wanted to handle the case herself at first.

The girl countered him. "No, she wanted me to fill out the application because we were talking to some lawyers and they said I was allowed—"

"They seem to be charging a lot of money," Bauer interrupted.

"Yeah."

"The lawyers that are telling you that are lying to you," said Bauer.

"I was allowed to get one?"

Bauer railed at the girl. "Mr. Gradess is speaking ignorantly. He doesn't know what I know about your posture and position and your ability to get a lawyer. And your position was you didn't want to get a lawyer. You made that clear to me. I don't know if you made that clear to him. And I don't force lawyers down peoples' throats when they don't want a lawyer. And I told you, you need a lawyer all along and I held off sentencing specifically for that reason."

With that, Bauer handed her the form for a public defender.

There is something unequivocally wrong about a seventeen-year-old girl having to beg for the form to show that she needed an attorney— after she had been found guilty. More important, she shouldn't have been conducting her own defense against a prosecutor, much less a judge.

When contacted six years later, Wagar was working as a driver for Federal Express. She described how her detour in Bauer's court had affected her. Back in 1999, Bauer finally got around to assigning her a lawyer, Art Glass, in time for sentencing. The punishment was a fine and community service. "I cleaned the city streets," she said. However, Wagar had missed too many classes while attending hearings because her request for a trial had dragged on. She ended up dropping out of high school when told she would have to repeat her junior year. This landed her a full-time job at the Price Chopper supermarket. Years later, Wagar went on to get her GED.

Bauer had helped cleaned up the city all right, but his court had regularly failed to take the elemental steps of deciding which defendants needed a lawyer, what had happened in a case, and whether a crime had actually occurred. And almost no attorney in Troy was willing to admit it. This was a tight-knit community; no one wanted to fess up. In the end, friendship and affability trumped the protection of rights. One attorney, a former prosecutor, when reached by phone, acknowledged that Bauer was lazy "and tried to make a full-time job part-time. He did some serious things," he said, "but he is also my friend." Then he hung up.

CHAPTER THREE

MISS WIGGS'S LIST

By law and by custom, a prosecutor has broad authority in prosecuting criminal cases, including the option to "screen out" or decide against pursuing a case at any stage. Soon after the police make an arrest, usually within twenty-four hours, the defendant appears before a judge, who determines whether the initial evidence indicates that this person has committed a crime. At this time and until trial, the prosecutor reviews the charges and makes a choice: prosecute, investigate, or go no further. The responsibility of making this call might be the most important one a prosecutor has. As it happens, many cases get screened out across the country for reasons that are hard to divine. For the most part, the exercise of "prosecutorial discretion" requires no formal process or oversight. A prosecutor does not have to explain his or her decision to proceed or dismiss a case and can even rely on gut instinct if he or she chooses. Though some offices report screened-out cases, classifying them as "dismissals," and keep track of "clearance rates," or the number of cases actually resolved, others keep no tallies or organized records. As Kenneth Culp Davis observed in his landmark book *Discretionary Justice*, "The plain fact is that more than nine-tenths of local prosecutors' decisions are supervised or reviewed by no one."[1]

Nonprosecution is rarely a subject of discussion let alone disapproval since the general public rarely hears about cases that are not prosecuted. Most crimes happen quietly—without dead bodies, burned-down buildings, sirens or even a visible sign that someone or something has been hurt. Domestic violence, child abuse, possession and sale of drugs—often these incidents need to be investigated. But if no one does investigate and in the absence of evidence of wrongdoing, it is hard to argue that a case should have gone to court. As a result, most people are oblivious to these cases, and so, of course, will not decry a policy of nonprosecution about which they know nothing.

But in Quitman County, Mississippi, cases that were vanishing after arrest had become a topic of conversation. I had initially come to Quitman to look into the county's role as the plaintiff in a highly unusual civil suit. The suit had arisen out of a murder trial in which the county had been required to pay two hundred and fifty thousand dollars in legal fees for the defense of the indigent defendants. Arnold & Porter, a big law firm in Washington, D.C., was representing Quitman against the state of Mississippi, arguing that the county was too poor to adequately defend the indigent.[2]

When I got to Quitman County, however, the circuit court where felonies are prosecuted had only a handful of cases. It seemed free of the caseloads and assembly-line system I had seen in indigent defense in places like Georgia. Nonetheless, Arnold & Porter's lawsuit had gotten tons of media attention, including a story on the front page of the *New York Times*.[3] But Ann H. Lamar, the state trial court judge who ruled on the suit, found no constitutional violation, adding that the county had not shown specific examples of defendants who claimed to have received ineffective assistance. (Quitman County went on to appeal the case to the state supreme court, but lost.)[4]

In spending time in the county, however, I learned that almost everyone, from the librarian at the checkout counter to the owner of a cell-phone store, seemed to have a story about justice gone wrong, but their complaints had nothing to do with inadequate defense. One story seemed to lead to another. The county is small. It occupies 404 square miles and, according to the 2006 census, has a population of 9,289. Most live in Marks, the county seat. The county has two national fast-food franchises, no movie theater, three attorneys, and outspoken people who lead a rural community life smack in the middle of cotton and soybean fields, about seventy miles southeast of Memphis. The rumor mill is big.

After only a few days, it led me to Judge Joe Brown, who, it turned out, had less concern about inadequate counsel for the poor than about nonprosecution. Brown sat on the bench in justice court, where most criminal cases begin. His job was to determine whether there was "probable cause" to believe that a crime had been committed and whether the defendant had committed it. If he found not enough support, he would dismiss the charges.

If Brown did find probable cause for a misdemeanor, he would try it in justice court; for a felony he would set bail and "bound over" or refer the case to grand jury in circuit court, where serious crimes are tried. A grand jury is a group of citizens who evaluate a district attorney's presentation of evidence that the accused committed the crime, including testimony from police officers, sheriff's deputies, and other witnesses. After hearing the statements, the grand jury votes on whether formal charges—called the indictment—should be filed.

But something was going wrong with Brown's cases: He had bound them over to a grand jury, but they had never gotten there. Sitting at the bottom of the legal chain, he couldn't tell whose fault it was. He suspected foul play.

"I am a Christian man and I cannot stand what is happening," Brown said to me in his office at court, a windowless, bookless space he had occupied for four years. The way he saw it, "It's who you know and whether you can get it swept under the rug" that determined whether a case would get tried. At Brown's home, he handed me envelopes from a locked safe. Sealed and signed and dated on the back, they contained records of cases that had never gone to the grand jury. He planned to give them to the authorities as soon as someone began an investigation, a day he was sure would come.

Brown did not blame the prosecutor, who was the one to move the case on to the grand jury, but the clerks in justice court. Brown, who was white, told me he thought the clerks, who happened to be black, were helping out their friends by tossing away files and entering false information into the computer. I found no evidence of this. Brown had no idea how many files in total had gone nowhere. He had made copies of only the few that had been brought to his attention by victims who couldn't figure out why their perpetrators hadn't gone to trial. But he did not have any legal reason to get more involved; the lower court has no jurisdiction over a case that has been bound over.

Following his lead, I went down the street to the "higher" circuit court (with a different clerks' office) to see Brenda Wiggs, the head clerk, who reportedly knew something about the nonprosecutions. She had saucer-blue eyes and powder-white skin and was known to sound off about the significant racial divisions in Quitman County. Of course, the Mississippi Delta has a long history of racial and economic disenfranchisement. Martin Luther King Jr. had wanted the Poor People's Campaign to start in Quitman because the economic distortions were so intense. At the time, increasing mechanization had brought about migration to northern cities and a drastic reduction of wages earned by day laborers.[5] In probably the most famous moment in the county's history, on March 18, 1968, Martin Luther King visited the town of Marks and toured the dirt roads with their shotgun houses mired in swampy water. At a schoolhouse, King saw a teacher pass out a slice of apple and a few crackers to some children for lunch. He couldn't believe that was all they got. King wept openly. Then, in the wake of his death in 1968, the Southern contingent of the campaign began its journey in Quitman with a train of mules that plodded its way to a June rally in Washington, D.C., to protest poverty.[6]

Today in Quitman County, thirty percent of citizens live below the federal poverty line. While the county is nearly 70 percent black, the leadership positions in the county are, by and large, held by whites, though the sheriff, an elected official, is black. People's views on the county's justice system began with race. Brown said he suspected that black clerks were getting rid of cases for friends, but many black people in the community surmised that the unprosecuted cases must have been black-on-black crime, presumably because such cases attract less interest. In the court clerk's office, where bound volumes line the walls, the gold-embossed word *colored* stood out on the spines like a tattoo. The marriage records for blacks and whites were kept in separate books until 1988, when Brenda Wiggs came in and changed things.

Everyone called her Miss Wiggs, a reference to her schoolteacher days, though she was in fact a "Mrs.," married for over forty years to Harold Wiggs, a retired postal worker who runs a catfish farm. She left court each day to make him lunch, and she ran a Bible-study group at the courthouse, where women held hands and prayed for strength in their marriages and families. Miss Wiggs was no radical. She taught for years at a private school, a virtually all-white institution. She had extremely traditional views of women. "We don't need a woman president," I heard her say over lunch to a table of men at the Rotary club. "Women are too emotional." At the same time, she took pride in being a leader. And Miss Wiggs was notoriously vocal about the strangely disappearing cases.

Over the years, Miss Wiggs had received many calls from angry victims wanting to know why their cases weren't being prosecuted. "You would be shocked," she said of the stories she heard. She was known to call the district attorney responsible for prosecutions in Quitman County, who resided an hour away in Cleveland, Mississippi. "I have asked and asked . . . and nothing happens," she said.

"I don't know where you would lay the blame," she said, and gestured to something taped to the wall by her desk: five pages of cases that were bound over but had never gone to trial or been pleaded out. There were names on the pages, some typed, others handwritten. The cases included assault, burglary, robbery, rape, aggravated assault, embezzlement, child abuse, statutory rape, "worthless" or bounced checks, drive-by shooting, breaking and entering an auto, disturbing the public peace, shoplifting, and drug cases, like the theft of anhydrous ammonia to make methamphetamine. "All of these people you see on this wall—I would estimate about fifty or more names—they all have been bound over to circuit court. And yet," she went on, when the grand jury convened, "we only had eight people" accused of crimes.

It was possible that a few of these cases would yet make it to a future grand jury, but probably not. Eventually, Miss Wiggs would take the list down and paste up new pages with more names. To her, the list was just names on a wall. The "only time that would change is when victims call and tell me about their cases."

The defendants, of course, never called. Even defendants who had posted bail but were not brought back to trial did not come to ask for their money back. "Usually," Miss Wiggs said, people "are so glad they have not been indicted that they get lost and let us keep the money." At the end of each calendar year, the county reaped from four thousand dollars to twelve thousand dollars from cases left in limbo, according to Thomas "Butch" Scipper, the county administrator, treasurer, and chancery court clerk, who worked down the hall.[7]

Working from Miss Wiggs's list, it seemed that the district attorney in Quitman County eventually brought to the grand jury 35 percent of cases bound over in 2002, 24 percent in 2003, and again 24 percent in 2004. The rest fell by the wayside. Where did Quitman County stand in comparison to other counties? It was hard to say. Nationally, statistics on nonprosecution don't exist. In a report published in 2008, the Department of Justice notes that, 68 percent of the cases in the nation's 75 most populous counties ended in conviction, but this figure does not convey the actual prosecution rates or how many crimes and arrests were dropped at different stages.[8] Locally, the other counties had no records similar to the ones kept by Miss Wiggs or at least couldn't put their hands on them without enormous difficulty.

"Ask Laurence," Miss Wiggs said when I wanted to know why the prosecution rate seemed low. She was referring to the district attorney for Quitman County, Laurence Y. Mellen, who worked out of a corner office in an annex to the Bolivar County Courthouse in Cleveland. The state is divided into twenty-two prosecutorial districts, and Mellen's encompasses four counties (Coahoma, Bolivar, Tunica, and Quitman), which, in 2007, had a total population of 85,541. Every month, Mellen would drive hundreds of miles to make appearances at grand juries in these four different counties (three of which had bigger populations and industry than Quitman). He had five assistant lawyers and three investigators. He didn't keep statistics on caseloads, but he liked to do big trials himself, as many as ten a year, which is quite a lot. He loved to tell trial tales that ended in victory. He would be stuck with an indictment, the story would go, and then he would live through some sort of ordeal, working as hard as he could to turn the situation around. "I don't prosecute anyone who isn't guilty," he said, his eyes squinting with joy. Mellen stands five foot six, but his charisma and energy made him seem taller.

Mellen became a district attorney somewhat by accident. As a young man he attended Mississippi State University with dreams of becoming a wildlife biologist. "I just love biology and all that," he said. He graduated with a double major in general science and industrial management and then served for two years as an officer in the 101st Airborne Division in both Kentucky and the Dominican Republic. During his duty, he saved money for law school, but not because he was dying to be a lawyer; he had lost touch with most of his college friends and feared he wouldn't be able to find a job. He felt a law degree would complement his industrial studies. Mellen attended the School of Law at the University of Mississippi in Oxford and remembered having no affinity for any particular subject. "Law school is hard. It's really kind of tough," he said. He did succeed in making connections, though. During law school, he joined the 20th Special Forces Group of the Mississippi National Guard. The commander of the unit, a lieutenant colonel, had a civilian job as assistant attorney general in the criminal division. Mellen's relationship with him resulted in a job at the attorney general's office in Jackson, the state capital. There he did appeals for a year before landing a position with a private firm in Cleveland, hours away from his family in Jackson. Mellen was grateful for the job. "I didn't come from a legal background. Some do and they'll go work in a big law firm where their daddy or uncle is this or that."

His father, Frederic Mellen, had discovered the first commercial oil field in Mississippi, the Tinsley oil field in Yazoo County, as an assistant state geologist in 1938. Nearly five hundred wells have since been drilled on and around the Tinsley structure. Eventually, Mellen's father became the state geologist. "He worked for the state, so he didn't get anything out of it, other than that he is famous for what he did," Mellen said. His mother worked in a state welfare department, "probably to help her children get through college."

Mellen stayed in private practice for five years before choosing to work in the public interest. "I kind of wanted to prosecute. Because it's doing right. And there's a lot of wrong going on." He decided to run in the Democratic primary for district attorney in 1983 in a contested election against both a white incumbent and a black assistant DA. The region is majority black so Mellen, who is white, said he had to campaign extra hard to win. "I beat him just barely," he said of his black opponent. Mellen then handily won the main election. Four years later, in the next election, he got 83 percent of the vote, once again defeating a black opponent. "After a while I had name recognition," he said.

In most states in the United States, chief prosecutors at the district, county, and municipal levels are usually elected. The model emerged in the 1820s as a way to make prosecutors more accountable to the people. It's part of an American political tradition that favors allowing the states to determine their criminal laws rather than the centralized government.[9] In communities across the country, prosecutors can run in elections that are highly combative where win-loss records are an issue. Skeptics insist that this pressures our leading law enforcers to deliver convictions, not the truth.[10]

But little has been written about another reality: an uninvolved electorate that doesn't vote, put forth an alternative candidate, or care about most convictions. Often, the public has little information with which to gauge a prosecutor's performance, at least in relation to his decisions about who to charge, when to plea bargain, and how to sentence. The public doesn't really have much on which to base its choice except what the prosecutor reveals come election time, which is often a conviction rate subject to manipulation. Sometimes the media, for some reason, decides to unearth a prosecutor's record. More often, prosecutors run unopposed, overshadowed by the more prominent races of other public officials; as a result, their records can lay unexamined.[11] In Mellen's case, after his first and second elections, he ran uncontested every four years for nearly two decades except for his sixth term in 2007, which he won narrowly. (The original pay was forty-five thousand dollars and is now approximately ninety-two thousand dollars.)

Over the years, Mellen's success rate in trials began to sag; the press took some notice, but the general public hardly noticed at all. In 2003, the *Clarksdale Press Register* in adjacent Coahoma County ran a story whose headline read: "Acquittals Trouble D.A.: 'Juries Don't Respond the Way They Used To.'" Of his early years, Mellen said, "We used to have a 92-percent conviction rate." According to the paper, by 2003, while the national federal conviction rate was about 90 percent, Mellen and his staff's rate had dropped to less than 15 percent in the county's last term of court. Mellen blamed his declining conviction rate on small-town juries that feared retaliation from drug dealers and gang members. He also believed that TV crime shows had created unrealistic expectations about the kind of evidence that should be presented.[12] This is not an uncommon complaint by district attorneys.

The people of Quitman County were willing to tolerate Mellen's low conviction rate. As one scholar remarked, prosecutors are not always held directly responsible for arrests that don't end in convictions, either because the public blames the arresting officers or just doesn't focus on the issue "because of some larger failure of electoral accountability."[13] The problem, however, is that without an interested electorate, the American prosecutor pretty much has carte blanche.

If the electorate fails to check prosecutorial power and abuse, grand juries are supposed to function as a backup. The institution can be traced to twelfth-century England, in which the government used a panel of local residents to help uncover crime and apprehend offenders. Locals understood more of what was happening in the community than the Crown's representatives and could better present charges. Also, the grand jury could refuse to indict if it found insufficient evidence that the accused probably committed the crime. The American colonies adopted the institution, and it soon became an important watchdog power. Grand juries could initiate criminal charges themselves and issue "criminal presentments" against royal officials to show their dissatisfaction with representatives of the Crown. At times they refused to issue requested indictments, flexing their muscle against royal commands.[14]

After the Revolution, the framers guaranteed the right to a grand jury in the first clause of the Fifth Amendment.[15] The clause was only intended to apply to the federal government, but all the original states had laws giving defendants a right to grand juries, anyway.[16] Even so, the U.S. Supreme Court declined to require the states to initiate prosecution by grand jury. Rather, states simply have to ensure that adequate safeguards against the arbitrary exercise of prosecutorial power exist. Only eighteen states, including Mississippi, plus the District of Columbia (as well as the federal system) require grand jury indictments for all felony prosecutions.[17] Others allow a prosecutor to file an "information" or written accusation to inform the defendant of the charges, and in most states this must be supported by a preliminary hearing before a judge to make sure enough evidence exists to send a case to trial.[18]

Although Mellen was required to bring cases to grand jury, he didn't have much faith in them and liked to invoke an old adage: "A grand jury would indict a ham sandwich." It is true that a grand jury comprises a group of laypeople who generally have no idea how legal standards operate; they hear a one-sided case delivered by a prosecutor who doesn't have to offer any exculpatory evidence and who speaks without restraint outside the presence of a judge; prospective defendants are not permitted to present any counter-evidence or participate in any way. Still, I interviewed four area prosecutors in Mississippi who said they preferred to present virtually everything to a grand jury, no matter how weak the case, in order to receive community input about what should go to trial. Passing the decision off to a neutral group of ordinary citizens politically insulates a prosecutor against any allegations of favoritism for one community over another, black or white, for example, or against allegations of a cover-up of police misconduct.

Presenting cases to the grand jury is also what Mississippi's chief law enforcement officer, the Office of the Attorney General, instructs prosecutors to do. In 2005 Mellen in fact wrote to the attorney general asking for guidance on the matter, and was told that "Each case bound over must be presented to the next grand jury," though a prosecutor can maintain that further investigation is needed or ask to continue the case at a future date.[19] A straightforward issue? Not exactly. The attorney general's instructions are advisory and become relevant only if someone successfully sues Mellen for not proceeding with cases that should have been prosecuted; but for various reasons, an individual successfully suing the prosecutor "never happens," said Michael Lanford, deputy attorney general and head of the opinions section of the office.

Mellen did not, in any case, appear to follow the opinion's directive. And here's perhaps why: If he brought marginal cases before a grand jury, the defendants would most likely have been indicted. Then Mellen would have been forced to choose among three unpleasant options: haggle with a defense lawyer to secure a plea; bring the case before a jury and perhaps lose (which would hurt his conviction rate); or request a judge to overrule the grand jury and dismiss the case. All three choices required a lot more work than just putting the case aside. "Why don't I indict?" Mellen said. "It's because we don't have the proof. People may not know it, but I know it. Okay?"

Even though Mellen's community did not appear interested in his conviction rate, it mattered enough to Mellen for him to refuse to move cases forward. He disdained overzealous prosecutors who wanted to indict on insufficient grounds. Still, there seemed to be no clear explanation for why particular cases didn't advance. Were his decisions driven purely by a lack of evidence, like Mellen said? Or was Judge Brown right about a racial conspiracy? Or was it that black-on-black crime simply got the short shrift? The interesting question was whether Mellen had a method to his nonprosecutions, whether he worked to uncover the truth about a crime before putting the case aside, or whether random or other circumstances determined which cases got dropped.

A good place to start looking for answers was the National District Attorneys' Association, the only national organization for America's state and local prosecutors. The association, based in Alexandria, Virginia, has established guidelines for nonprosecution that are meant to be suggestive, not binding, since each office operates as its own fiefdom with its own budgetary and political constraints.[20] The guidelines suggest, ideally, that in order to determine which individuals should be charged with crimes, the prosecutor should establish standards. With an explicit policy in place, a prosecutor can explain the screening program to victims, witnesses, officers, and investigators so that not only is justice done but the people involved understand the outcome.[21] In deciding whether to exercise discretion in screening, a prosecutor may consider:

a. Doubt as to the accused's guilt;

b. Insufficient admissible evidence to support a conviction;

c. Reluctance of a victim to cooperate in the prosecution;

d. Possible improper motives of a victim or witness;

e. The availability of adequate civil remedies;

f. The availability of suitable diversion and rehabilitative programs;

g. Provisions for restitution;

h. Likelihood of prosecution by another criminal justice authority;

i. Aid to other prosecution goals through nonprosecution;

j. The age of the case;

k. The attitude and mental status of the accused;

l. Undue hardship caused to the accused;

m. A history of non-enforcement of the applicable violation;[22]

n. Failure of law enforcement agencies to perform necessary duties or investigation;

o. The expressed desire of an accused to release potential civil

claims against victims, witnesses, law enforcement agencies and
their personnel, and the prosecutor and his personnel, where
such desire is expressed after the opportunity to obtain advice
from counsel and is knowing and voluntary;[23]

p. Any mitigating circumstances.

Factors that should not be considered in this decision include:

a. The prosecutor's rate of conviction;
b. Personal advantages which prosecution may bring to the prosecutor;
c. Political advantages which prosecution may bring to the prosecutor;
d. Characteristics of the accused legally recognized to be deemed
invidious discrimination insofar as those factors are not pertinent to the elements of the crime.[24]

Finally, a prosecutor should keep a record of the screening decision
and reasons for the screening disposition of each matter, and be willing
to share information and reconsider new information.[25]

Mellen was not able to articulate a policy for his screening process
nor did he keep records. Unlike what was needed in a big city, record-
keeping seemed unnecessary in counties like Quitman, he claimed,
since his staff often knew most of the law enforcement officers by first
name. Mellen also had three experienced investigators whose jobs
were to make sure that the charges were justified by reviewing evidence or by learning more about the facts of the case. These investigators usually did the initial screening, often involving "send backs," in
which they returned a case to the police, asking for more information
after arrest. If they considered the charge too high, they could reduce
it, or drop it completely if they felt that the arrest was based on skimpy
evidence.

During the time that I looked into cases in Quitman County, the principal investigator for the area was David James, who had a sense of rectitude about his job. When anxious, his stony face would crack into a grin, though, as he liked to say, "It's not a smirk, I am praying." James went to church three or four times a week, "maybe more," he said. He would toss out bits of oratory in the middle of conversation. "A man no matter how much land he owns never owns the land. The land owns him." When asked why this was relevant to his job as an investigator, he said, "I am a Christian man and I give all glory to God. No matter what you do in life, it's not about me. It's about God and whatever it takes to glorify him."

James, who is black, hailed from Rosedale in Bolivar County, where he grew up picking and chopping cotton on somebody else's farm. His parents picked pecans and drove tractors, and his mother also worked in landowners' homes. After graduating from high school, he served in the military for nine years. He took correspondence courses for his Bachelor of Arts degree while he traveled to Honduras and Panama and served in the army during Operation Desert Shield. James said he worked on communications in intelligence. "A lot of things I can't tell you," he said mysteriously. Afterward, he ended up in charge of soldiers doing guard duty at a military base in Germany and then as a chauffeur for generals and a weapons instructor in Fort Stewart, Georgia. He once drove in a motorcade for President George H. W. Bush. Later he came back to Rosedale, where he took a job as a police officer and finally as an investigator for Mellen, who ultimately fired him in January 2007 after twelve years when James decided to run for sheriff of Bolivar County. James said Mellen didn't want a black sheriff: "It was purely racist." Mellen laughed at the allegation. "That is absurd. He was on mighty hollow ground in his work anyway," Mellen said. According to Mellen, running for sheriff was a full-time job and James couldn't do both his job and compete for office at the same time. (James eventually lost his bid for sheriff and was not hired back by Mellen.)[26]

In his job as investigator, James bore an enormous responsibility. Though not a lawyer, he often acted as the gatekeeper to prosecution.

He would review the files and, if he deemed a case worthy, pass it on to an assistant district attorney or to Mellen himself, who would decide whether to take it to a grand jury. If a case had problems, James was supposed to get approval from a lawyer to put it aside, but this didn't always happen. When asked who oversaw him and where the buck ultimately stopped, he said gravely, "It stops here. I can review a file and determine if it goes to the grand jury or not—yes or no."

His reviews of files upset people throughout the county, including Judge Larry Lewis. Lewis was a circuit court judge for the Eleventh District, which encompassed Quitman County. Before being elected to the judgeship, he worked for nearly three decades handling cases in the justice court as the county prosecutor, a position that operated independently of the district attorney because it was funded by the county and not the state. However, at times Lewis was required to assist Mellen, not only to assess when cases should go forward to a grand jury but also when they went to trial.

Lewis noticed that some cases he thought prosecutable never made it to the grand jury. He lived in town, and victims of crime would give him an earful, asking for his help to track down their cases. "Some people think that the DA is asleep when it comes to Quitman County," he said.

During the five years I visited Quitman County, I watched as Lewis tried to do something about the nonprosecutions. First he had Miss Wiggs draw up names for all the nonprosecuted cases she knew about. Then he confronted Mellen, who came up with an excuse for each one, mostly blaming the police or the sheriff's office for not producing evidence. Meanwhile, officers and deputies took offense, claiming the prosecutor's office had the necessary reports. "While this finger pointing has gone on, the system has collapsed," said Lewis.

Still, Lewis didn't know exactly who or what was actually causing the problem. He theorized that at times David James was calling the shots and that Mellen had too easily accepted the investigator's assessments that there was not enough evidence to prosecute, when in fact no one had actually investigated the cases enough to turn up evidence one way or the other. Despite having been sued by James, Mellen said he had no reason to believe James had not looked into cases and kept his office informed.

How could Lewis get the information necessary to prove a pattern? On an ongoing basis he could review Mellen's decisions not to prosecute. But the U.S. Supreme Court has long suggested that judges are not equipped to review prosecutors' decisions. A judge would have to take each case and determine whether there was reason to justify nonprosecution. To verify, for instance, that a victim was unwilling to testify, a judge would have to bring this witness into court for questioning or else knock on doors himself. The U.S. Supreme Court pointed out in *Wayte v. United States* in 1985 that a court's decision to backtrack and examine the prosecutor's decision "delays the criminal proceeding, threatens to chill law enforcement by subjecting the prosecutor's motives and decision making to outside inquiry, and may undermine prosecutorial effectiveness by revealing the Government's enforcement policy."[27]

Nevertheless, to make the process more visible, many jurisdictions have provided that a judge can force the prosecutor to explain his reasons to decline prosecution, but only *after* a grand jury has already approved it. But even this limited requirement has become boilerplate: the prosecutor may simply say that nonprosecution is "in the interests of justice." In essence, this provision safeguards nothing.[28]

Lewis could have asked for an inquiry into indictment practices by the state attorney general. But without enough evidence to discredit Mellen, the attorney general would not be likely to step in. Additionally, if Lewis was wrong, his reputation would suffer. "What can I do? If I step up to the plate and commence an investigation and ruin my relationship with all these people I've known my life long, and if the investigation turns up nothing—then what? I say I'm sorry? This is not some large place. You run into the people all the time."

For Lewis, the amount of work it would take to fault Mellen and the political fallout if he failed made his involvement unlikely. "You got to be right when you stand up. You can't spew facts if you don't know the truth," he said of his thinking at the time. Still, he tried to address Mellen's claim that the police were failing in their investigations so that the prosecutor would no longer have this excuse. The police were clearly overwhelmed, he was told, and needed an experienced investigator who was properly trained in order to do the leg work. So Lewis went before the Board of Supervisors, which allocates money, and explained the need to hire an investigator or two. But, as Lewis put it, "nothing happened." The county had other priorities, like schools and roads. No one, really, had any incentive to go after the facts.

Over the course of one year, from September 2001 to August 2002, Miss Wiggs recorded ninety-five cases involving ninety people that had not gone to grand jury. I decided to study six. Each one involved a defendant who had been identified but not punished. Each had come to a stop at a different stage of the process. In reviewing these cases, I got more than I bargained for: a tableau of breakdowns and circumstances that were all capable of derailing a case when the prosecutors, in addition to police, sheriffs, and state law enforcement, apply their own standards of right and wrong. No one did anything that strictly qualified as corrupt, nor did anything I found reach the level of a Constitutional violation, like selective prosecution of people based on race; if Mellen were forced to justify his decisions in court, his reasons would have certainly been upheld. Yet the systemic mismanagement and blundering I encountered was enough to make you think that the American prosecutor has too much hidden discretion.

■ ■ ■

The first case on my list that had failed to reach the grand jury involved a woman, Jody Clifton,§ who said she had been beaten by her boyfriend, Anthony Washington.§ In Quitman County, eleven out of three hundred

§ Victims of domestic-violence and sex crimes have been given pseudonyms to protect their privacy. Fictitious names are also used for criminal suspects who were never formally charged. The pseudonyms are denoted with a symbol. Any similarity between these names and those of living persons is accidental.

and one cases during a three-year period (bound over from justice court) involved domestic-violence charges. Only two had made it to a grand jury, which had indicted both. But both times the victims were not available to give testimony at trial and the cases were nol-prossed, or dropped, according to Miss Wiggs. "Since I have been here, there has been no domestic violence cases prosecuted," she said of her twenty-one years in office.

"I don't have a lot of success in domestic violence cases," Mellen said. "I don't have much success in getting them [to the grand jury]." The reason, he said, was because, "the woman comes in and says, 'I don't want to do it.'" The victims don't want to testify, male or female. One man told Mellen his girlfriend had intentionally given him AIDS. Mellen was willing to try the case so long as the man was willing to testify. "Well, we indict and he says, 'I don't want to do it. We are back together.' Then he comes back and says, 'I do want to do it.' What happened? 'Well we are not back together.' He switched about three or four times. Last time he came in I said, 'Get out.' . . . I said, 'I am very sorry for what you went through but you can't mistreat the prosecution. You can't just come in and abuse our time.' That illustration is extreme. But that is what I run across a lot of the time."

Generally, the victims are overwhelmingly women, not men; but the sentiment that the victim is to blame remains the same. Even if a victim does agree to testify, juries in the Mississippi Delta often will not deliver a guilty verdict. Juries are especially loath to convict when couples reunite, because they believe the accusations were exaggerated or that the victims might have committed criminal acts themselves. In one case a woman poured hot grease over her lover's face and the jury came back with a not-guilty verdict. "I guess he deserved it," Mellen said wryly.

Mellen's reluctance to prosecute domestic-violence cases represents a national problem, deeply rooted in American culture and legal history, and one that may be just as prevalent in big cities as in small towns. The criminal justice system has historically not treated domestic violence seriously. As late as the eighteenth century, a husband was allowed to subject his wife to corporal punishment because she was considered property with which he could do what he wished—"so long as he did not inflict permanent injury upon her."[29] As views of marriage changed in the nineteenth century, women's rights advocates helped push for laws that made sure a husband no longer had the authority to beat his wife. Judges intervened only intermittently, more often acting against immigrants and black men.[30] For the majority of cases, judges chose to protect the privacy of the family and to promote "domestic harmony."[31] In 1852 a North Carolina judge wrote in an opinion:

> We know that a slap on the cheek, let it be as light as it
> may, indeed any touching of the person of another in a
> rude or angry manner—is in law an assault and battery.
> In the nature of things it cannot apply to persons in the
> marriage state, it would break down the great principle
> of mutual confidence and dependence; throw open the
> bedroom to the gaze of the public; and spread discord
> and misery, contention and strife, where peace and con-
> cord ought to reign.[32]

Domestic violence began to be treated as a "real" crime after the women's rights movement brought it to national attention in the 1970s. Reforms were based on the idea that the relationship between the parties is irrelevant to the allegation of abuse; and that domestic violence victims deserve the same protections as other victims of violent crime because abuse is unacceptable no matter the circumstance. Advocates have lobbied to change stereotypes held by police and prosecutors, who always seemed to find reasons to stop following through on charges, including the one cited by Mellen: the victim changed his or her mind. They have argued that police and hospital reports could provide enough evidence to convict, just as prosecutors do in other cases, like murder, where the victim isn't available to testify. This sort of reliance on evidence that doesn't require the victim's cooperation (the possible use of a 911 tape or testimony from neighbors, for example) is called "victimless prosecution" or "evidence-based prosecution." In 1994, Congress passed the Violence Against Women Act, which established several programs to improve local reaction of police and prosecutors to domestic violence crime.[33] In 2005, a re-authorized version of the act allocated money to train law enforcement and to provide shelter, which helps keep victims safe.

But pouring money into the system hasn't yet changed the fact that jurors, law enforcement, victims, and judges alike still consider women complicit in their violent relationships.[34] At the urging of activists, numerous jurisdictions have now adopted "no-drop" policies by which a prosecutor cannot drop a case on grounds that the victim won't cooperate.[35] However, a study of four "no-drop" jurisdictions that questioned the feasibility of prosecuting a case without the victim showed that the offices involved did not prosecute every instance of domestic violence that came up.[36] This reveals little (since it is doubtful that any district attorney's office in the country pursues every case brought to its attention, no matter what the crime) except that "one-size-fits-all" policies that completely eliminate discretion are objectionable to some prosecutors. The National District Attorneys Association has asserted that "[i]t is essential that each instance of domestic violence be evaluated and resolved on a case-by-case basis."[37] Even some traditional feminists and women's advocates have argued that a no-drop policy ignores the individual experience of victims, some of whom are likely to be subject to retaliation from a batterer trying to maintain control.[38]

Despite these drawbacks, many women's rights advocates still support the no-drop policy and wish it were in place nationwide. It is "our dream," said Michele Carroll, former executive director of the Mississippi Coalition Against Domestic Violence in Jackson. Carroll said that Mississippi doesn't keep statistics on domestic-violence prosecutions, but she has watched police and prosecutors fail to do the necessary legwork. "I don't know if they are lying or if the reality is that they really do think it is a family issue and not their business . . . They really don't want to fool with it."

Certainly in the case of Anthony Washington and Jody Clifton, it seemed as if law enforcement did not want to fool with it. Washington's file included a Polaroid photograph showing Clifton wearing a yellow mesh athletic jersey, slumped in a chair, with a red towel around her shoulders. Her puffy face was bruised and her eyes were swollen shut. According to the court file, two years earlier a justice court judge had found "probable cause" that Washington, who had the relationship of "boyfriend to victim" had "purposely, knowingly and feloniously caused bodily injury to another with a deadly weapon a tire iron by hitting her in the face a means which was likely to produce death or serious bodily harm . . . (sic, punctuation)" The case had been bound over to circuit court, but the district attorney had not presented it to a grand jury.

I decided to visit Jody Clifton to see why her case had stalled. She lived in a tan-colored trailer at the end of a wide dirt road. When I showed up, she was on the couch watching TV. We sat together in the steamy living room. Several fans blew strongly. When I told her I had come to talk about Anthony Washington, she was dismissive. "He's been in jail for two years. They got him on the assault." Strangely, she thought that her case had gone to court. "They locked him up for it," she said. She didn't realize that her ex-boyfriend had never been prose-cuted for aggravated assault. Her new boyfriend was milling about, so I asked her if we could talk outside.

It was true that Washington was in prison, but not for beating her up. He had been on probation when he was arrested for the attack on Jody Clifton. Several years before, he had pleaded guilty to "uttering forgery" for issuing two false checks (one for eighty dollars; the other for forty-five). Because of his arrest in her case, a judge had revoked his probation and he went to prison for two years to serve the remaining sentence for forgery. He had served no time for the aggravated assault charge, and was to be released in seven months.

Clifton, in the middle of trying to heal her injuries, feed her chil-dren, and get back to work, had heard from relatives that Washington was in prison and had concluded that the system had taken care of her case. "They didn't tell me nothing else," she said. "I don't know. I just left it alone." She looked across the road at the weedy lawns and water tanks of other trailers. A wasp circled our heads. Then, barely moving her lips, she said, "I haven't heard from him since."

At the time of the crime, she was twenty-eight and living with Washington in nearby Tunica County. They had been arguing to the point that her mother had predicted the assault, saying that one day he would make her pay for her refusal to succumb to his wishes. But there had been glimmers of goodness. Washington was doing his farm work plowing fields, and he bought her three children school clothes (one was his biological child). The fights had been getting worse, though, ending in violence. Clifton wasn't strong enough to win, just to defend herself enough to stop the situation or run away.

The pair had been charged with domestic violence before, she said (though I couldn't find a record of it in either Tunica or Quitman counties, where she had residences). For that charge, she said she had paid a one-hundred-dollar fine to get out of jail and that the experience had taught her a lesson: "Last time I had to go to jail and pay, so I didn't fight [him] this time." The fact that she was discouraged to protect herself is one reason why the National District Attorneys Association strongly discourages "dual arrests," and advises that an officer should thoroughly investigate to see whether one of the parties was acting in self defense to a "predominant aggressor." In other words, dual arrests shouldn't be a substitute for investigative work.[39]

On the night of June 14, 2001, Clifton was out at a nightclub with her friends. She had been sitting at a table when she heard the disc jockey call out her name. Washington was waiting outside. He wanted to talk to her. She didn't want to see him, so her brother went and told Washington to leave. "I knew how he was," she said. "He would have tried to put me in the car then and take me home."

Early the next morning, at three a.m., Clifton's girlfriend was driving her home and yielded at a stop sign. The vehicle behind them, a Nissan pickup truck, sped ahead and parked in front, blocking their way. Washington flew out. He opened the car's passenger door and pulled Jody Clifton out. He shoved her into his truck and the friend left. "She thought he was going to take me home," Clifton said. In the backseat were her four-year-old daughter and her six-year-old niece. Washington drove away and then stopped the truck under a bridge. As he got out, Clifton tried to roll up the windows and lock the doors, but Washington got hold of her before she finished. As the daughter and niece watched, Washington's fists knocked her backward. She lay on the ground while he beat her. She wasn't sure which he used first, but she remembered a hammer, a lug wrench, and pipes pounding her head, hands, neck, legs, and back.

Washington then put her back in the truck and drove to a dirt road. Just when she thought it was over, he dragged her out again and attacked her with a pipe.

Clifton's daughter had been hollering loudly. Suddenly a switch went off for Washington. He said he was sorry. "And he drove me home," Clifton said.

She couldn't see through her swelling eyes, so she held onto Washington's shirt as they entered their home. He passed out on the bed. She lay beside him, awake until around six a.m. when her mother knocked at the door. Clifton's sister, who also lived with them, had found traces of blood on the floor and phoned their mother to come over. Washington stood up in his underwear. Seeing Clifton's face, her mother shoved him back on to the bed and took her daughter to Quitman County Hospital.

Jody Clifton stayed in the hospital for two days, according to the medical report.[40] Her left eye was "bleeding slightly" with "marked swelling of the left upper and lower eyelid. Patient cannot open her eye." Hospital staff noted "numerous areas of bruising" and "multiple contusions to upper and lower back." After leaving the hospital, Clifton and her three children moved into her mother's trailer. She never went back for her things, abandoning clothes, appliances, housewares, and a whole freezer full of meat, which her family could have used. She used to work as a housecleaner at a casino in Tunica. Now she couldn't hold a pocketbook on her shoulder, much less bend over.

When I interviewed the arresting officer, Marvin Furr, two years after the crime, he remembered Anthony Washington as "manipulative," "a thug," as well as "a con man who could talk you into anything." If called to testify, Officer Furr would do so. But he and the prosecutors didn't coordinate a lot. He would rarely reach out to the prosecutor's office to follow up on cases he had put in motion. With all his cases, not just domestic violence, he saw his responsibility as a small, distinct one: to hand in a report that a crime occurred, and put the prosecutor on notice. "We can't push it," he says. "What they do from that point on is out of our hands."

His work didn't seem complicated or filled with unanswered questions begging for resolution, like with the investigators or police on TV who never give up on a case until the culprit is brought to justice. "Some people are going to get help and some aren't," he said. At first Furr insisted that Jody Clifton's case had gone all the way to a plea deal. He then had a different recollection: "I think the girl bailed on us. . . . [she] backed out on us and wouldn't testify." Even more surprising, he said that she had gone back to live with Washington. This would have made his lack of follow-up reasonable since it would most likely have weakened the case.

Furr had no records and so was unable to check his files. Officers kept their paperwork individually, and since he had moved from the sheriff's department to work for the city, he threw out his old files. He had interviewed Jody twice—once in the hospital and once at the police station. Afterward, he wrote his report, which was filed in justice court.

> On July 14, at approximately 1046 hours, I, Deputy Marvin Furr received a call to go to Quitman County Hospital E.R. and talk to a [Jody Clifton]. On my arrival [Clifton] advised me that she had been assault [sic] by her boyfriend [Anthony Washington]. [Clifton] advised me that she was staying with [Washington] on Tibbs Road in

Tunica County. [Clifton] also stated that [Washington] brought her to Highway 315 in Quitman County under a bridge and assaulted her with a tire iron and kicking her in the stomach and beating her in the face with the tire iron [sic]. [Clifton] stated that this incident happen[ed] Friday night and she did not remember the time. At this time I advised [Clifton] that [Washington] would be arrested for aggravated assault/domestic violence and a warrant would be issue [sic] for his arrest. End of report—

In its vagueness, the report provided the prosecutor and his investigator with no road map to go back to the precise scene of the crime to gather evidence. The report mentions a tire iron, but Clifton had also recalled a pipe and a hammer, which had remained at the scene. Furr never went to the crime scene himself; he didn't need to, he explained, because he only did the initial work and it fell to David James, the investigator for the prosecutor, to do the rest. "We're not going to do as much as he is," Furr said.

Here began a problem. Furr expected the prosecutor to gather evidence once he had written an initial report, while James, the prosecutor's investigator, expected policemen like Furr to do the on-the-ground work. Surely neither genuinely held these expectations, or else no evidence would ever be gathered for any case in the county. But according to national experts, this sort of tension between police and prosecutors is not unusual. "Often the police department says, 'We have the basic facts for you, you figure it out,' and the prosecutor is thinking 'Duh, did you interview the witness?'" said Joshua Marquis, who is on the board of directors of the National District Attorneys Association and is chair of the media committee.

The fact is, neither Furr nor James appeared to know much about the case. James claimed to have reviewed the papers and knocked the charge down to a misdemeanor that involved neither serious injury nor weapons. He said he had talked to one of the officers "who said it was simple assault in nature." James sent the case back to justice court. No longer a felony, it wouldn't go to grand jury, and Mellen wouldn't have to prosecute it. (But the case wasn't prosecuted as a misdemeanor, either; and I saw nothing in the file to show that James had actually sent it back to the justice court for adjudication.)

One had to wonder how such an alleged beating would not qualify as a felony. The seriousness of the pounding—the hammering of her hands, buttocks, and legs—had left Jody Clifton unable to do all kinds of work. I pressed James. "There are pictures of her with her face as bloody as the red towel around her neck."

Mellen, who was there with us, said, "Red because she's angry?"

"No, red with blood. She can't see because her head was beaten with a hammer," I said.

"Well, why did he do that to her?" Mellen asked. "She's in Sledge? Call over there and find out," he told James. Mellen was getting uncomfortable.

"The hammer—this is the first I heard of it," James said.

I gave him directions to Jody Clifton's trailer.

When I went back to see her myself, I reported what Officer Furr had said—that the case wasn't prosecuted because she hadn't wanted to cooperate and had decided to go back and live with Anthony Washington.

"That's a lie," Clifton said.

"A big one," her mother, Sara Clifton,§ added.

Jody looked away and muttered, "They telling stories."

"I brought and carried her home," Sara insisted, and her eyes sharpened to black dots. "I got her out of the hospital and she stayed with me until last year," she added.

A silence followed. As demoralizing as it is to be overlooked by the justice system, encountering its ineffectiveness directly is almost worse. Jody and her mother felt that the people who worked in the courts were liars and hypocrites who would say anything to protect themselves. Sara finally punctured the silence, saying, "I'm glad I didn't have no gun. She looked like a monster."

Afterward, Sara Clifton and I went to lunch at Western Sizzlin restaurant in Batesville, where she barely touched her food as she tried to figure out how her daughter's case against Washington had evaporated. She was not exactly unacquainted with the justice system. In 1987, her husband was murdered. He had been shot in the chest at a bar. The killer had pleaded guilty to manslaughter and was serving eight years in prison. "I don't know who it was, the prosecutor maybe, that asked me if it was enough time and I said, 'No,' " she recalled. Still, she thought she understood how the law worked, that one person might rob a bank and do more time than someone who commits murder. "It depends on who you are," she said.

Sara Clifton had learned her lesson. Her husband's killer had gone to jail, but not for long enough, while her daughter's assailant had not gone to jail at all, at least not for the crime that had virtually ruined Jody's life. "If something happens and they are supposed to get back to you, you better investigate it," she concluded. "Because they don't do nothing."

No one from the prosecutor's office ever contacted Jody. Years later, returning to Quitman County, I reminded Mellen of Jody Clifton's case. Among the steps he could have taken to try it successfully was to put her on the stand before a jury. She had received a cruel beating. Even if she refused to take the stand, there was medical evidence. Perhaps law enforcement could have built a case on that. There was also proof left at the scene—a pipe and hammer with Jody's blood on it, perhaps Washington's fingerprints. And her family had seen her immediately after the crime. But Mellen's office had not gathered the evidence, leaving the police and his investigator to point fingers at each other for why the case had gone nowhere.

Now, six years after the assault, Mellen pulled out a yellow notepad as if he was finally going to follow up, even as the evidence was surely lost and memories had faded. What's more, Washington had died in a motorcycle accident, according to his mother.

What did Mellen think? Even without knowing that Washington was dead, he reverted to his standby defense of nonprosecution when it comes to domestic violence: "I understand that there are people who have extremely strong feelings about domestic abuse—it's kind of a favorite topic, as child sexual abuse has been," he said. "I don't know what to do about [these cases]. They just aren't successful."

■ ■ ■

If Mellen's failure to prosecute the assault against Jody Clifton was rooted in a cultural-historical prejudice against a certain kind of crime, his overlooking another case on Miss Wiggs's list seemed to spring from pure distrust of the victim, Lewis F. "Rusty" Gurley, Jr., who owned a small convenience store on the corner of Martin Luther King Drive in Marks and another in Lambert. The stores were among the few places in the county that were open late for sandwiches, fried chicken, and soft drinks. They also sold beer. Strange characters would wander in and commit small crimes. Dozens of cases—charges of stolen snacks and beer, false checks and embezzlement—had piled up. "I have caught over three hundred people stealing last year alone and not one has spent a night in jail," Gurley claimed. This seemed like quite a lot and left me wondering whether he was exaggerating out of annoyance. At the end of the week, Gurley, sandy haired, tanned and handsome, in his late thirties, was tallying earnings on a large ledger. When asked about the cases, he barely looked up from securing a wad of cash: "All the paperwork was 'lost.' If you call the prosecutor's office or circuit court they'll say they don't have it."

Gurley had given up. "I honestly don't know what the failure is, if it's the buddy system or what," he said, referring to a cronyism that he imagined could make cases disappear. The police would write up a report. They would make arrests. The defendants would be taken to jail and charged officially in justice court. Then nothing.

Gurley had talked to the local prosecuting attorney, who said, "It's out of his hands," but he had never talked to Mellen himself. "I have heard other people say it's just wasting time," he said with an air of complacency that appeared odd, given his frustration at having been denied action so many times. So I brought up Gurley's situation with Mellen, who seemed peeved. "I am not going to start doing his work for him. He needs to hire the right people as they pass through and clean up his act. I ain't got time to be all twiddling around doing all this for someone hiring someone who is stealing."

In Mellen's opinion, Gurley wasn't as much of a victim as he claimed to be. He might have been swindled, but he'd walked into it with his eyes open. People like him, Mellen said, "want me to help them out. And I tell them that I am not a collection agency."

According to the National District Attorneys Association, Mellen is within reason to refuse to take on such cases. As the association's guidelines put it, "The availability of adequate civil remedies" is a valid reason to screen out [criminal] cases." Mellen also considered the crimes less important because they involved damage to property, Gurley's store, and not to his person. "I don't have time," Mellen said. "I have people who are hurt."

But there's more to the story. Rusty and his father, Lewis F. "Frank" Gurley, Sr., who had founded the convenience-store chain, had recently been in trouble with the law. In 1998, the two pleaded guilty in federal court to conspiring to conduct an illegal gambling business in several stores, bribing a Panola County sheriff with five thousand dollars, and possessing a firearm. They were each sentenced to three years of probation and a fifteen-thousand-dollar fine.

In a religious town, gambling was not only illegal, it was also a sin. "I don't even go in there," said an assistant circuit court clerk of Gurley's stores, as if any right-minded person would know better. Gurley's father lived on Gurley Road, where he owned several houses and a stretch of land adorned with a lot of exuberant, oversized sculptures— a shoe that you could walk into, a thirty-foot-long dinosaur, a huge Noah's ark, and a little train—all deemed extravagant and weird in this conservative, struggling community. In short, Mellen didn't trust Gurley or believe that a jury would trust him, particularly in light of his efforts to bribe a sheriff.

Obviously, some victims appear more trustworthy than others. And there's nothing wrong with a prosecutor deciding to disregard people he finds unreliable. For the sake of argument, though, let's assume

Mellen had a personal bias against Gurley. Only if this bias were "illegitimate," i.e., based on factors like race, national origin, sex, political activity, or membership in a political party, would Mellen's refusal to prosecute violate the Fourteenth Amendment. Gurley could have a case for discrimination against Mellen if he could produce a similar storeowner who had received better treatment, for example, if someone had shoplifted at Gurley's store with impunity and then crossed the street to steal someplace else and faced criminal charges for the latter crime. Of course, in a small town, this kind of discrimination is nearly impossible to show. As long as the prosecutor says he's acting rationally and there's no evidence to the contrary, the prosecutor's decisions are well within his lawful discretion.

Moreover, the U.S. Supreme Court has ruled that the "worth" of a victim can be taken into consideration when deciding whom to prosecute and what damages to bring, especially in cases where there's been a violent crime. For example, when it comes to sentencing a defendant in a capital murder case, a prosecutor can give a "victim's impact" statement about the victim's laudatory qualities.[41] Some victims will undoubtedly be more worthy than others: a heart surgeon, for example, may have more value than a killer or a drug dealer.

Though Gurley was no saint, he was no killer, either. Even if Gurley had spoken up about the nonprosecutions, Mellen could argue that he didn't think the crimes were serious enough to warrant the expenditure of scarce resources the case would require. Gurley's cases weren't violent, after all, and could end up being prosecuted as misdemeanors in justice court. Yet Mellen acted as if Gurley deserved any crime against his property that could have been prevented. And Gurley, like so many victims, may not himself have felt worthy of speaking out against Mellen and instead simply fell into line. In 2008, Gurley said that a week or two earlier someone had come in and stolen his air conditioner and heating unit, worth five thousand dollars a piece. Tired of being a victim, he wanted to close up shop. But last time I checked, Gurley was still operating his store.

■ ■ ■

In the domestic-violence and property-theft cases, Mellen had deemed both unworthy of prosecution even before the investigation had begun. The decision seemed worse in the case of the domestic violence because it was steeped in a bias that refused to take into account that Jody Clifton had been badly hurt. Mellen's rationale for not pursuing Gurley's complaints was somewhat reasonable insofar as a prosecutor might not have the time to act as a collection agency. However, the other basis for not prosecuting—that a jury may not trust that a convicted gambler could also be a legitimate victim—was shaky; even a convicted gambler is entitled to protection of the law.

The next case I looked at dropped out later in the prosecutorial process. It involved the statutory rape of an eleven-year-old girl.

In statutory rape, the victim's "worth" is ostensibly determined by his or her age, which is the first indicator that something criminal has transpired. Statutory rape criminalizes sexual conduct between people that would be legal if not for their age: if a victim is underage and the perpetrator is a certain number of years older, for example. Despite the fact that there is a clear-cut liability component—an underage person having sex with an older person is by definition a criminal act—statutory rape is notorious for its sporadic enforcement. It is a major illustration of the problem of law in theory versus practice. Today, prosecutors mostly use the law to convict in cases in which there is insufficient evidence to sustain a general rape conviction, or to add on years of imprisonment to a rape conviction.[42]

Statutory rape law came to America from English common law, which aimed to preserve the economic value of young unmarried females (not males) whose families stood to gain from their marrying well and who thus wanted "undamaged" property fit for marriage. If a man had sex with a girl under a certain age, the man would be liable for statutory rape—whether or not the victim consented, looked older than the age of consent, or even initiated the contact. However, the statutory rape law initially applied only to virgins. What mattered was not preventing underage women from having sex but preserving virgins. For this reason, a man accused could use the victim's sexual history as a defense: even if she were ten years old, a girl who'd lost her virginity did not need protection.[43] The victim's experience was crucial, even beyond the issues of age and protecting children from abuse.[44]

The age of consent, originally ten, was gradually raised to eighteen in the nineteenth century after reformers campaigned to change the rape laws, arguing that the lack of legal protection against sexual force made women a sexual underclass. The feminists "exposed the state's complicity in what otherwise appeared to be wholly private acts of oppression," including so-called "'consensual' sexual contact . . . [that] took place within the family, or in dating, or acquaintance relationships marked by violence, coercion, pressure, or fraud. . . ."[45] The law favored men. Women were expected to be chaste before marriage, but girls over age ten were fair game for sex and abuse.[46]

In the twentieth century, women's rights activists tried to change the landscape of rape law even further by amending statutory rape law. As they saw it, the existing law reinforced sexual stereotypes by recognizing only two kinds of underage women: "bad girls" who had a sexual history and who could be exploited at will; and "good girls," or virgins, who merited protection. They also argued that males and females should be protected equally, and that laws which aided only girls perpetuated the idea that women were weaker than men. Most states eventually revised their statutory rape laws to make them gender neutral. Boys could be victims, too.[47]

In addition, states eventually did away with the caveat that a minor had to have been a virgin in order to prosecute her rapist. Instead, a prosecutor merely had to prove that one person had sexual intercourse with another person who was under a particular age, varying from twelve to eighteen years depending on the state, at times also requiring that the defendant be a minimum age or a certain number of years older than the victim.[48] Under Mississippi law, a person eighteen years or over who has sex with a child under fourteen years can be imprisoned for life "but not less than twenty (20) years."[49]

So there's the law in theory, which seems straightforward enough, and there's what prosecutors generally do with the law in practice, which is still to separate victims into "good" and "bad"—those whose cases can be won and those whose can't. "Good" victims might have little or no sexual history and not know the assailant at all, while "bad" victims are familiar with their assailants or have had sexual relations in the past. According to several sociological studies, prosecutors who want to estimate the likelihood of a conviction still consider factors like the victim's background, character, and behavior, his or her relationship to the suspect, and his or her willingness to cooperate as the case moves forward. This "perceptual shorthand" of "real" crimes and "credible" victims reduces the prosecutor's chances of losing before a jury.[50] Mellen concurred. "Hardest case to try is a girl who is willing," and by this he meant an underage girl who "consented" to sex with an adult. "I just look at them and say it won't do any good to indict. Juries won't convict." He couldn't win.

Mellen was not just speculating; his track record with statutory-rape cases in Quitman County was grim, and he had come to the conclusion that the community was too close-knit to provide jurors who would strictly follow the law when determining guilt or innocence. "It's a really political county," he said. "There are always these sinister little connections. They know one another and talk too much." In Quitman, sexual activity among young girls had become so common that jurors had become particularly "hardened."[51] Mellen compared the county to a war-torn country where ordinary citizens get used to seeing bodies on the street. "Jurors will say I don't care about what the law says. I know how life is."

Sometimes though, juries surprised him. Cases he thought would go well—with a "flat chested," "country" girl and a stranger—would go to trial and a jury would find not guilty; on the other hand, a "very healthy, you know, robust" girl who had sex with a male acquaintance who bought her snacks would result in a guilty verdict. Already in the way he spoke of victims, Mellen categorized them by culture, not law. He seemed to have incorporated stereotypes into his way of thinking.[52]

I met with a school administrator who showed me a list of cases involving children and teenagers participating in sexual activities with adults. I investigated a few of them and found the circumstances so chaotic that I could see why they had never been prosecuted, and maybe how Mellen might have developed such stereotypical notions. One mother and her thirteen-year-old daughter swore that the girl's uncle had raped her at knifepoint, but a DNA test of the sperm taken from her vagina the night of the alleged rape didn't match her uncle's. There was no accounting for the discrepancy. "We were always concerned that somebody switched the DNA. What else could it be?" asked Judge Larry Lewis, looking at the case in the light most favorable to the girl, who had seemed so believable to virtually everyone.

In another fraught situation, a fourteen-year-old had testified under oath in a civil action that she had been raped in a bathroom she was using during band practice at the high school. The culprit, she had alleged, was an inmate from the Mississippi Department of Corrections, who was there doing work after hours as part of a contract with the county. The girl had filed notice of a claim that the inmate had "forcibly" raped her and that she contracted a venereal disease from the incident; the girl and her parents charged gross negligence by the county Board of Education, Board of Supervisors, the governor, and the Department of Corrections and sought ten million dollars in damages. The girl had already given a deposition, her parents told me, when they discovered that she had agreed to meet the man in the bathroom. The girl then testified that she had previously lied under oath about the incident being a onetime, violent rape with a stranger. Not that it should have mattered. Her young age is precisely the reason why the law attempts to protect girls like her from sexual relations. She wasn't old enough to be on an equal footing with a prisoner working at her school. Once she admitted lying under oath, however, her credibility went out the window, as did her civil case and apparently any criminal charges.

In this mess of incidents, I came across an appalling case that showed how indifferent prosecutors and police had become to these sorts of allegations. Eleven-year-old Bernice[§] lived with her grandmother in a small house on the black side of Marks. She had a womanly body at one hundred eighty-four pounds, and a wide, pretty golden face, but she was slow-witted, unable to read properly or assert herself as much as her grandmother would have liked. She could be overfriendly. She seemed to want to be loved and feel close to people. "Can you ask my grandmother if I can sleep with you at your hotel tonight?" she asked me the day we met. She took medication for seizures, which made her foggy and tired.

One lazy spring afternoon, she and three girlfriends wandered over to the home of a friend's boyfriend to watch TV. The house was filled with children who were using the computer, watching TV, playing bingo, dominos and Monopoly, and venturing into different rooms. Bernice, according to her written testimony to police, decided to go to Frederico Laplatte's[§] room; he was nineteen years old and her friend's brother. She knew who he was, but was not his friend, per se. Her girlfriends left her alone in Laplatte's room, where, she said, he whispered into her ear, "Man you scared." The next part felt like a dream, as she pulled down her pants and he pulled down his. He put a condom on and climbed on top of her. After they finished, they put their clothes back on and Bernice left the house.

According to her own written report, right after the sex, Bernice crossed the street to a different home. There she had sex with another boy—a twelve-year-old whom she described as her "best friend" in sixth grade. "He asked me to have sex," she wrote in her report, which because of her age was unsurprisingly filled with spelling errors. "At first I said no . . . Then I said yes. Then we went into his borther rom. He put on a condom. I laid on the bed. He started kissing me before we had sexz. We started having sex. After I finish we put own clothes on and I left."

"I don't know why I did it," she said later.

The girl's grandmother, Emma Hollinger,[§] heard about what happened from a neighbor. She called the sheriff's department and wanted the nineteen-year-old prosecuted for statutory rape. The twelve-year-old couldn't be prosecuted because there was not enough of an age difference between the pair.

Frederico Laplatte said that he had never had any sort of sex with Bernice. "She wanted me to have sex with her and I said I didn't want it," he said, which echoed a statement he had written in his own report to police. He knew to reject her advances, because "she was eleven and I was nineteen" and he had learned about statutory-rape law in high school. He seemed to be traumatized by the whole event, saying that he had developed seizures from the stress of it all. "It messed me up pretty bad," he said, though when I talked with him six years after the incident, he seemed to be doing well. He had a three-year-old daughter with his girlfriend and was working as a bricklayer in Oxford. He still lived with his mother in the same house near where Bernice lived with her grandmother. "When I see her," he said, "I go the other direction."

With only Bernice's allegation against Laplatte, the case needed the other children at the scene to testify that they had seen the pair go into a room alone for a period of time and close the door. Instead, the kids offered up incoherent statements with major flaws. Reports from five of the boys are so similar they appear to have been contrived. The teenagers parroted Laplatte's written statement that Bernice had begged him to have sex and that he had refused. In young handwriting with creative spelling, they all purported to have overheard the same conversation.

A girl reported, "[Bernice] said no I want to have sex with [Frederico Laplatte] then he said know you to young for me."

Another: "The girl did as[k] [Frederico Laplatte] to have sex with her, but he told her he was to old for her and he didn't want to go to jail."

And this from a seventeen-year-old boy: "[Bernice] did ask [Frederico] to have sex with her, but he told her he was to old for her, and he didn't want to go to jail."

More so-called exoneration from a fifteen-year-old: "Then Bernice said that . . . I want [Frederico Laplatte.] He said, girl you're too young you need to leave."

Another fifteen-year-old wrote that she saw them go into the room together. "I was standing at the door with my ear on the door. I heard [Bernice] ask [Frederico] to have sex with her, he told no to get out my room. I ran out side to the window. I looked in the window he was trying to get her out his room he grab her by the arm a thru her on the bed he walk out the room."

Trying to interview the children was frustrating and absurd. I found one boy, eleven when the incident happened, on the main drag in town. He claimed to have had his ear to the door. He said sex "sounded like you moaning," and he didn't hear that. He did say two interesting things, though: that Bernice and Laplatte had been in the room for about a half hour, and that after he wrote his statement, "I had to go back and rewrite it." Indeed, in one of the statements to the police, someone had scribbled, "this is the story not the other one," at the top, suggesting that the reports were not spontaneous.

There was little proof that Bernice had sex with Laplatte. Though the medical report showed her hymen was torn, the second alleged sex act with the twelve-year-old boy could have been the cause. Still, a few of the statements mentioned that Laplatte had been watching "a sex tape" in his room, and that Bernice had watched it with him, according to one fourteen-year-old girl. Law enforcement never seized this sex tape. Others mentioned boys chasing the girls, which could intimate pressure, and that there were "a lot of girls running around the house."

Months went by and Laplatte wasn't arrested. Hollinger's earthy face flashed with rage that her granddaughter's case hadn't been taken seriously. "I had the devil working in me saying go and take justice into your own hands. I had to think. It was a hurting moment. I had to give myself to the Lord. I prayed and prayed. I prayed to the Lord and said leave it alone. He'll take care of it."

The police seemed to be waiting for a nod from the prosecutor's office before making an arrest. But when Hollinger called the prosecutor's office she got "the runaround." David James told her that the case was under investigation.

Hollinger went to see Judge Lewis, who was still the county prosecuting attorney in justice court at the time. He decided to look into Bernice's case. At the very least, he thought it deserved a decent investigation. To pressure law enforcement, he filed an official charge in justice court, which is what police or citizens usually do before an arrest. "I made the charge myself because nobody else would do it," Lewis said. The next day Laplatte appeared before Judge Brown, who found probable cause that he had committed the crime. Laplatte was arrested and given a fifteen thousand dollars bond; he paid the required fifteen hundred dollars and was released pending trial.

Emma Hollinger finally thought the case was on track. A month later, though, she was in the beauty parlor when she heard that the case had been dismissed in court that day. She called David James. "He couldn't tell me nothing," she said.

She ran down to court only to find that the case had been closed by justice court Judge Archie Cook. "I talked with Glenn Rossi of the district attorney's office. He stated that this case will not be prosecuted," Judge Cook's remarks read. In the meantime, Lewis had become a circuit court judge, a powerful position that let him rule on Laurence Mellen's cases, but not advocate for a single case or pressure the prosecutor to take a case. So Hollinger got in touch with Mellen, who was tired of her calling. "It got to be a pain in the neck," he said and asked her to meet him in court later that month.

"The case is over," Hollinger recalled him saying to her.

"What do you mean over with? This is an eleven-year-old-girl!"

Mellen explained that the case lacked evidence. "Your granddaughter wasn't brutally raped," he told her. "She consented."

By law, Hollinger's granddaughter could not have actually consented, since "consent" is irrelevant when one is underage. The fact that Bernice was also intellectually challenged probably made her more vulnerable than the average eleven-year-old, and even more hungry for attention and confused about the difference between sincere affection and whatever it was these males—the nineteen or the twelve-year-old—were offering her. Of course, in an ideal world, a teacher or psychologist would have taught her something about bodies, their needs, the risks of sex, and the kind of trust that ideally accompanies sexual intimacy. But in the real world, Mellen would have probably lost her case because jurors would conclude that she asked for it or would question her credibility because of her mental limitations. "I just don't know where in the world we could find a jury that would [convict]," he said.

Unfortunately for Hollinger, the only man who could provide her day in court was Mellen. But it was his prerogative not to prosecute if he thought it a waste of time. Hollinger wondered why she hadn't gotten this answer earlier. She had been given the run-around for months only to be told in the end that the facts didn't merit pursuit from the start. She was left whirling. She went on local radio talk shows and fired off letters to nineteen state agencies, the state attorney general, a congressperson, two U.S. senators, the Federal Bureau of Investigation and the Justice Department in Washington, D.C. "I wrote everybody I could write," she said of her campaign, which, in the end, accomplished nothing.

■ ■ ■

Emma Hollinger was not the only one who had trouble getting a straight answer about what had happened to her case. Other victims experienced the same frustration. People's perception of justice comes from whether the prosecution of a crime is speedy and whether the public is kept informed about what has happened in their cases. When this does not take place, citizens presume injustice, even though, as in Quitman County, a prosecutor has made decisions that are defensible from a legal standpoint. Take seventeen-year-old Kevin Roach, whose father owned a crop dusting business. On Christmas Eve, 2001, he had been driving to his girlfriend's house when he stopped to help a man whose car was stuck in a muddy ditch. The man asked him for a ride. Roach said no but offered the man his cell phone to make a call. According to Roach, the man then tried to pull him out through his car window. Roach pressed on the gas, but the man's grip was so tight that he stayed with the car for what seemed like minutes. "Finally, I got him almost off my car and he was still holding onto me by my jacket and I couldn't keep my car on the road and my car spun around in a circle and slung him off," Roach wrote in a written statement. He called the sheriff's department.

Michael Knox Jr.[§] was later found crawling through a field near where Roach had been stopped. A photo showed Knox with his pants down and open abrasions on his knees, presumably from being dragged by the car. An officer scribbled the word *mental* on an arrest report. Roach identified Knox as his carjacker; Knox was arrested and charged with carjacking. How could this case be anything but clear-cut?

Roach's mother, Cathy, wanted to see justice in court. She called the clerks, the sheriff, and the district attorney at least once a week, she said. A maelstrom of confusion followed. "They kept on telling us that we would get a subpoena in the mail, but the subpoena never came." Finally, a clerk gave Mrs. Roach a date to come to court, but when the family arrived, the case wasn't on any docket.

Eddie Roach, Kevin's father, sent a registered letter to Jimmy Miller, the local prosecuting attorney in justice court:

> We are grateful that our son was not injured; however we fear this person may be successful the next time and someone could be injured or killed. Please advise us how to proceed with this matter.

Miller had never heard of the case. So he wrote a letter to Mellen, Sheriff Oliver Parker, Miss Wiggs, and justice court clerk Eloise Figgs, as well as the two justice court judges, Archie Cook and Joe Brown, asking them for information.

> Could any one of you provide me a report concerning the status of this case? Frankly, I have no recollection of the matter, but I did tell Mrs. Roach that I would make an effort to determine the status of this case and report back to her. Please provide me with any information which you have and I will report it to Mrs. Roach.

Miller could not recall anyone getting back to him.

At the next grand jury, held twice a year, the Roaches went to court on the off-chance they might be able to nail down some answers. But David James told them the case wasn't going to be brought up because it was still "under investigation." Given that the assault had occurred six months earlier, and had involved only one witness, who was their son, they couldn't understand what was left to investigate.

The family then decided to focus on the DA himself. They left three messages for Mellen, who called back to commend Kevin Roach for being such a "smart young man." However, he said, there was nothing to do because the defendant was "mental."

"He was nice, but it wasn't what I wanted to hear," said Cathy Roach.

So what happened to Michael Knox Jr.?

Quitman, like so many poor rural counties, does not have resources to handle the mentally ill. With twenty cells that can house a maximum of forty defendants, the jail does not have the space or the manpower to watch the extremely disturbed. During my last visit to the county, an inmate had just hanged himself with his own pants from the window bars. "We have a very small jail built in 1980 or '81 and no cameras to monitor each cell," said Butch Scipper, the clerk of chancery court, which handles mental health matters on the civil side, such as having people involuntarily committed because mental illness made them a danger to themselves or others. "Crazy people don't belong in jail. They belong in a treatment center provided not with jailers to watch them but people who are trained in mental health."

Judge Archie Cook, who had ordered Knox's release, didn't remember the case years later but said he could have let Knox go without talking to the DA. "It was probably for a period of time until [the case] went for grand jury," he said.

Indeed, the release didn't have to mean the end of the case. Whether or not a person like Knox may be prosecuted depends on two legal issues. The first is whether he is competent to stand trial. Competency has been defined as the ability to understand the proceedings and to assist one's lawyer in representation. A person found incompetent is committed to a mental institution and treated until he or she becomes competent. At that time, the defendant may be tried. If it becomes clear that someone will never regain competency, the person remains in a mental institution so long as he is a danger to himself or others.

As for the second legal issue, the person's mental state at the time of the offense, states define "not guilty by reason of insanity" in different ways. But usually it means that the defendant did not realize the wrongfulness of conduct because of a mental condition. Someone who burns down a house because of a mental illness that causes him to believe, incorrectly, that enemy soldiers are occupying it would be such a person.[53]

To determine competency for trial, most states today have evaluation systems that screen defendants. Only those defendants who are found incompetent or for whom there is serious doubt as to competency are sent on to the hospital. The others go to regular jail. In Mississippi, evaluations are done at the state hospital at Whitfield, which has notoriously scarce resources. The entire state has thirty-five beds in the mental health wing for a population of nearly three million. The waiting list is from three to eight months and, if the county doesn't do the paperwork properly (which often happens), it can be even longer. During the months spent waiting to be admitted for an evaluation, the defendant remains in jail and the county must bear the burden of sheltering the inmate and providing food, medical care, and drugs. Antipsychotic medication may cost from six hundred to eight hundred dollars a month. "That is mega bucks," said Butch Scipper, who is also the county treasurer.

Inmates know that counties don't want the hassle and economic burden of keeping them in jail. At times inmates might act crazy just to be released. "It's counterintuitive," said Dr. Reb McMichael, service chief of forensic services for Mississippi State Hospital at Whitfield. "If you flood your cell and throw feces at the guard they are going to let you out so you can go back to your bayou and wander around." (Of course, release depends on what an inmate is accused of doing. A serial killer or anyone who is dangerous probably would stay in jail.)

To Mellen, the issue again came down to whether he could try the case. If Knox had a mental problem, there was no point questioning him. "Why indict him if they are going to send him down there [to an institution]? The problem is it scares the poor young kid, I know that. Why indict him—I don't think anybody is hurt."

But how did he know Knox was mentally ill? "There was something. It's not like I just say he's just acting crazy so we don't try [the case]," he said. Maybe that word "mental" scribbled on the police report was enough.

If Knox had been sent to Whitfield, the facility would have evaluated him for competence to stand trial. At a prehearing, Knox's attorney would have probably argued that he was not competent. And if a judge had agreed and also found, either then or later, that Knox was not restorable to competence, charges could have been dismissed or civil commitment could have occurred, or both. If, on the other hand, Knox was found competent and trial took place, the defense attorney would probably have argued that he was insane at the specific time of the crime. So Knox might either have ended up civilly committed to an institution, which would not exactly have been a "victory" for Mellen in terms of convictions, or found not guilty by reason of insanity, which also would result in hospitalization, not conviction and punishment. The upshot: a lot of work and a likely waste of time for an overwhelmed prosecutor.

Still, someone in the system could have let the Roach family know that Mellen was loathe to take on a case like that. Instead, the family spent hours making phone calls and running to court hearings that never occurred. In my conversations with Mellen, he seemed to regret the situation. While releasing a defendant who is mentally ill because the case is too hard to prosecute might be the general rule, he wasn't proud of it. Nor did he want to articulate the practice as a general policy. "The fact is . . . we should have found out and just told [the Roaches] we weren't going to do anything. But that is a difficult thing to do."

In the end, it may have made sense not to prosecute Knox's case. When reached by phone five years later, Knox explained that at the time he'd been suffering from depression. He didn't go places. He stayed home. But on the day of his arrest he had been traveling to see his psychiatrist when his car went out of control and ended up in a ditch. Knox remembered flagging down someone but, "I couldn't get my words like I wanted to," he said. He began pounding on the window because he needed help but couldn't speak. "It happened sometimes when I got real stressed." After his parents picked him up from jail the next day, he worked at his father's cotton gin for a few months and his life turned around. He landed a position cooking at a casino in Tunica, where he has worked for five years. He also got married and had two children. "I am going to keep on striving," he said.

■ ■ ■

When I asked Miss Wiggs about which kinds of prosecutions usually did make it to court, she pointed to drug cases. Once the Mississippi Bureau of Narcotics, which works with county officers, gets involved, investigations seem to whiz right through the system. Indeed, pages of the bound volumes in Miss Wiggs's office were filled with sale- or possession-of-controlled-substance cases in which the defendants had pled guilty and been convicted. However, several cases involving attempted "theft of anhydrous ammonia" were stuck on Miss Wiggs's list. Anhydrous ammonia is a colorless liquid gas kept in large tanks on farms as an agricultural fertilizer or industrial refrigerant. It can be a key ingredient in the manufacture of methamphetamine ("meth"), ordinarily thought of as the poor white man's drug of choice because it is cheap. Meth can be snorted, swallowed, smoked, or injected. The less potent form is a powder, but what prosecutors are calling "a national plague" is the manufacturing and use of crystal methamphetamine, which looks like rock candy and is, as experts say, a drug like no other. It is smoked and has an immediate, intense and long-lasting high that is so addictive and destructive that people become prone to psychotic behavior and suffer organic brain damage from protracted use.

The liquid gas required to make the drug is not available to the public. Farmers and industries are required to have a license to purchase anhydrous ammonia, and it is sold in enormous quantities like one thousand gallons—enough to fertilize a crop. The gas smells so bad that farmers inhaling it have been known to throw up, collapse, or jump off a tractor to escape its fumes. People who want to make meth sneak onto a property and unlock the tank valve to fill up a quart or gallon of an Igloo-style cooler. Then the gas is taken back to a makeshift lab and combined with ephedrine or pseudoephedrine (found in cold medicine), lithium, ether, and hydrogen chloride gas to create or "cook" meth.

One of the cases on the list involved Tom Cole,[§] believed by federal agents to be at the "top" of a loose organization that manufactured, sold, and used meth, and Frank McNally,[§] who lived such a transient existence that my numerous attempts to find him failed. Early one morning, back in 2002, at two forty-five a.m., a car drove up to Tackett Farms where a large tank of anhydrous ammonia sat in the middle of a field. The vehicle turned its headlights off and parked two hundred feet away from the tank. Deputy Sheriff Tommie Bryant had been staking out the area and monitoring the tank for recurring thefts and saw the car stop.

Officer Bryant approached the car and found Cole and McNally, whom people describe as skinny with a sunken face, small eyes, and pale skin. The two men had been watching the tank through night-vision goggles, presumably to see if the coast was clear. After a search of the car, the police found a hose that might attach to the valve opening of the tank, a pipe wrench that could be used to open the valve, and a tall Igloo thermos. The two men were charged with attempted theft of anhydrous ammonia.

The problem was that to prosecute someone for attempted theft in the state of Mississippi, a prosecutor needs an affirmative act toward the commission of that theft.[54] Mere intent or preparation to commit a crime is not enough. Was stopping on a deserted public road with a container part of the process of stealing the anhydrous ammonia?[55] The answer would decide whether the case merited prosecution. Mellen thought it didn't. There had to be an overt act, he explained, and McNally hadn't done enough. He wasn't caught walking up to the tank. He hadn't tapped the tank. "What in the world have they done? They sat on a dusty road," he said. "They could say we were looking at deer. It could be 'I just had the cooler in my car.'"

So Mellen declined to prosecute. According to Deputy Bryant, however, the tank was the only thing out in the middle of a vast countryside with a mile of barren "plowed-under" land on either side. "If they would have kept going north they would have hit the tank," he said. At the very least, the position of the car, in the middle of nowhere, directly south of the tank, combined with the cooler, the hose, and the wrench, all set to go in the middle of the night could show an affirmative act, which would allow for prosecution. Just driving right up next to the tank at two forty-five a.m. could arguably have been an affirmative act. "It's not like they were sitting in the coffee house," said one district attorney who mulled over the facts. "They have taken steps to accomplish the crime."

On the other hand, every prosecutor knows the attitude of potential jurors and whether they are likely to convict at trial. While other prosecutors might bring a case like this, Mellen knew he had to have extra proof to successfully prosecute a drug case. Jurors in his jurisdiction were extremely wary of law enforcement. Also, judges tended to excuse a lot of "good citizen" jurors who had full-time jobs, leaving people who may well have used drugs themselves, who might be scared to convict drug dealers known to them, are skeptical of police practices, or who might have had brothers or sisters sent to jail for drugs and thus empathize with the defendants. Said Mellen: "[Jurors] used to be people who were conservative. Now you have people in there who see drugs being sold in the neighborhoods. They are tolerant of crime." Here, Mellen's experience differs from what lawyers generally report: Jurors are so sick of seeing drugs in their neighborhoods that they can't wait to convict.

Officers wished Mellen were more willing to try difficult cases. An incident like this wasn't a slam dunk, though it was typical of meth cases. Several prosecutors said they had prosecuted and won many like it. There would be "no doubt in my mind that these guys were up to no good," said one area prosecutor, adding, "I would have to let a jury decide."

"Study the case, get the witnesses to prepare, come up with a strategy, and present that strategy to a jury!" said an officer who worked on both men's cases and didn't understand why Cole had not been tried. If the defendants chose to testify, the prosecutor could cross-examine them and ask, "But why did you come to *this* location and stop your car?" "The same type of people that are in grand jury will sit on a jury trial," this officer said, referring to the likelihood of getting an indictment. "They are good people with a common sense smart enough to know the difference between right and wrong, good and bad."

Frustrated with Mellen, specifically his nonprosecution of drug-related crime, state drug agents tried to work through the U.S. attorneys in the Northern District federal court in Oxford. That office had worked on similar cases and had even won an award in 2006 from the Organized Crime Drug Enforcement Task Force for dismantling the largest methamphetamine distribution operation in the Northern District of Mississippi.

Cole ended up pleading guilty in federal court, not for the Tackett Farms incident but for one in nearby Sunflower County (after state drug agents discovered him on a three-wheel all-terrain vehicle with a headlamp in the middle of a farm at two fifteen a.m.). Cole pleaded guilty to posesion of a firearm and, having three previous felonies for firearm possession, he was sentenced by a federal judge to sixteen and a half years in prison.

Meanwhile, McNally, who had been with Cole at Tackett Farms, was able to evade justice. "Everyone knew he was making multi-ounces," meaning more than a little, "and was probably one of the biggest cooks," said a former federal narcotics agent. And yet when McNally's case went to the federal prosecutor, the agent was asked for "fresh" evidence because the investigators' findings in Quitman County were deemed insufficient.

Locally, McNally had been arrested three times (in two adjacent counties) for possession of "precursor chemicals," or key ingredients for manufacturing meth. He had racked up a heap of misdemeanor convictions (trespassing twice; driving with an expired tag or no tag; driving with no insurance; driving on a suspended license; driving without proper safety mechanisms or child restraint; seatbelt violation; reckless driving), according to court records. Then, in December 2003, a twenty-five-year-old man was found dead in his car from a drug overdose a little more than a mile from McNally's house. Scotty Alan Meredith, the chief medical examiner/investigator for Coahoma County, went out to the scene as part of the research for his autopsy report and wrote that bystanders saw McNally go up to the car where the young man was slumped in the driver's seat, purple from the neck up with one leg hanging out. He removed two bags and took them back to his house. The local newspaper reported the death and one reader wrote in: "When is enough enough? How long are these key players going to be allowed to roam the streets?"[56]

In 2006, farmers reported hearing strange noises on Bland Road in Lambert, a town in Quitman County. The Mississippi Bureau of Narcotics traced the tracks of a four wheel all-terrain vehicle over some matted parts of a wheat field back to McNally's family's house. To the side of the house, in an old cotton gin (used to separate cotton fibers from seedpods) belonging to someone else, officers found farm equipment, some anhydrous ammonia, and an empty soda bottle with two holes drilled on either side for tubes to make meth. Walking back to the house, the officers also found a cooler leaning against a dog pen, ephedrine pills, and a tea pitcher filled with engine starter fluid (which contains ether).

Outside, two people pulled up to the front of the house in the four-wheeler. The couple claimed to have just come back from the cotton gin. "They said they weren't doing anything," recalled one officer. But in the little trunk in the back of the four-wheeler, investigators found a plastic bowl filled with crystal meth with a T-shirt wrapped around it. Inside the house, McNally and another man stood sopping wet, toweling off. McNally was arrested and charged with theft of anhydrous ammonia and manufacturing meth. Leslie Flint, the assistant district attorney assigned to the case, said she didn't think she could prosecute any of the four men for possession, much less theft or manufacturing. McNally and his companion claimed to have no knowledge of the meth. "I need more to show that they knew," she said.

Mellen pointed the finger back at investigators for not getting him what he needed. As he said many times, "I want the investigator to do his work. And then I want to pick up the file and I want to win." He would prosecute the cases when officers gave him better evidence. The officers, on the other hand, thought their job was to provide the basic facts and that Mellen should try his hand before a jury and stop thwarting their work. As for McNally, he moved out of Quitman County and down to Jackson, the state capital, according to his mother, Judith.[§] He was trying to start fresh. "He's clean now," she said.

■ ■ ■

No matter what the case, the road to prosecution always begins with the police force, which in Quitman County, like in so many places, is underfunded and undertrained. In order to receive training, an officer must already be employed or sponsored by a police department, sheriff's office or state agency, which then sends the officer to the Mississippi Law Enforcement Officer's Training Academy. The academy requires a high-school equivalency diploma and mandates a ten-week course and four hundred hours of training, which is slightly below the national average of five hundred hours most states require, according to the Albion, Michigan-based International Association of Directors of Law Enforcement Standards and Training (IADLEST), which assists states in establishing standards for employment and training of peace officers.[57]

In a poor county in a poor state, where education, like all other services, needs more money, those who are well-educated tend to take jobs in more lucrative fields than police work or they leave the field quickly. In Quitman in 2006, deputy sheriffs made $23,000 to $31,000 a year, and Sheriff Oliver Parker earned $56,400. The facilities are also underfunded. Sheriff Parker didn't have enough money to hire a full-time cook at the jail. On weekends you could see him with a set of over-sized keys in hand, lumbering to the courthouse to whip up breakfast for the inmates. Of course, insufficient resources do not mean officers can't be good at what they do. If their basic work is competent, their level of education becomes irrelevant in court on the stand. "Jurors appreciate plain talk," said one area prosecutor.

Good police work is central to a successful prosecution. When I tried to isolate what the prosecuted cases had in common, a decent investigation was almost always in evidence. Other aspects, like reliable eyewitness testimony, helped. But the participation of the police was the biggest determinant. When Mellen declined to prosecute, he tended to blame the officers and poor police work, calling them idiots. Justifying his view of officers, he recounted a child-rape case outside of Quitman County, in which a police chief kept some bloody clothes for two weeks in his car in the sun. Over time, blood "mildews, molds, and petrifies," Mellen explained. So he had no clothes to introduce at trial. "He was just so stupid," Mellen said.

Clearly, this officer needed some guidance and supervision. He is not alone. Poor relations between prosecutors and the police and ineffective or shoddy investigative work collapse cases across the country. Unlike the federal system, in which the attorney general has authority over both the federal prosecutors and those investigative agencies housed in the Justice Department (like the FBI), state systems "generally lack even this small degree of structural coordination."[58] Prosecutors, sheriffs, and police chiefs operate independently of each other. In New Orleans, a 2005 report penned by Paul Schectman, a former director of the New York State Division of Criminal Justice, for national consulting firm Linder & Associates, noted the dysfunctional relationship between the district attorney's office and the New Orleans Police Department (NOPD). "Both ADAs and NOPD officers do not believe that either group 'knows what they are doing.'"[59] The report suggested a new unit be established as the liaison to ensure that more arrests be prosecuted with a reasonable prospect of conviction.[60]

Deputies are not always trained to acquire evidence beyond the need to make an arrest. The necessary standard to make an arrest (probable cause) requires considerably less evidence than a conviction in court (guilt beyond reasonable doubt). So prosecutors are often required to send police back for more. I had only to look at one child-molestation case on Miss Wiggs's list to see how an important prosecution could be ruined if the police are not being properly directed. This case had the fattest, most complete file of hospital records, social-work reports, and medical tests, yet it still fell through the cracks.

It concerned five-year-old Malissa,[§] the daughter of Eleanor Johnson.[§] One night in June 2001, Eleanor was cooking dinner. Her daughter and some young cousins were sitting on the floor in a circle. Malissa's legs were apart. She was wearing shorts that were pushed to the side so that her underpants showed. But instead of clean white fabric peeking through, the crotch area had a greenish-yellow stain. The day before, Eleanor had noticed the same dark color, only she had thought nothing of it. But now the tinge didn't seem normal. Eleanor took Malissa away from the game. Malissa started to cry. "I peed on myself," she insisted.

"Why do your panties look like that?" Eleanor asked.

"I can't tell," the little girl said, gulping down tears. If she told, Malissa said, she would get "in trouble." Something "bad" would happen to her younger sister.

Eleanor started to cry, too. She was sure that someone had been hurting her child. "I always tell my kids this is a private spot, nobody is going to touch you 'there,'" Eleanor told me.

So she asked her daughter if someone had been touching her "there." Yes, her daughter said. Who? Eleanor wanted to know.

Malissa said, "Cortez."

Eleanor knew most everybody in Quitman County. She had never heard of anyone named Cortez.

"Is Cortez big or not?" Eleanor asked. "He big," she remembers the girl saying.

"Who is he? Is he in your classroom?"

During the summer her daughter had attended a class at Quitman County Elementary School to prepare for kindergarten. Malissa went with her cousins in the morning and she seemed to like it. "Her teacher was always saying how good she was doing and how smart she was," Eleanor remembered.

"He's around the school. He cleans up," the five-year-old said, according to her mother.

Eleanor asked if Cortez put his penis inside of her. Her daughter said no, but that he rubbed himself in between her legs.

Eleanor took her child to Quitman County Hospital's emergency room. To her extreme relief, a doctor found that there had been no penetration of the girl's vagina. However, he found "moderate vaginal secretion," which is unusual for a five-year-old unless she has an infection. The hospital did some tests and released her that night. Two weeks later Eleanor Johnson was at home when the phone rang. The Department of Human Services was following up on her daughter's hospital visit. The test results were back. "Your daughter has herpes," the voice said.

Eleanor dropped the phone.

When Lambert Police Chief Tommie Doyle was assigned the case, he thought it auspicious. "I had been knowing the family since I was a little kid," he said, explaining that he felt that he had Eleanor Johnson's trust right away. In addition, he had a good relationship with Glenn Rossi, the then-assistant district attorney in charge of the county.

Chief Doyle was a tall, strapping man with a large shaved head. He had spent the first twenty years of his career in the military and his lips emitted gravelly, assertive words that owned responsibility for his role in the case. "I put a lot of work in," he said.

The first time he questioned the little girl at the police department, the five-year-old was full of energy, running here and there. She talked of a man she knew as Cortez who had rubbed his penis between her legs and against her buttocks twice. She described him as a potbellied, rabbit-toothed man, small and fat, like a butterball. And he wore a white T-shirt.

Next Chief Doyle asked Eleanor to take her daughter to the school to see if she could find Cortez without anyone knowing what she was doing. Doyle had already walked through the halls and talked to the child's teacher, who said that it wasn't impossible that a child could have slipped away unnoticed for any length of time. He saw several men who worked at the school but in particular noticed a janitor who fit the description of Cortez. The man, Jerry Rivers,§ stood five feet four, weighed about one hundred eighty pounds and wore a white T-shirt. Doyle told Eleanor not to leave until Malissa took a good look at Rivers.

A teacher gave Eleanor a tour of the school. She remembered walking through other classrooms where bigger boys were tutoring, and passing several janitors before Rivers started walking toward them. Malissa froze and cried, "I can't tell you. I can't lose my sister."

Eleanor became stern. "You can't let him hurt someone else. Now which one is it?"

Malissa said he was the one walking. "I said, 'Right there, the one right there with a white T-shirt and the bald head?'" Eleanor asked before calling Chief Doyle and telling him of the identification.

When Malissa's allegations were made, the school decided to move Rivers to another job, in a bus repair shop, where no children were present. The precautionary measure, taken in case Rivers was convicted, would also help to insulate the school from future charges of negligence or recklessness.

Chief Doyle first questioned Rivers at the police station.[61] "He acted like he didn't have a clue as to what I was talking about," Doyle wrote in his report. At the same time "I thought I had a good case," Doyle said. "I can think of no kid dreaming up something like that and putting it in the school."

Jerry Rivers, with his lawyer's approval, got tested for herpes. When the test came back, it showed that he had a very high count of herpes antibodies, which could indicate a current or recent infection. The police arrested Rivers, charging him with molestation or "indulging his depraved, licentious sexual desires" and "rub[bing] in between [Malissa's] legs with his penis, [Malissa], a child under sixteen years of age." A justice court judge held a hearing and bound over the case to circuit court for grand jury.

But the grand jury never heard the case. Over the next year, more investigation followed. Chief Doyle wanted Malissa's underwear tested for sperm to see if they matched Rivers' DNA. He sent the underwear to a major laboratory in New Orleans, which was unable to find any sperm. The laboratory deemed the results "inconclusive." By this time, prosecutor Glenn Rossi had left Quitman County and moved elsewhere. Without his point person to communicate with, Chief Doyle felt disoriented. "There wasn't anyone lawyerwise to talk to," he said, explaining that trying to talk to Laurence Mellen was like hoping for "an act of God" because you could never get him on the phone. "When I lost Glenn, that was it," he said.

Doyle, however, still thought that he had enough evidence for the state to secure a conviction. He had the little girl's description, which matched Rivers and he had the herpes test. Doyle waited for a prosecutor to contact him. A whole year after Eleanor Johnson had first made her complaint, Doyle received a summons beckoning him to testify, not at circuit court for felonies, but at justice court, where misdemeanor cases are adjudicated. After the case had been bound over to circuit court, the district attorney's office had changed the charge from molestation, a felony punishable by two to fifteen years in prison and one to five thousand dollars in fines, to simple assault, a misdemeanor that merited a maximum of six months in county jail, and a fine of five hundred dollars. "It was insulting," Doyle said grimly. "There was a five-year-old with herpes."

Doyle rang up the district attorney's investigator David James.

James said he had reviewed Malissa's case and explained that the evidence did not point to "capital rape"—which he said Doyle's affidavit and report had claimed was the crime—so he sent the case back down as simple assault. ("Capital" referred to the fact that the rape of a child can merit the death penalty or capital punishment). Doyle's heart sank. Nothing in the papers he had sent over implied that the crime was a rape, which, in Mississippi, required "sexual intercourse," or penetration, or proof of some sort of tearing of the genitals.[62] This case was about molestation or improperly touching a child without penetration.

Doyle tried to set James straight. He urged the district attorney's office to interview the girl, and Doyle thought that James had agreed to do so. James even fired off a letter to justice court implying that the case was still open and justice court should stay out of it and not to rule it as a misdemeanor yet: "[Jerry Rivers] has been charged with the crime of sexual battery. This case is currently under investigation by this office with the assistance of Chief Doyle of the Lambert Police Department," the letter, dated June 2002, read in its entirety.

But nobody from the district attorney's office ever called Eleanor to interview her daughter. In fact, just the opposite happened. After months of unreturned phone calls, Eleanor Johnson cornered James at the courthouse. Did he want to interview her daughter? What was happening with Malissa's case? "He said they didn't have enough evidence," Eleanor said. The case was closed.

With that, Malissa's mother packed her things and moved to Chicago. She had sent her daughter to live with relatives because three months after the incident Malissa had been suspended from Quitman's elementary school because of behavior problems. At first, she had stayed at the same program and had been doing well. One of her teachers had sent home a note in September saying what a "good girl" Malissa was. She had done her work quietly, had taken a long nap, had eaten her lunch, and "listened so nicely during story time." The note ended by saying that Malissa had been determined to behave. "She is a very happy, smart little girl. I enjoy having her in my class. You should be proud of her!" the teacher wrote.

But just one month later, the first grader was suspended for three days. According to the suspension form, the child was sent home for being "rude/discourteous," for "excessive talking," for being "disruptive/uncooperative," for "fighting," as well as being "harmful to self/others." "Student discards my notes to parent," the principal wrote, claiming that she had also telephoned Eleanor to discuss Malissa's problems. The school principal, Eunice Jordan, who at sixty-six is retired and teaching as an adjunct professor at a local university, said the girl "would yell out in class, jump out of her seat, and climb on the tables in lack of consideration of the other kids."

Eleanor disagreed, insisting the school had suspended her daughter only after her lawyer had notified the school that Eleanor was planning a civil suit for gross negligence in providing a safe place. The school, Eleanor thought, was retaliating. Even if her daughter was disruptive and having problems, perhaps because she had been molested, the school couldn't be bothered to help her.

In the meantime, Doyle remained determined to fix the case. He attended a seminar with some of the state's best experts in handling sexual-assault cases. He learned that he had made several mistakes. First, the herpes test, a serology test for the herpes antibody, was of little value. It did not distinguish between the kind of herpes that affects the mouth and genitalia and it needed to be redone.

Moreover, national experts agree that serology tests are notoriously unreliable to prove herpes. Only a special culture for herpes from the skin of both Rivers and the girl could determine if either one had the disease at all, according to Dr. Margaret Hammerschlag, director of the department of pediatrics at SUNY Health Science Center at Brooklyn and a consultant for the Center for Disease Control for the STD Treatment Guidelines. "I could tell you stories of peoples' lives being ruined by doing the wrong tests and real cases of abuse go out the window," she said. "Because of the issue of resources and education, people are using the wrong tests." Most likely, only a court order would enable Doyle to retest Rivers, who had hired a lawyer by this point.

Second, Doyle should have interviewed the girl in a special forensic setting where their conversation would have been videotaped. He also never should have suggested that the mother check out Jerry Rivers at the school because that could have been considered a suggestive identification. "I did everything I thought I could do, but I didn't have enough training," he admitted.

Doyle decided to press for the case to be reopened, and when Eleanor and her daughter came back to town for a visit, he called David James and asked that he interview the girl as promised. Doyle never heard back from him. In his defense, James pointed to his overwhelming workload. He claims he wouldn't have made a decision either to close or reopen the case without talking first to an assistant district attorney. "But the bottom line is if there was a case they felt should have been prosecuted, and if they felt that Glenn Rossi or myself should have looked at it differently, then [Chief Doyle] should have gone to Laurence Mellen," said James.

But Doyle knew that Mellen wouldn't prosecute a case unless the police did the hard work for him. "It's your responsibility to push your case. . . . And if the DA says he needs more, you have to see if you can get it," Doyle said. In the end, he realized that the only thing to be done was to push David James on his promise to reinterview the girl, and to seek another herpes test from a judge. But he gave up. No matter how hard he tried, he wouldn't get the girl justice, he thought. Instead, Doyle resigned and took a job as a probation officer in nearby Clarksdale. He had been an officer for eight years, six as chief, and he felt defeated. People in the town blamed him, he thought, when their crimes weren't prosecuted. The "pitiful" pay (twenty-four thousand dollars a year as chief) didn't help. And serious cases like Malissa's hung heavy on his heart. "It hurt," he said.

He thought they had made mistakes, he said, of the district attorney's office, "but they will never stand up to it. They will put it on everybody but themselves."

When I interviewed David James in an office with Mellen, he said little to prove Doyle wrong.

"[Jerry Rivers]," he began. "They sent the file here as capital rape."

I disagreed. The papers in the court file alleged sexual molestation, not rape.

"Molestation or capital rape—either one of the two because of the age of the victim. Five years old—" he continued.

"Yeah. But they sent it to us as what?" Mellen wanted to know.

"Capital rape," James said.

"Are you sure?" Mellen said.

"If I am not mistaken, yes, sir, because that is what I have got on here," he said, pointing to the computer printout of his case summaries. "And I do it exactly from their affidavits."

James knew, or should have known, that there was no capital rape charge. Doyle claimed to have told him many times. Perhaps James had incorrectly read or transferred the seven-line affidavit, which cited the molestation statute. Regardless, had he understood the case, he would not have thought that the charge was rape.

James then pointed to the DNA testing, which, in his view, ruled out Jerry Rivers. However, the DNA report said that testing was "inconclusive due to insufficient or excessively degraded DNA." Nothing pointed to another defendant.

Only a very small percent of legal cases rely on DNA evidence to resolve them. Most require old-fashioned evidence, which means pounding the pavement to find facts and link them to law. For example, the herpes test needed refining. But James and Mellen showed no interest in redoing this, either. "That is not going to tell you that [Rivers] was the one," James said.

This was true. Even if a new test had specified that both girl and janitor had herpes type 2, it would not have sealed the deal. There was no semen on her underwear, no useable DNA. So basically all the district attorney had was the girl's testimony and a shared disease that a lot of people have.

Not enough evidence, as yet, existed to prosecute. But neither James nor Mellen seemed to concentrate on the case, either. It was never properly charged. The little girl was never interviewed by the district attorney's office. Nor had anyone pursued the herpes test and learned what to look for. Meanwhile, Jerry Rivers desperately wanted to clear his name. "I tell you this," Rivers said in his tidy home near the court. "The child could walk up to me right now. I wouldn't know who she is today."

James, faced with an overwhelming number of cases and a great many angry victims and puzzled officers, had grown accustomed to brushing people off. That dismissiveness, coupled with a lack of over-sight, proved a disservice to the people of Quitman County. A very young child had been sexually abused by someone, possibly at school; a man had been accused as a sexual predator—and then left in limbo. What had actually happened to this little girl? No one had done a proper investigation to find out. Everyone was harmed by the shabby handling of an incident that was undeniably grave.

■ ■ ■

Miss Wiggs had her own explanation for all the nonprosecuted cases. Hushed, as if someone were listening, she said, "In great big letters, it's the L-A-Z-Y mentality. If you had *any* compassion for people—a little child! A woman who was beaten senseless!" The people on the list, she said, were like "dusting to a housewife," a low priority chore that never did seem to get done.

Of Mellen she said, "He chooses the high-profile cases, perhaps media cases, and he performs for them. But for the people who really need justice, who takes their cases?"

Miss Wiggs herself did not have a solution in mind. "In a sense, my hands are tied . . . It's hard to do something. You can't push it any further. It would take someone who was brave enough and strong enough to be vocal to say, 'This is what is happening and this is wrong' and be able to take the flack. That person would get a lot of persecution."

I was not certain I agreed that laziness was the overriding problem in Quitman County. If it were, then Laurence Mellen could simply fix the problem. But he couldn't fix the problem. He alone could not teach an officer how to write a decent report. Or help the sheriff attract decently educated police officers when the pay is so miserably low. Or undo years of apathy and bias. Mellen may have to shoulder some blame for not pursuing cases he might have won at trial and for letting so many cases founder for lack of guidance, but he could not be blamed for an almost institutionalized mentality. That was:

- We don't prosecute victims of domestic abuse because they don't give us wins.
- We don't prosecute a case where we don't like the victims or we consider them unreliable.
- We don't follow up on mental health cases because they don't give us wins.
- We don't prosecute cases that require a lot of hard work to establish the facts and in which a jury might turn us down, even if we think the defendant is guilty and jailing him or her would protect the community.

Why does law enforcement get away with this? The foremost reason is that there is no systematic way for the voters who elect their prosecutors to monitor the system's workings. Mellen himself didn't realize at times that no one was going after the facts. And individual victims had no way to prove him wrong even though patterns had developed. On the other hand, one could imagine that a crime committed by an unreliable victim could have unduly drained resources. So could a tough drug case. Or a defendant with mental illness.

For now, prosecutor's decisions are not transparent, except in those major trials that make it to court. Prosecutors are not accountable and rarely have to justify their actions or identify the facts that contributed to them. With too little oversight on potentially momentous decisions that are made behind closed doors, prosecutors have no incentive to be neutral, fair, or to seek justice. Instead, they measure themselves by wins and losses, which is, in the end, a minor part of what their job means to the people who are victims of crime or to the communities that expect their protection.

CHAPTER FOUR

SHOW TRIAL

Thomas M. Breen is a trial jock. He is sixty-two years old with a mop of white hair, long legs that stride with purpose, and a deep, cigarette-tinged voice that easily captivates the attention of a jury. He's a well-known attorney in Chicago, the type whom businessmen and politicians call on when they get into trouble. Glass-framed front-page stories of his victories adorn his office walls, and he has received numerous awards for excellence in public service for his pro bono work. The secret, his colleagues agree, is that he throws himself into his cases, working passionately and intensely. Then, when it comes time to go to trial, Breen is a great communicator.

Although his career has been a study in success, it began with a failure so profound he carries it with him every day of his life. Breen started out as a prosecutor. In 1972, at age twenty-five, he took a position in the Cook County state's attorney's office and quickly proved he could handle big felony cases. In his first three years alone, he prosecuted about thirty murder trials. He was young and ambitious and what he lacked in experience he made up for with vigor. At twenty-nine, he landed a case that most prosecutors only dream about: high stakes, a lot of media attention, a potential career maker.

It was January 14, 1976. Lisa Cabassa, an alert, lively, nine-year-old girl, had left her home on South Saginaw Avenue on the Southeast Side of Chicago to tag along with her eleven-year-old brother, Ricky, as he walked a friend home. Midway there, she turned back, saying she had a headache. Ricky saw a car honk at her as she crossed the street. A neighbor saw her walking. She was wearing a red plaid coat, blue jeans, and a white, yellow, and blue scarf. Lisa never made it home. The next morning a man parking his car found her in an alley several miles from where Ricky had last seen her. Lisa was dead. She had been raped and strangled.

The Chicago police went full force trying to find a suspect, checking the whereabouts of known sex offenders and recent inmates. Detectives hunted door to door for clues and questioned teenagers and adults who had known Lisa. Weeks passed. More than a dozen men were arrested and let go.[1]

Then, a month and a half after the crime, the police had a witness: Judy Januszewski, a mother of two young children, claimed to have seen Lisa's abduction while walking home from work. Januszewski identified seventeen-year-old Michael Evans, who wore platform shoes and his hair kinked up in an afro. Michael was then charged with kidnapping, murder, and rape. He had never been in trouble with the law. He was a high-school dropout with learning disabilities who was attending vocational school; and he had a girlfriend with whom he had a son. Those who knew him described him as happy and easy going. His lawyer described him to the media as "retarded."[2]

Breen was assigned the case, along with his trial partner, Terry Ekl. They tried it twice. Both times, the accused's lawyers put on what Breen in retrospect called "a brilliant defense." Ultimately, though, Breen and Ekl prevailed, sending Michael and a second seventeen-year-old boy,

Paul Terry, to prison for a term of two hundred to four hundred years. The two boys, now men, ultimately spent twenty-seven years in prison.

A case like this one, involving the rape and murder of a child, inevitably draws public outrage, a cry for justice, and the fiercest possible demand to try the culprit and deliver a conviction. Although prosecutors might see such cases as a gift to a career, these situations are also a magnet for injustice and overzealous prosecution. In a tragedy like the death of Lisa Cabassa, the inordinate amount of pressure to win at trial can cloud an attorney's ability to weigh the truth. Unfortunately, these are the trials that resonate deeply with the citizenry. We see them on TV. They are the very image of American justice, the wellspring of all the *Law and Order* episodes where investigators won't stop pursuing a lead until the case is closed. Prosecutors want the dramatic closure of order prevailing over crime, and they know that conviction in a high-profile case is what registers with most citizens. And since citizens often elect both the prosecutor and the judge, the pressure is on.

Overzealous prosecution in high-profile show trials is directly related to the kind of underprosecution practiced in Quitman County, Mississippi. Always bearing in mind what will play before a jury, a district attorney assesses hundreds, if not thousands, of smaller, less visible cases. In Mississippi, Laurence Mellen, with his negligible funding, made his decisions based on whether he could land convictions. A fear of losing and further tanking his conviction rate drove his decisions to chuck cases. In both under-and overprosecution, pressures and incentives to win can override a prosecutor's good judgment when it comes to deciding whom to charge with a crime. In a case like Lisa Cabassa's, the prosecutor's responsibility to assess the truth is arguably even higher because it involves the vindication of a little girl's death. Yet there is virtually no check on the prosecutor who acts in this quasi-judicial role. Instead, the system puts its faith in his professionalism and the belief that the defense or a jury will catch his mistakes.

Breen's victory in the trial of Lisa Cabassa's murder showed he could win a weak case. Yet despite his success, he left the prosecutor's office to become a private defense lawyer. He settled in the Monadnock

Building on Jackson Street, a haven for his former prosecutor friends. He went about his business for nineteen years, hardly ever mentioning Lisa's case. But in the winter of 1995, Breen decided it was possible he'd convicted the wrong men. He asked a colleague who investigates wrongful convictions to look into whether he could have made a mistake prosecuting Michael Evans and Paul Terry. As Breen said in an interview later, "The factual situation never made a lot of sense to me."

As a result of his speaking up, the case became the nation's oldest conviction to be overturned on DNA evidence. Even after Breen voiced his doubts, it took another eight years to exonerate Michael and Paul, which meant each had spent twenty-seven years in prison. Michael, nicknamed "Smiley" for his exaggerated cheerfulness, stumbled into the free world without a compass, at a loss. The other convict, Paul, went mad waiting. He had entered prison as a fastidious mama's boy and walked out with his hair in unkempt clumps and his mind delusional, haunted by imaginary guards always yelling at him.

As horrible as it is, Michael and Paul's case is not that unusual in Illinois. Their exoneration followed thirteen cases of inmates on death row who had been cleared of murder charges. These wrongful convictions caused such alarm that the governor of Illinois decided to establish a moratorium against the death penalty in 2000, and to commute the sentences of all 167 men and four women on death row to life in 2003. But Michael and Paul's case stands apart. Its reversal was instigated by the very prosecutor who had put them in jail in the first place. Breen's turnaround raises so many questions. How, after so many years, did he realize he had gotten it wrong? Why did he wait so long?

■　■　■

The miscarriage of justice that sent Michael and Paul to prison for twenty-seven years was born of the union between the prosecutor's drive to convict and the police who wanted to produce a defendant. In the early 1970s, the Cook County state's attorney's office was just the right place for an aggressive young lawyer like Breen. He had hoped to enter Northwestern University School of Law, where his father went, but his grades were low and he had botched the law school entrance exam. So he attended Loyola University's Chicago School of Law, which admitted him on the condition that he earn good grades in his first year. He performed brilliantly, ending up sixteenth out of one hundred and twenty students, he said, and after that, "I assumed my role being right smack in the middle of the class."

Loyola regularly fed the state's attorney's office with recent graduates. In 1972, a new state's attorney, Bernard Carey, a Republican and an Irishman, had just been elected. He was only thirty-one years old. Streams of the old assistant prosecutors, mostly Democrats, were leaving. Carey hired a slew of new attorneys, many of whom, like Breen, were Irish Republicans.

By going to work for Carey, Breen joined a strong tradition of sons of cops or law enforcement agents who went into criminal law and would become career prosecutors. (Breen's father had been an agent for the Federal Bureau of Investigation before he became an attorney who did mostly civil work.) Many had attended Catholic high schools, and went to the same colleges and law schools—a common set of references. "What parish are you from?" was a common ice-breaker among new hirees. "Even the Jewish guys would tell you what parish they grew up in," joked Lee Schoen, an assistant state's attorney at the time. The shared background created a quick, strong bond among the one hundred or so attorneys, mostly in their mid-twenties, single and male, who worked for Cook County.

The office itself was intense. The atmosphere was filled with a sense of competition, not just to convict defendants but to beat out the other prosecutors. According to a report in the *Chicago Tribune*, the attorneys tallied their wins and losses on a chart pinned to the wall: a green sticker for victory, red for defeat. Every prosecutor had a record.[3]

"There wasn't much room for a critical evaluation of all attitudes of the accused, or of whether everything we were doing all the time was right," said Lorna Propes, one of the few women who worked for the state's attorney. "I don't want to say that we were being unfair. But the focus was winning and not being critical of the methods. I don't want to be quoted as saying the methods were wrong. We were young kids in a highly charged battle. Right and wrong. Good against evil."

Theoretically, a prosecutor and his staff aren't supposed to be so concerned with winning. They are supposed to pursue justice. The ideal is perhaps best described by Robert H. Jackson as U.S. attorney general before he became a supreme court justice:

> The qualities of a good prosecutor are as elusive and as impossible to define as those which make a gentleman. And those who need to be told would not understand it anyway. A sensitiveness to fair play and sportsmanship is perhaps the best protection against the abuse of power, and the citizen's safety lies in the prosecutor who tempers zeal with human kindness, who seeks truth and not victims, who serves the law and not factional purposes, and who approaches his task with humility.[4]

Even people trained to search for the truth, however, face conflicting demands within the adversarial system. Prosecutors are supposed to act in favor of the victim, protect the defendant from having his rights impinged, and adhere to the law while reflecting local customs and values. It's an extremely complex position to be in. The defense attorney, by contrast, simply has to advocate as best he can for his client. And because prosecutors serve at the pleasure of their bosses, who are usually elected, they are heavily influenced by conviction statistics. Losing a case can mean bad press and missed votes in a community where a tough law-and-order image is often necessary for budget negotiations with the county.[5] Plus, the type of lawyer drawn to trial work is inherently competitive. There's an old saying that a good trial lawyer is a frustrated jock looking for a new arena in which to compete. "We were all competitive with anyone," said William J. Kunkle Jr., an assistant state's attorney at the time.

"What that atmosphere created among prosecutors was a zealousness that could be taken too far," said Robert Egan, also an assistant state's attorney in the 1970s. "The perception was that we weren't just fighting criminals, we were fighting defense attorneys and judges, and it wasn't a fair fight." The office motto, "Do the right thing," was supposed to inspire a sense of moral responsibility among the young attorneys. However, it often came to mean that it was better to push the bounds of the law and be slapped down by the appellate courts than to stick to the rules and lose. "There was definitely a saying at the office that you can't be reversed on the appeal if you don't win at the trial," said one former prosecutor. "To some people, it was a win-at-all-costs, let-them-sort-it-out-on-appeal sort of atmosphere."

Given the polarity the prosecutors had established between them and the defense—good against evil—lawyers in the DA's office naturally stuck together. They were fighting to protect citizens against the underbelly of society, "bad" people, like murderers, robbers, and rapists, people who hurt other people on a routine basis. And they did this work without getting paid as much as their counterparts in the private sector who earned maybe five times more. Most did not yet have families or spouses. After work they would go to bars to get flying drunk—places like Jean's, a dive across the street from the courthouse virtually closed to the outside world. Breen would sit for hours at Jean's with a Jack Daniel's in one hand and a cigarette in the other. Even judges went. "It was like another college fraternity," Lee Schoen remembered.

There were frat-like antics, as well. For instance, the famous "two-ton contest," in which some prosecutors competed to see who would be first to convict defendants weighing a total of four thousand pounds. In a procedure that had no legal meaning, defendants—mostly black—were weighed on a scale in the back of a courtroom. Lawyers referred to the behind-the-scenes sport as "niggers by the pound."[6] However cruel this might seem, Schoen said of his colleagues that had they been truly prejudiced they wouldn't have represented the victims—who were also mostly black—so vigorously. He tried to cast the contest as "juvenile athletics" and "a sports thing, winning and losing."

Breen didn't remember anything unsavory about the office. In fact, just the opposite. Echoing several former prosecutors, he told the story of a bum convicted of murdering a woman in Grant Park. He was arrested, charged, and convicted of murder. Shortly after, another man confessed to the murder, creating doubt for the prosecuting attorney Thomas R. Fitzgerald (now chief justice of the Illinois Supreme Court). Fitzgerald, no longer believing he had the right man, marched into court and requested that the original defendant be released on the basis of innocence. "That is what I learned in 1972," Breen said of the office.

Breen's colleagues describe his talent and playful sense of humor, which made him "the darling" of judges and journalists. He had the respect of many an attorney too. As Lorna Propes put it, "Tom Breen was without question the most popular and one of the . . . most highly regarded, emulated prosecutors. There was no one [else] who most epitomized what was good and fun about the office." He had loads of friends who sought his company but rarely discussed anything emotionally sensitive or personal with him. Robert Egan, now sixty, and until recently deputy chief of the public interest bureau of the state's attorney's office, pulled out a pile of photos from his desk drawer. They showed several prosecutors looking every bit like frat boys out to play. First: one of Breen trying to push in on a photo of Ekl (his trial partner in the Cabassa case) and his wife. Then: Breen sporting a Beatles bowl haircut with a cigarette dangling out of his mouth as he looks boldly into the camera; another with him in a Red Sox hat drinking beer with friends. "This guy is a judge now," Egan said of Dennis J. Porter, sitting next to Breen. (Coincidentally, Porter was the judge who eventually released Michael Evans and Paul Terry.)

If Breen was one of the guys in most respects, in court he was slightly different. He was a "comer," a top prosecutor known for his vigorous, bold tactics. He loved to make a judge smile, a jury laugh. He bordered on the outrageous, doing things slightly differently and informally. He yelled at witnesses in a way that didn't seem berating. Jurors wanted to talk to him after court and tell him what a good job he did. Or how much he reminded them of a favorite uncle or brother.

In preparing for trial Breen was known for the color-coded file system he used to keep things neat and organized. But in the courtroom he found an emotional outlet. He thrived in the atmosphere of intensity and competition. Brought up, as he claimed, with "the Irish sense of personal guilt," he felt the courtroom was the one place he could shrug off the imperative to love thy neighbor. It was his job to demolish the other side. "Trial is an adversarial proceeding where you have to be in combat, you can't take a blow and say, I will take that. You have to be on guard, not unlike in a boxing match"—a sport Breen had taken up in college and been extremely successful at. His colleagues noticed how his personality changed in court. "With Tom, you see anger and emotion in the courtroom that you have never seen in real life," said one, "and it never comes off as fake or whiney." Said Lee Schoen, "There's an innate sense of decency to him."

Colleagues described Breen's gift for cross-examination. "He knows when to stop," said William Martin Sr., who had worked with him over the years. "He knows when he has landed a right hook." According to Propes, "He didn't hide things or do bullshit things that prosecutors can do." When it came to the Cabassa case, however, he did not fully get the chance to play fair because by the time he was assigned to it, the police had already cut corners to make the arrests.

The police who put together the case against Michael Evans and Paul Terry hailed from Area 2. The office covered the South Side of Chicago, where many police officers had grown up and later raised their families but had since abandoned because of an influx of crime. "People now policing the area were policing people in their old neighborhoods who had ruined [them]," said Richard Brzeczek, former superintendent of the Chicago Police Department.

Many defense lawyers and public defenders had heard tales of the police mistreating suspects and residents on the South Side. Prosecutors had a sense of this as well. Egan remembered working for the felony review unit, which screened and approved felony charges, and heading down to Area 2 to talk to cops. He saw a man chained to the wall. "He's just in for his monthly beating and oil change," the cop said. Maybe the cop was trying to be funny. But "the fact of the matter was [that the cop] was treating abuse of prisoners lightly," Egan said.

Prosecutors have an incentive to turn a blind eye to police abuse, in large part because the relationship between them and the police is symbiotic. Without the cops, the prosecutors would not have their cases, and without the prosecutors, law enforcement investigations would go nowhere. Breen said he had heard complaints about Area 2 from defense attorneys, but as a prosecutor he trusted his officers. "Many of the policemen were very hard-working," he said. "I liked them. They were good policemen."

Defense lawyers disagreed, among them Sam Adam. He was something of a radical. In the 1960s, he'd been a freedom rider, protesting abuse of civil rights in the South. He'd heard about the way police would go down to the South Side and arrest a bunch of innocent black kids. Especially in Area 2, cops would threaten young men unless someone confessed. The interrogation room had hooks for beatings. If a client had been brought in on a homicide charge in Area 2, "He was in for an ass whupping," Adam said.

Sam Adam was the man Michael's family turned to when they decided to hire a lawyer, and he was ready for the fight. When Adam interviewed Michael, he was surprised to find that except for some lashings with a metal belt in the van on the way to jail, the police had not given him an Area 2–style beating, possibly because, as Adam put it, "He was so meek and so mild."

From the outset, there were problems with the police case. Michael was arrested because Judy Januszewski claimed to have witnessed him abducting Lisa. Michael's family lived not far from Januszewski, a white woman of Polish descent, who worked at Lamplighter Real Estate as a secretary several blocks from her home. Januszewski knew Michael not only from the neighborhood, but because he used to come to the real-estate office to visit his volunteer mentor, an agent who helped with his school work.

Januszewski, however, waited five days before coming forward as a witness, and even then she did not immediately name Michael as a suspect. The delay seemed strange to Adam, since she had two children of her own who played in the same playground as Lisa. Logically, concern for the other children, not to mention her own, would have compelled her to speak up earlier. And when police first interviewed her, she was quite unclear about what she had seen. She thought perhaps she had witnessed a brother dragging his sister home by her arm. Then she said she saw two men pulling a young girl toward the alley. She described them as "negroes," in their late teens to early twenties, both about five feet eleven. As the men were pulling the girl, Januszewski heard her say, "No." A third man stood about ten feet away, but Januszewski wasn't sure the three men were together, according to the police report.

Forty-one days passed after Lisa's disappearance before Januszewski identified Michael, even though she knew him. She said she had been harassed by phone by a man and had received a threatening note. Fear had kept her from coming forward, she claimed. But when the intimidation didn't stop, she decided to tell police that Michael had been the one in the alley. At this point, she could not positively identify the second man; and though she recognized the third man as someone whom she used to see at her office and on Saginaw Avenue, she called him "Earl Jones," a name no one else in the neighborhood knew. Thus police had only Michael as a suspect.

Area 2 officers insisted that when they arrested Michael, he made a statement or confession about Lisa's murder. This statement, Adam noticed, was missing from the police report. Instead, the report summarized a confession taken by Officer Melvin Duncan.

> He [Michael Evans] observed Lisa walking with another
> little girl. The other little girl left and the victim was alone
> in the alley. Evans observed a man known to him as Earl
> put the victim in an auto (Earl's) and at that time Michael
> got into the car. At this time the victim was in the back
> seat of the auto, a 2 door green Chevy or Ford. They then
> went to 75th St. and parked the auto on a street two blocks

east of Stony Island. At this time Earl got into the rear seat of the auto with the victim and began having intercourse with her. The victim was asking him to stop and he continued to have sex with her. He at first began "sucking" on the victim and then put his penis in her. The victim was making a lot of noise and then Earl began choking her. At this point in the assault Evans stated he went to a neighborhood store and bought a PayDay candy bar and some chewing gum. When Evans returned to the car the victim was dead. Evans also stated that he thinks that Earl put some acid in the wine that they were drinking and that he then got drunk and does not remember more.

Evans later recanted this statement given to Officer Duncan.

In fairness to the detectives, had they wanted to frame Michael, they would have left his recantation out of the police report. Adam thought that in all likelihood Michael had confessed. He did not have a forceful personality and had been held for eleven hours. "I just knew that he had made a bad statement," Adam said.

Adam wanted to see the confession in which Michael had supposedly admitted to the crime. He never received it. Adam believes that officers had lied about Michael's confession. "Area 2 was so corrupted," he said. "The way to clean up crime was to grab a bunch of black kids and say one of them confessed." Instead, the police gave him a transcript of an interrogation which never even mentioned the alleged earlier confession. Adam also advised Michael to stop talking to police. So, at the top of the transcript of that conversation, Michael scrawled in nearly illegible handwriting: *On advice of my attorney Sam Adam I not sign this, MLE.*

Adam remembers the transcript as "the strangest criminal statement I had ever seen." It had been conducted by a representative from the state's attorney's office with an investigator from the homicide–sex unit. Much of the talk was sexual or concerned Judy Januszewski. Inexplicably, no one asked Michael whether he had confessed earlier or whether he was with Lisa the night she was killed. It was so vague and indirect that it lacked an actual confession. The following are excerpts:

"Michael, was this real-estate woman [Judy Januszewski] trying to hit on you?" the state's attorney asked.

"Well one time she was, you know, the way she acted, you know."

"Would you tell me, please, how she acted?"

"Well, she acted like when I go in there, you know, I tell her, you know, like I got to go and stuff, you know. And she would give me a cup of coffee and stuff, you know, I have cigarettes and stuff, you know, she offer me, take one. And I would smoke one and she say, take a couple more. I say, no, I got my own cigarettes."

"Did she try to be close to you, Mike? Was she trying to make you?"

"Something she was trying to do."

"You think she was trying to make you?"

"Yeah, and then like, you know, like when you see her at night she would be waving at me and stuff. So I just wave back, you know."

"Did she have a nice body, Mike, she have big tits?"

"Yeah, she kind of stacked."

"Kind of what?"

"Stacked."

"Stacked. Did she ever move on you?"

"Nope. I never, you know messed around, you know. Only thing I ever did was talk to her."

. . . .

"You ever go in there just to bullshit with her?"

"Yup, I always go in there, read books, drink coffee."

"You've been in there more than three times, is that correct?"

"Yes."

"Would you consider her a friend of yours?"

"Yup, but she act like she wanted to make it, you know, wanted to make it out of something else, you know, smiling and stuff, but I never did, you know."

. . . .

The questioners then asked if he knew Lisa.

"Mike, do you know if Lisa was putting out for any of the black kids in the neighborhood?"

"What you mean?"

"Was she giving any pussy?"

"I don't know about that."

"Or was she sucking any dick?"

"I don't know."

"Did you ever fuck Lisa, Mike?"

"No.

"You think any of those black dudes were fucking her?"

"They probably—probably did, I'm not sure you know."

"You think it was the older guys?"

"Probably."

"Why do you say that, why do you say probably?"

"Because I don't know."

"Just because they were playing?"

"Yeah."

"Did you ever hear any talk in the neighborhood that she was playing around with the older boys?"

"No I never heard it, I saw it."

"How many times did you see it?"

"About one time."

"About one time for sure?"

"Yeah, yeah."

Michael also proceeded to recall things in such detail, they could not possibly be true six weeks after the murder. Whatever he was asked, he kept coming up with answers, like a poor student trying to satisfy his teachers. "He had a tendency to agree with whatever you said," Adam remembered (which is also, he said, why he refused to put Michael on the stand).

For example, in the interrogation, Michael said on the day of the murder he was home with a chest cold, having orange juice. He had left his house for his "auntie's" at around eight-thirty p.m.—he had checked the time—to hang out with his cousin and his friends "cause they had some reefers." He stayed with them until about nine-thirty, ten p.m., when he came home. Yes, he remembered that the street was slippery; how long he stayed at his auntie's house (an hour and a half, two hours); exactly who he saw when he came home (his father, mother, and sisters); which channel he was watching when he heard the news that Lisa had been killed. Yes, he knew Lisa by sight from playing with other kids in the neighborhood, but he "didn't know her by name," and yes, he had seen her earlier that day when she was walking down the street going to school, the same school his niece went to.[7] He remembered other seemingly hard-to-recall details: that he bought some chips and RC Cola and paid with a one-dollar bill to a clerk wearing a black jump suit; he played with his little niece who was wearing pink pants and a black jacket that day, he himself was wearing a gray hat (which Januszewksi had reported seeing on one of the abductors). Also, he recalled a conversation with Januszewski—a "friend"—about what a "shame" the murder was.

The transcripts did not seem to implicate Michael in the least. The purported confession he had given to Officer Duncan was never found, just a third-hand account, and all that was left was this bizarre interview that recorded Michael's refusal to endorse it. The prosecution had no real confession and no evidence besides Januszewski's eyewitness testimony. Still, Adam thought the case would be difficult to defend. The murder was so horrible that jurors might be moved to convict just to hold someone responsible. "There are some cases where you know from the beginning that the problem with the case is the heinousness of the crime and not the evidence," he said.

For this reason and others, in Illinois a defendant can waive a trial by jury and ask for a bench trial in which a judge decides guilt or innocence. (Only a minority of states give the defendant the unconditional right to trial without a jury. Most states require both the prosecution or the judge, or both, to agree.) Adam decided a reasonable judge would be less likely to be swayed by the horrific facts of the murder and rape than ordinary citizens on a jury with little experience. "This case, without a confession and depending upon the word of this woman, cried out to me that a good judge would toss [it]," said Adam. But that would depend on the judge to whom the case was randomly assigned.

Adam said he thought he had gotten a windfall when Earl Strayhorn, a black judge, landed the case. Strayhorn had a reputation for being fair to defendants, the type who wouldn't be swayed by public opinion and who was "his own man." Adam asked for a bench trial without a jury.

At the start, Strayhorn seemed to make rulings that favored Michael. He suppressed the odd interrogation as well as other statements that would have supported the prosecution. He also acknowledged evidence of police misconduct. For instance, Michael's mother, Lillie, tried for twelve hours to see her son but was rebuffed by police. "During those hours, [she] was no more than a few feet from where he was being held, but she was not permitted to see him," Judge Strayhorn said in a newspaper account of the trial (the 1976 court transcript is incomplete), adding that police had promised Mrs. Evans, who was illiterate, that she could see her son if she would sign papers allowing a search of her house.[8] The police conducted the search but did not keep their promise to let Mrs. Evans see her son. With this sort of misconduct, before a judge like Strayhorn, both sides thought the case would be thrown out.

And yet at the conclusion of the trial in June 1976, to everyone's astonishment, Strayhorn convicted Michael on all counts. If not for new evidence posttrial, the verdict would have stuck. As it turned out, the state had failed to disclose that it had given Januszewski $1,250 to relocate her family. The payment was common practice: the state's attorney would often offer a witness of few means the option to move for safety so as not to jeopardize the case. "It is one of those unfair things in the practice of law," Adam said. "If I did this for an alibi witness, they would indict me for bribery." After the conviction, Adam argued in a motion for a new trial that the money had given Januszewski motive to lie. She wanted out of the neighborhood in which she had lived for over ten years—it was changing from predominantly white to black and Hispanic.

Adam also discovered after the trial that Januszewski had first come forward not to the police but to a citizen offering a five-thousand-dollar reward and anonymity in exchange for information about the crime. She never collected the money, for reasons unclear, and she seemed to have waived her anonymity because the police interviewed her the next day. Adam said Januszewski was motivated by greed to testify and by a need to get out of the neighborhood. He argued that not turning over such evidence was a violation of *Brady v. Maryland*, which established the prosecution's obligation to turn over any exculpatory material to the defense.[9]

Today, Chicago courts would likely discipline prosecutors for such errors. "It's serious business," said Egan. But Strayhorn decided in September 1976 that the mistakes were unintentional; though he reversed his conviction, he found that the prosecutors deserved another shot. Strayhorn granted the prosecution's motion for a new trial.

Upon hearing that the convictions were overturned, Lisa's mother, Carmen Cabassa, sobbed. Breen, too, was brought to tears, according to a newspaper report. "We'll do it all over again . . . all over again," he assured her.[10] In the lag between trials, police continued investigating. After all, Januszewski had said that she had seen *two* men abduct Lisa and a third who stood by whom she called Earl Jones, but whom the police could not find.

In early November, police interviewed a sixteen-year-old boy, Keith Jones, who said that Michael Evans had shown him Lisa's body on the night of the murder. He then signed a statement that he had not been threatened by police or coerced into giving information. He identified four new suspects, all friends of Michael's. One was Paul Terry. The others were Sam Parker, nineteen; Columbus Thomas, twenty-two; and James Davis, twenty-four, whom Januszewksi had named Earl Jones, though no one called him that. All were arrested.[11]

Based on Keith Jones's statement, given ten months after the crime, Januszewski pointed to Paul Terry in a police line-up as the person who had abducted Lisa alongside Michael. But less than three weeks after the murder, on February 2, 1976, police had asked her to look through a high-school yearbook that contained Paul's photo. She had picked out a different boy, who was never charged. And in previous accounts, Januszewski claimed to have seen the man for ten to fifteen seconds on a dimly lit street, but she insisted he had very distinctive eyebrows that stood out in her mind. They were "dark and neatly trimmed" as if "penciled over," police reported. Paul's eyebrows were nondescript. Like Michael, Paul had never been in trouble with the law. He was a quiet boy who rarely went out and who was teased at school for his punctuality and fastidious attire.

Nonetheless, James Davis, Paul Terry, and Michael Evans were charged with murder, rape, deviant sexual assault, and aggravated kidnapping. Sam Parker and Columbus Thomas were charged with concealing a homicide.[12]

It seemed like the police had cracked the case, but Keith Jones recanted his statement the following month and then gave a sixty-two page statement to Adam describing how two unidentified investigators had encouraged him to lie. "They were hollering at me, and stuff, like I really knew something. So I went on and put a lie together just to free myself."[13]

Joseph DiLeonardi, Chicago police homicide commander, denied that the witness had been intimidated. He said that Jones had voluntarily come to the station with his mother. "At no time during the interview by the prosecutors did the witness or his mother complain that anyone had intimidated the youth," DiLeonardi said to the press. In addition, a civilian court reporter, as well as Terry Ekl and Tom Breen, had all been present during the interrogation, according to a newspaper report.[14] Still, based on the recantation, the charges against Parker and Thomas were dropped and the case against James Davis was also dismissed just prior to the second trial. Only Paul and Michael remained as defendants because Judy Januszewski had identified them.

For the new trial, Judge Strayhorn recused himself and had the case reassigned, which was standard procedure in a bench trial. He was replaced by Judge Frank W. Barbaro, who had a reputation for favoring the prosecution. "He was going to do whatever the state's attorney tells him to do," Adam remembered. Adam asked for a jury trial.

In the meantime, the state's attorney's office was well aware of the weaknesses of the prosecution. In fact, even though it was a high-profile case, no prosecutor really wanted the job. Higher-ranking prosecutors and supervisors tended to prefer ones that were easier to win; the tough ones went to less senior prosecutors like Breen and Terry Ekl.

The two were great friends. Ekl was dark haired, fit, a former starting guard football player at Northwestern University and, according to Breen, the best athlete of the group. Ekl prided himself on his logical approach, and was known for a no-holds-barred attitude. "A real hard charger," is how one fellow prosecutor described him; "a one note, one speed, one vision guy," said another. He was so committed to the case that even though he had left the state's attorney's office prior to the second trial, he returned to work on it. Ekl explained that he hadn't been in private practice very long, maybe a month, and he "had a good sense of the facts," without which the prosecution would have had a lack of continuity. Besides, the Cabassa family were "really sweet nice people and I had developed a really nice relationship with them," Ekl said.

Newspaper clips from the case show that the new trial had become a campaign issue in the race for Cook County state's attorney. Bernard Carey, the state's attorney, faced criticism that the prosecution had blown the case. "This is yet another example of Carey seeking headlines at the cost of a successful prosecution," his democratic opponent Edward J. Egan said, to which Carey replied that Egan was making the police and prosecutors' jobs harder. "The grief that surrounds the Lisa Cabassa case should not be exploited for political advantage," read an editorial in the *Chicago Daily News*.[15] (Neither Breen nor Ekl remember the political pressure today.)

In Ekl's opening statement, he focused on Judy Januszewski's testimony. "This case is a case of credibility," he said. "Either you are going to believe Judy Januszewski is telling the truth and find these defendants guilty or you are going to conclude that she is a liar and then you would find them not guilty. There is no middle ground."

He described how Januszewski had been walking home after work at eight p.m. when she approached the corner of Eighty-sixth and Saginaw and saw Michael and two other men with a little girl. Two of the men, including Michael, had their hands underneath Lisa's arms. Lisa was bending forward and saying, "No."

He said Januszewski had learned of Lisa's abduction and rape the next morning on the way to work, but that she didn't tell anyone what she had seen, not even the neighbors who had told her about the crime. Afraid for herself and her family, "Judy Januszewski did not want to get involved."

She waited five days. Then she went to a local citizen who promised her anonymity and a five-thousand-dollar reward for coming forward. But as she was not interested in anonymity, the police were notified and they questioned her the next day. At the time, she refused to say she knew Michael Evans. Instead, she gave what Ekl called "a detailed and accurate description of Michael Evans and Paul Terry." As for why Januszewski didn't own up to recognizing Michael earlier, Ekl said she had been through a lot. Citing Januszewski's claims of harassment, Ekl pointed to the series of phone calls she had received threatening her, her children, and her sister. Menacing visits from Michael at her office also kept her quiet. "You will hear her fears for herself and her little children," Ekl said. "You will have to judge the reasonableness of that explanation."

Only after a .25 caliber bullet attached to a note arrived at her house did Januszewski feel that she had to speak up. "[T]he threats against herself and her children became unbearable."

"Ultimately, a twenty-four-hour police guard was placed on her," Ekl said. She was given money to relocate by the Illinois Law Enforcement Commission. "You will see, ladies and gentleman, the tragic effects upon her life."

Sam Adam, in his opening statement, also chose to focus on Januszewski, though he tried to paint her as completely unreliable—a victim herself of a desperate police force twisting the evidence and coercing her testimony. From the start, her statements made little sense, he said. At first, she thought the abductor was a brother taking his sister home. "A brother. Not brothers. Not three people," he said, trying to emphasize facts that would later change.

He pointed out that when the officers interviewed her and took her to an artist for a police drawing, she then described two abductors—no longer just one. These two had medium complexions, men between nineteen and twenty-five. The officers also kept her until early morning at the station house while her husband didn't know where she was.

Then Sam Adam revealed a crucial piece of information. The Cabassas had first reported that Lisa had gone missing at six p.m. Januszewski, in her original written statement given a week after the crime, said she remembered leaving work at six thirty-seven p.m., which meant she could have seen the crime. One to three weeks later, it came to light that Januszewski had actually left work at eight p.m., according to her time card. The Cabassa family then changed the time Lisa went missing to eight p.m., which accommodated the police by allowing Januszewski to remain a witness. The implication was that the family, witness, and the police were conspiring to get a conviction because they thought that they had the right guys.

Finally, it had taken Januszewski ten months to identify the other man who allegedly carried Lisa away, Paul Terry, who looked nothing like the composite sketch Januszewski had come up with. Attorney T. Lee Boyd, who had been hired by Paul Terry's family for this trial, said of his client, "It is my suggestion to you that that there has been a gross mistake of identification."

After opening arguments, the case proceeded simply. There were no motions, no scientific evidence (DNA testing had not yet been developed as a method of proof), and there was nothing on Lisa's body that could be used to help identify her assailants.

During the trial, Carmen Cabassa explained how her daughter had left home after eight p.m. after watching most of a favorite TV show, *The Bionic Woman*. She also cried heavily on the stand as she identified her daughter's tattered, bloody coat. Her weeping was "doing nothing but creating prejudice and sympathy for the jury, which is unnecessary," objected Adam to the judge. He was overruled.

Adam decided not to cross-examine her. Even though she had changed the timeline of her daughter's abduction to accord with Januszewski's testimony, he didn't want to call the mother of a murdered girl a liar. "I was put in the position of trying to impeach the mother of the child."

To admit the time discrepancy into evidence, Adam needed a cop to testify that Lisa's mother had given police two different time frames. The original police report had mysteriously disappeared but Adam was able to get one officer, who had taken pictures at the crime scene, to testify that Lisa was first reported missing at "6:37." The officer said his partner, who wasn't in court that day, had made a note of the time. Adam thus got the discrepancy admitted, but its potency was diminished. It seemed like a pebble in a mountain of testimony. To compensate, Adam needed to go full throttle on Januszewski.

On the stand she explained how, on the day of the abduction, she knew it was Michael from ten to fifteen feet away.

Terry Ekl asked why she had not called the police immediately.

"I was afraid," Januszewski replied.

She then reconstructed the different incidents of harassment and threats toward her and her children that she claimed had kept her from coming forward. In one phone call to her office, a voice—she believed it was Michael's—said, "If I told the police about anything that I had seen on the corner that night, the same thing would happen to me in the same fashion as it did to Lisa." She claimed to have received other calls, as well as visits from Michael, who at one point told her that she "would be a nice fuck." At home she received the note with the bullet tied to it, and it read, "The next time you talk to police, you will get the real thing," which was delivered by the never-to-be-found "Earl Jones." And the next day she heard a pounding on the north side of her house, which she attributed to Michael, whom she had seen leaving the premises. This last incident forced her to give the police his name. "I just felt I couldn't hold back anymore," she said.

Sam Adam, on cross-examination, began by mentioning that

Januszewski's children were ages three and five, intimating that if she really feared a child rapist and murderer were in the area, wouldn't she have wanted to protect her own children by turning him in immediately? At the very least, not coming forward betrayed a strange lack of empathy for Lisa and her family. Januszewski hadn't even told the police that she knew Lisa from the playground. "I didn't want the police to know everything that I knew," she said. When asked to identify the clothes Lisa had been wearing, she said only that they could have been worn by the girl she claimed to have seen abducted.

Was her vague answer "an attempt to lie to the police or mislead them?" Adam asked.

"Yes, it was," she said.

Januszewski had also contradicted herself regarding the citizen who had offered a reward, Adam pointed out. First she claimed she wanted anonymity, not money, then she said she knew the police would be contacted and that she was actually not concerned with anonymity at all.

Working with the police sketch artist, she had described an offender who in fact did not look like Michael. He had a round chin, she had said. Michael did not. He had a flat nose, she had claimed. Michael did not. This, too, she now explained, was an attempt to mislead the police. In the cross-examination, Adam asked Januszewski whether was telling the truth now. "Yes, sir, I am telling the truth now and I was misleading the artist."

She also conceded that Paul Terry's eyebrows were not "the way I saw them that evening." She had described them as looking penciled in. Now they appeared regular.

Adam then focused attention on Januszewski's interrogation by the police, arguing that after a full day of police questioning, she had begun to lie about the assailants just to get out of the precinct.

"Would you characterize your entry into the station that night as being against your will?" Adam asked.

"Yes, sir, it was," Januszewski said.

. . . .

"Did you ask permission to call your husband?"

"Yes."

"Did [the officer] give it to you?"

"No."

"Wouldn't let you call your home?"

"They told me that they didn't have a pay telephone."

. . . .

"And you knew that your children and your husband were home and didn't know where you were, right?"

"That is correct."

. . . .

"And you knew that in the police station, in the second largest city in the country, they have all kinds of phones?"

"That's right."

"And you knew they were lying to you when they told you you couldn't make a pay phone call?"

"Well, they told me they didn't have a pay phone in the station and so I assumed they weren't going to let me make a phone call until they wanted to let me."

"So you knew they tricked you or forced you to be there?"

"Yes, sure, they did."

Adam continued. "You were fooling them about telling them you didn't know who committed the crime?"

"No, I wasn't fooling. I was lying."

. . . .

"You believed at that time they were not going to let you out of there until you told them something, didn't you?"

"I didn't know what they had in mind. I know that I wanted to go home or at least call up and let my husband know where I was and what was happening."

"And they wouldn't let you, would they?"

"No."

"And you knew if you were going to get out of there you had better tell them something, right?"

"No, I didn't surmise it that way in my mind, I didn't know what to do or how to get out of there."

"Were you scared?"

"Yes."

"Nervous?"

"Yes."

"Upset?"

"Very."

"Upset not only about yourself but your children?"

"Especially my children and my husband as to what his reaction was going to be about all of this."

"So you went ahead and made a statement?"

"Yes."

"And in that statement you told one lie after another, didn't you?"

"Yes, I did."

Adam seemed to have scored a major success. Next he needed to prove that the cops had changed the time to fix the case. He quoted Januszewski's original report saying, "I left my office at approximately 6:37 p.m." He asked Januszewski if she remembered making that statement. She denied it.

"So you did not say I left the office at 6:37?" he asked.

"No, sir."

"[The officer] made that up, then?"

"Yes, sir."

"At no time did you ever say you left at 6:37?"

"[The detective] made that up out of his own head, he brought up the time 6:37."

"He made it up?"

"Yes, sir."

In retrospect, the weakness of Januszewski's testimony seems painfully clear. She had lied from the moment Lisa Cabassa was killed and perhaps had never stopped. And it seemed likely that the prosecution knew it or maybe should have known it. And yet on an April day in 1977, Breen showed no signs of doubt about his star witness as he completed the state's closing arguments. He was full of confidence. "Ladies and gentlemen of the jury. I have sat back now for two hours and heard a continuation of a con job, a sham and an absolutely fraudulent and non-evidentiary defense. I'm not going to stand up here and tell you stories, I happen to be a very rotten storyteller. I'm not going to stand up here with hat in hand, with palm open, asking for anything. I'm not going to offend you to this degree. I'm not even going to thank you as jurors."

He did, however, thank the jurors for being attentive but then boldly leapt to the Cabassa family's loss. "I don't ask for any sympathy because I don't give a damn what you do," he told the jury. "Mr. and Mrs. Cabassa will never see their daughter, Lisa Cabassa, again. That is a fact of life."

Breen then flung in the type of comment that has little to do with the facts but which trial attorneys have been known to use to sway a jury and many would characterize as misconduct. "You should have seen all the evidence we kept out of this offense," Breen said, adding that "[b]ecause of the law, we are handcuffed. There is a lot of things we would like to present to you; we can't do it. We have to do it on direct evidence, not hearsay, not immaterial or incompetent type testimony, but direct evidence."

Breen was not supposed to interject this kind of information into a closing argument. The U.S. Supreme Court does not allow prosecutors to refer to specific evidence not introduced or excluded at trial because doing so can lead a jury to convict. Unseen evidence "carries with it the imprimatur of the government, and may induce the jury to trust the government's judgment rather than its own."[16] In this particular circumstance, Breen was permitted to mention evidence left out of the trial that specifically related to Michael's past conduct because, the judge said, Sam Adam had "opened the door" during his own closing—that is, he had mentioned Michael's unblemished criminal background and good character. Breen later said he didn't remember exactly what "evidence" he was referring to, but he felt sure he had good reason. "I thought there was an incident with a girl running from him in an alley but I don't know the truth. I don't remember." As Sam Adam later pointed out, had Breen been in possession of such evidence, he could have brought it in during trial, once that door had been opened. "They had nothing," Adam said. "Michael had never had any trouble in his life. It was one of the most unfair arguments I have ever heard. And Breen did it deliberately."

Regarding the competing time frames Sam Adam had raised, Breen told the jury they were not an issue. "Now, from the beginning, what the heck is the defense? Is the time problem a defense? Is the fact that six thirty was originated in some police report, because a police officer or police officers spoke to . . . a frantic mother? Is that their defense? That it couldn't have happened at eight o'clock, that it had to have happened at six thirty? That is just a crock. That isn't even logical."

Breen tried to explain away Januszewski's lapses. "It's the 'don't get involved' or the 'fearful attitude' so many of us have, unfortunately," Breen said. "She delayed. One delay begets another delay . . . Many, many crimes are witnessed by but one, and it takes a pretty gutsy person, that one, to stand up alone."

He admitted police were forceful with her. "She wasn't treated as royalty." But "these are experienced police investigators. If you were sitting down with a woman who you knew knew so much more than she was telling you, wouldn't you kind of push her to the point . . . Maybe it wasn't the best treatment in the end, but police didn't break her, Michael Evans broke her through consistent threats. . . ."

He vouched for Januszewski's character. "I don't say you would want to break bread with her or have coffee with her; you may dislike her, you may want to call her a coward. But I know she happens to be a very real person."

In words that would eerily apply to himself many years later, Breen added, "I can't as a law enforcement officer and representative of the People of Cook County, I cannot justify people not coming forward because of fear, I can't justify it, but my God, I think I understand it because I see it so often, as we all do." And then, relaying the words that Januszewski might have thought about having to testify, he cried, "Oh, my God, oh my God, don't let it be me to stand up."

It took the jury almost fourteen hours to reach a verdict.[17] A newspaper report quoted one woman juror empathizing with Januszewski's plight. "We['ve] all had the same kind of fear . . . sometime, something had happened to us that was so frightening we could visualize ourselves feeling the same way," she said. She asked not to be identified because she too feared threats of reprisals.[18]

Another juror, forewoman Barbara Bartolotta, suggested that many of the jurors felt compelled to come to a decision because they were under the misimpression that otherwise they would have to hear the case again. If she had known differently she "would not have signed a verdict of guilty, but would have informed the court that it was impossible for the jury to have reached a unanimous agreement."[19]

The jury convicted the two boys. At the sentencing, Adam maintained his client's innocence. "Somewhere, somehow, sometime, the real fiend and fanatic and maniac will be caught in this case," he said.

Judge Barbaro thought the defendants didn't seem like they could be rehabilitated. He "observed no remorse" in them and that both "walked into the court with a swagger." After noting Michael's "sort of a grin" that very morning, he sentenced the seventeen-year-old boys to what was then the maximum: two hundred to four hundred years. (At the time, the death penalty had not yet been reinstated by the U.S. Supreme Court.)[20]

After the verdict, Sam Adam let Breen have it. Breen had gone too far. His comments during closing and his use of Januszewski's testimony despite her own admission of lying seriously calls his judgment into question. "Those guys were innocent. You just gave two hundred to four hundred years to two innocent boys," Adam railed.

The verdict was appealed. Tony Pinelli, perhaps Breen's closest friend, said Breen had discussed the case with him in the months prior to the appellate court decision. "He didn't really know if he had the right guys," Pinelli recalled. "Unlike other crimes he had tried, there was something disquieting about this case. I don't mean he said anything like, 'Oh my God, we put away two innocent guys.' [But] I think he had doubts."

Yet the appellate court found no error and upheld the verdict, though it did censure Breen's improper remark regarding evidence kept out of the trial. "While such a comment is not to be condoned, it was not of such magnitude as to require reversal," the court wrote, adding that Adam's immediate objection, which was sustained by the court, minimized any prejudice for the jury.[21]

With his legal avenues now closed, there was little more for Adam to do. On a regular basis, however, he would see Breen in the hallways of court and remind him that Michael and Paul were innocent. His persistence bothered Breen. It was extremely rare for a defense attorney to insist on a client's innocence outside the adversarialism of the courtroom. Perhaps to ease his conscience, Breen offered Adam an opening: "If you ever have anything to show me, bring it to me. The door is open. You know?"

But there was nothing to show. The case was closed and the boys stayed in prison.

They would have stayed there, too, serving life sentences, if a circuitous set of events had not led Tom Breen to voice doubts, many years later, about the validity of their conviction. His decision to come forward may seem simple: the evidence against Michael and Paul was shoddy, admit a possible mistake, and move on. But such an admission is costly. Prosecutors do come forward when offered proof that someone else committed the crime or confessed to it, but they rarely step up on a hunch or gut feeling, especially nineteen years later. To do so exposes the prosecutor to scrutiny. And it goes against what social scientists call "confirmation bias," or "the tendency to seek or interpret evidence in ways that support existing beliefs, expectations or hypotheses."[22] When presented with information that challenges a belief, prosecutors are motivated to defend their convictions in court to reinforce an initial viewpoint.

But Breen did the opposite. He triggered an investigation that challenged his past and reversed an appalling conclusion: Two innocent boys had been put away for life. If Breen hadn't spoken up, Michael and Paul would have languished in prison until someone tried to find DNA evidence, which by then might have disappeared, or they'd have stayed there for life. Rob Warden, executive director of the Center on

Wrongful Convictions at Northwestern University, was hard pressed to think of another example, besides Breen's, of a prosecutor coming forward without pressure. "He's a great hero," said Warden.

■ ■ ■

The year after the conviction, Breen was promoted to a supervisor in Cook County circuit court and wasn't trying as many cases. He started to get bored. Three months later he received a prime appointment to take on a big prison riot case as a special prosecutor at the state's attorney's office in Livingston County. In 1981, following three years of research, Breen launched a seven-and-a-half-month trial against ten prisoners and sought the death penalty for nine who were accused of murdering three guards at the Pontiac Correctional Facility in 1978. At the time, the case was reported as the biggest civilian death penalty trial in American legal history.[23] It didn't go well. All but one of the witnesses were convicted felons or gang leaders whose credibility—already dubious—suffered as they got into more trouble in the period following the riots. Breen lost the case and, after the verdict, walked into an elevator and punched the wall so hard that he broke his hand. A month later, he dropped the charges against another six defendants and felt he had had enough as a prosecutor. He decided to switch sides, opening his own criminal defense firm. "I found prosecuting to be somewhat monotonous," he said.

He was still partying hard with friends, however. In fact, over the years, Breen's drinking had become legendary. He bar-hopped regularly. On at least one occasion, he slept in a judge's chambers. He even suffered a scrape when he crashed his car, busted his nose, and ended up in the hospital. "We were all a bunch of alcoholics. Some of us slowed down. He didn't," said a friend from the prosecutor's office. Never married, Breen dozed in his car some nights, arriving late to work the next morning, disheveled and hungover. Witnesses waited angrily. Lawyers were outraged. But they all forgave him. "The old Tom always apologized and performed beautifully. He didn't show the wear and tear like some of us did," said Pinelli, who worked at the public defender's office.

The big shift toward sobriety and reflection for Breen began when he started work on the Gary Dotson case, the first DNA exoneration of a convicted man in this country.[24] In 1977, sixteen-year-old Cathleen Crowell was found muddy and desperate by the side of a road. She told police she had been abducted by three men and raped by one. The rapist, she said, had tried to carve a word into her stomach. She had scratches to prove it. She also had semen in her underwear.[25]

Crowell identified Dotson from a mugshot book. Even though inconsistencies plagued her testimony (Crowell described her attacker as having no facial hair; Dotson had a mustache, not to mention four alibis for the period during which the rape occurred), the prosecutor decided to try the case before a jury, which found Dotson guilty. He received twenty-five to fifty years for rape, and concurrently twenty-five to fifty years for aggravated kidnapping.[26]

Amazingly, five years later, the "victim," now Cathleen Crowell Webb, came forward and admitted she had made up the story. She had become a born-again Christian and, as part of her conversion, admitted to the lie. In truth, she said, she had been having consensual sex with her then-boyfriend and thought she might be pregnant. Worried that her parents would find out, she had invented the rape and carved the letters into her stomach herself, inspired by similar events in a romance novel called *Sweet Savage Love* by Rosemary Rogers. When prosecutors showed no interest in revisiting the case, she took her story to the media. The public responded with petitions to free Dotson.

In the end, the protest in Dotson's favor was so big and the political climate so sensitive that Illinois Governor James R. Thompson decided to step in, perhaps because it would deflect attention from the various political problems he had at the time.[27] Thompson took the rare step of calling his own hearing to listen to a clemency plea filed by Dotson. It was a risky move. The public clamor required that the governor give Dotson some relief, but should new evidence later emerge to implicate Dotson in the rape, or if Dotson committed some other crime as a free man, Thompson would have to pay the political price.[28]

Before camera crews, Thompson led a three-day hearing by the

Illinois Prisoner Review Board. A *Chicago* magazine article asserted that the governor stacked the deck against Dotson and the inquiry was lacking. The governor controlled approval of the witnesses and steered clear of anything that might embarrass his administration's forensic operation.[29]

To add to Dotson's difficulties, Cathleen Crowell Webb's former boyfriend David Beirne testified that he couldn't have had sex with her on the date in question because they saw each other only on weekends. The prosecutor in the case also claimed that her recantation defied "everyday experience and common sense" and asked why she would have injured herself so extensively had she wanted only to convince her parents that she had been raped.[30]

In the end, the Prisoner Review Board voted unanimously to deny clemency but, perhaps in a nod to the public outcry, Thompson commuted the sentence to time served on grounds that six years was longer than most other Illinois prisoners served for rape convictions. Practically, this meant that although Dotson was released, he was on parole and still under the watch of the prison system. If he got into trouble for any crime, no matter how small, he could be thrown back in prison for his remaining sentence. To stay out of prison, Dotson had to maintain "good behavior."[31]

By the time Breen got on the case, Dotson was messing up wildly. He had a drinking problem. In prison, he used contraband to make his own alcohol. Now, enduring taunts from passersby who recognized him, he would wake up and have a six pack. He married a woman, a bartender at a pub he frequented, had a baby, and tried to stop drinking, but he couldn't. One night in August 1987, he got into a fight with his wife in a car, slapped her, and stormed off with the child. On the basis of her complaint, Dotson was arrested and held without bond for violating his parole, though his wife tried to withdraw the complaint and charges against Dotson were dropped by the prosecution.[32]

Civia Tamarkin, then a reporter for *People* magazine who had also covered the Dotson clemency hearing for *Chicago* magazine, was now obsessed with the case. She couldn't believe that prosecutors wouldn't admit a mistake once the victim changed her testimony. Now, Dotson could end up spending his life in prison for violating his parole on a charge that stemmed from the tragedy of being convicted for a crime he didn't commit.

Tamarkin felt that the lawyers representing Dotson needed to be replaced. She approached a respected defense lawyer who didn't have time for the case but who referred her to Tom Breen. After meeting with Dotson, Breen agreed to take it on. He lost a first battle immediately: The Parole Board revoked Dotson's parole and reinstated his original sentence.[33]

Breen spent the next two years dealing with an unmanageable Dotson and trying to win a new trial, even though Illinois law said the time period for a new trial had expired.[34] Dotson now faced the possibility of being in prison until 2008.[35] With public disapproval still rampant, on Christmas eve 1987, Governor Thompson announced that he was giving Dotson "one last chance" by ordering his release from prison for the parole violation. Dotson, though free, was depressed and angry and, in an explosion of fury, he got into an argument with a sixty-seven-year-old waitress about whether he had ordered peppers on his sandwich. He refused to pay, hit the waitress, was arrested and charged with theft, battery, and disorderly conduct, then thrown back into the system for violating his parole. His wife filed for divorce.[36]

Tamarkin noticed that Breen was particularly concerned about Dotson's alcoholism. Still drinking heavily himself, he tried to convince Dotson to stop. "It was interesting," Tamarkin said. The same month Dotson assaulted the waitress, Breen had gone to a bar with five friends and ended up lying in a curb in his overcoat. A neighbor took him in. "I had embarrassed myself for the last time," he said. The next day, he announced that he was going to stop drinking. "It came out of the blue," said Tony Pinelli. Likely, Breen had been nearing rock bottom for a while.

In the months that followed, people began to notice a shift in Breen's behavior. The banter was gone. He wasn't as social. "He wasn't as much fun," said one friend, voicing a sentiment repeated by many. Breen became more serious. He talked of believing in a higher power and became openly vulnerable. Sam Adam remembered razzing him about his drinking. Whereas before, Breen would parry with a sarcastic retort, now he was hurt and told Adam so. "You were supposed to be my friend," Breen said. Adam apologized.

Two months before he got sober, Breen had read an article in *Newsweek* about the discovery of a technique that could extract DNA from a semen or hair sample and potentially link criminal suspects to a crime.[37] The method was reputed to be highly accurate. Though the testing was still in the initial stages, Breen pushed for it in the Dotson case. A first test on the semen found in Crowell's underwear gave him no cause for optimism because the sample had degraded. But a second, more advanced test by Edward Blake, a California forensic scientist who used a technique called PCR (polymerase chain reaction), excluded Dotson as a match for the semen and included Crowell's then-boyfriend as a possible source.

Breen formally asked the governor to grant unconditional clemency based on actual proof that Dotson was innocent. Governor Thompson, however, would not grant a pardon. He was waiting for the Prisoner Review Board to look at the new evidence and assure him the PCR test was accurate. Nine months after the DNA test came back, the Prisoner Review Board still hadn't acted on the case.

Breen filed a new petition for post-conviction relief based on the PCR results, asking for a new trial. The Cook County state's attorney— his former employer—publicly vowed to oppose the petition, despite the new evidence. "It's a cover-your-ass situation," Breen said. "They don't want to admit they are capable of making mistakes." Breen made a motion for a new trial before Judge Thomas R. Fitzgerald, then presiding judge of the criminal division of the Cook County circuit court. "It is my belief that had this evidence been available at the original trial the outcome would have been different," said Judge Fitzgerald in granting the motion. The state's attorney's office decided not to reprosecute the case. After twelve years in prison, Dotson was free.[38]

According to Tamarkin, the Dotson case was a watershed experience for Breen. He was opening up to the idea that prosecutors who had been operating in good faith could still have other agendas that blinded them to the truth. "You saw him become philosophical," she said. "He was a late bloomer. It was his awakening." Even so, Breen didn't think the case was representative of a larger problem or that the prosecutors' refusal to reconsider the evidence suggested a problem with the way justice was carried out. Journalist Rob Warden, who also did groundbreaking reporting on the story, remembered Breen saying, "It's isolated. It's an anomaly in a well-functioning system." In the *Los Angeles Times*, Breen was quoted as saying that "a rare, rare event has occurred in our judicial system. An innocent man was convicted of a crime that never even occurred."[39]

■ ■ ■

Throughout the Dotson case, Breen had been running a weekly self-help meeting in his neighborhood at a halfway house for boys. One evening, as he left the building, he caught a glimpse of a man walking up the stairs. Breen realized he was one of the defendants in the Pontiac prison riot case, a man he had charged with murder and for whom he had sought the death penalty.

"How are you, Ben?" Breen said calmly. He threw his arms around the man and wished him well. Over the years, he encountered several other defendants in the riot case. Once, he realized that a clerk in the public defender's office at juvenile court had also been a defendant he had tried to put to death. Breen found it significant that he kept running into these men. "I am not a religious nut. I am not particularly gung ho about the death penalty. But four people in *my* neighborhood that *I* prosecuted in a capital murder case?" He had called them the worst people in the world, and they now walked in the same circles as he did. "I actually met them on the street. They were people to me. People who might be able to get better." As a child, he had been taught to see people as either good or bad. Now he was trying to cultivate a more nuanced approach. "When you prosecute someone in a case, you take their worst act on their worst day and judge them by that," he said. "It was difficult when you saw them on better days when they are doing the right thing."

In 1990, Breen received news that further humbled him. His mentor Judge Frank Wilson was under investigation for taking bribes from a witness in a famous criminal case. As a young prosecutor, Breen had been close to Wilson, whose "reputation was perfect, that of a prosecution-minded jurist not loath to return guilty verdicts in tough cases."[40] Judge Wilson and Breen's father had known each other from the same parish. "He treated me like a son," Breen said. Many a night Wilson and Breen had ended up at the same bar. "One of the reasons Tom was a drinker was because he was assigned to Frank Wilson," said Bill Kunkle, who had worked at the state's attorney's office with Breen.

When the accusations against Wilson reached the papers, the judge had already retired to Arizona. Breen called him up to offer his support. A few days later, Wilson shot himself in the head.[41] Wilson's suicide led Breen to think about the consequences of not owning up to your mistakes. "This was a pretty good guy under horrible pressure," he said. "And he decided to kill himself instead of facing up to whatever it was."

Breen was edging toward a change in his perception of the legal system and of himself in that system that was further developed four years later when he began work on the Rolando Cruz case. The Cruz case may have done more to raise concerns about the death penalty than any other event in Illinois, even in the United States. Cruz was convicted in the rape and murder of ten-year-old Jeanine Nicarico, who had been sick at home alone when someone broke the door down, abducted her, raped her, and left her dead in the woods.

The evidence consisted of Cruz's alleged confession, which came in the form of a "vision statement" of what might have happened had he been at the scene of the crime, though he denied ever having made it. Police had no notes from the officers who took the statement or any recordings to prove that Cruz had confessed. There was no physical evidence linking him to the crime—no blood, clothes, hair, fiber, semen, fingerprints, or other forensic proof. However, a string of street kids and informants had testified at trial that they heard that Cruz or his co-defendant Alejandro "Alex" Hernandez was involved.[42] Plus, Cruz and Hernandez had talked too much to officers; they each had made several statements claiming to know who had done it.[43] The evidence was sketchy and filled with things that didn't jibe, but Cruz still got convicted and sentenced to death along with Hernandez in 1985. (The jury was hung on a third defendant, Stephen Buckley, and charges were eventually dropped.)

In their book on the case, *Victims of Justice*, authors Thomas Frisbie and Randy Garrett interviewed the jurors about how they could have convicted on so little evidence. Cruz's "smug" air and a parade of police officers pushed several unsure jurors over the edge. "There was a strong feeling someone had to pay for this," said one juror.[44] At the sentencing hearings, Hernandez testified that he had made up stories in hopes of recouping a reward. "I lied about everything," Hernandez said.[45] Nevertheless, a judge sentenced them both to death.

In November 1985, a man named Brian Dugan admitted to the crime months after an arrest for a separate rape and murder of a woman as well as a seven-year-old girl. Dugan knew details about Jeanine Nicarico's murder that had never been publicly revealed, although he did get some of the minor facts wrong. In exchange for confessing to the murder and killing of Nicarico, he wanted immunity from the death penalty. But instead of reopening the Cruz case, DuPage County prosecutors simply declared Dugan a liar.

Three years later, the Illinois Supreme Court overturned the Cruz–Hernandez convictions on grounds that the two men should have been tried separately. At a second trial in 1990, the judge allowed testimony that Dugan had admitted to the crime but excluded evidence that he had confessed to six other known sex crimes and had committed them alone. Cruz was convicted again, this time on the theory that Dugan might have helped him rape and murder the little girl. Cruz was given the death penalty, though Hernandez, in a separate trial, was convicted and sentenced to eighty years.

Lawrence C. Marshall, then a law professor at Northwestern University School of Law, signed on to do Cruz's appeal. Marshall was only thirty-one at the time, not yet a full professor, but he had experience with the appellate courts, having clerked for a U.S. Supreme Court justice. He

produced twenty-one legal grounds on which to appeal, the most important of which was the fact that Dugan's modus operandi and track
record—as a solo rapist of women and little girls—had been excluded.
Nonetheless, he lost the appeal. A year later, when the composition of the
court had changed and Cruz was granted a rehearing, Marshall secured a
reversal of Cruz's conviction. But Cruz still stood accused of the crime,
even though his conviction had twice been overturned. So, seven years
after the original conviction, Cruz had to endure a third trial. Most
people assume that someone can't be tried for the same crime twice. In
fact the "double jeopardy rule" stated in the Fifth Amendment only bars
a retrial for the same crime when the defendant has been found not
guilty or convicted with no subsequent reversal. Here, the appeals court
reversed the lower court, so the double jeopardy rule did not apply.

Marshall knew he didn't have the experience needed to pull off a
complicated trial like this, so he polled Chicago's top legal brass to see
whom they would hire in his position. Tom Breen's name came up consistently. Marshall went to Breen and told him he would receive no
compensation for taking the case and would have to contribute tens of
thousands of dollars in time. "That's a big deal for a lawyer," Marshall
said.

Breen looked at the trial transcripts, interviewed Cruz, and agreed
to become part of the legal team. He thought the prosecution had taken
advantage of the inflammatory nature of the case. "I couldn't figure out
how in the hell they could convict this guy on such short evidence—
other than the fact that you have the bereaved parents of the victim in a
monstrous case," he said. "There is no burden of proof." One might assume that jurors tend to raise the burden of proof in a case where the
consequences are so grave. But when it comes to accusations of heinous
crimes like pedophilia or child murder, jurors don't want to be responsible for putting a dangerous criminal back on the street who might repeat
the crime, so they are willing to convict defendants on little grounds. For
a criminal lawyer, Breen had woken up late to a rather commonplace
problem, though one that many longtime professionals never consider at
all. "I should have seen it a lot before that," he said.[46]

Almost a year into the job, Breen had become completely engrossed in the Cruz case, working until one a.m. most nights with a team of lawyers and students who, as Marshall said, "had been doing this intense bonding." One night, he and Marshall were sitting in a room filled with documents. Marshall was ruminating about how all-or-nothing prosecutors had to have certainty in a case to pursue a death sentence, and put a question to Breen: "Do you ever wonder if you convicted someone who was innocent?" Breen reacted immediately. "No, no. We did things differently back then. We used to drop cases. We didn't care about convictions. We cared about justice."

That same night, however, Breen thought of the Cabassa case. Out of all the hundreds he had prosecuted, why had this one stuck with him? In part because he had tried it twice, so it was prominent in his mind. It had also been a "heater," a front-page case. In addition, Sam Adam continued to remind him about it year after year. Finally, the defendants' plight was eerily similar to Cruz's. Both cases involved the rape and murder of a little girl, a crime appalling enough to sway a jury inappropriately. Both killings had allegedly been committed by at least two men, although, over the years, Breen had learned that crimes of pedophilia are generally carried out alone. And neither of the accused had ever properly confessed or pinned the crime on the other. "Guys like this are the weakest souls you could imagine," he said. "They have no allegiances. Why wouldn't one talk about the other?" Breen already had the answer: Because they knew nothing about the crime.

Despite his suspicions, he still could not think of a concrete reason to reopen the Cabassa case. As hard as it might be to believe, he couldn't pinpoint anything specific that he or Ekl had done wrong. He didn't think the police had lied or fabricated evidence. He still considered Januszewski a good witness. But the next night in the Cruz war room, he got to talking with Jeanine Bell, Marshall's secretary, the de facto paralegal on the case. A strict Catholic with a soft manner, she had a strong sense of right and wrong. The pair had been spending a lot of time together and were, apparently, in the early stages of a romance. In the late hours of that night, he explained what was bothering him. Did he have to say something to Larry Marshall? "You've got to do it," Jeanine told him.

So Breen raised it with Marshall. He did not think he had wrongly convicted a man but, "given what I now know," he said, "there is one case that I am more uneasy about." Breen went on to suggest they go back and look at the Lisa Cabassa files. "I was sure we had the right guys. . . . But [it] gives me pause."

Marshall knew that Breen was serious and agreed to look into it once they completed the Cruz trial, "the case of a lifetime in the heat of battle." He was working on several other death penalty cases at the time as well, in addition to his full-time teaching job at Northwestern. "I initially just made a mental note," Marshall said.

■ ■ ■

In September 1995, prior to Cruz's third trial, DNA evidence excluded him as the source of the semen found in Jeanine's body and implicated Brian Dugan in her rape. But prosecutors still refused to drop the case, which made Breen furious. "No individual person in the executive branch ever stood back and analyzed it properly," he said. "There were too many other things in the mix. The victim's family, the horrible nature of the crime, the politics involved, and the ego that overrides the ability to admit a mistake, even when the mistake is shown to you."

The trial began a month later and ended after two weeks with a bombshell. Police Lieutenant James Montesano had never taken the stand before, but he had testified in an earlier hearing that he had heard about Cruz's confession or "vision statement" from other officers on the night that Cruz had allegedly made it. However, he now realized that he had been on vacation at that time and could not have actually heard anything. He had lied under oath, though he said the mistake was inadvertent. With no one to verify that the confession even existed, a judge threw out the entire case for lack of evidence and ordered a verdict of not guilty. After ten years in prison, Cruz was a free man.[47]

The verdict changed Breen's life. He could no longer ignore the must-win attitude of the prosecutor's office, nor the fall-in-line conduct that trawls in its wake. He became gravely depressed. From the moment he had quit drinking, he had been working nonstop. First had been the Dotson case, which took a toll on his private practice. "I don't know what he was living on," Tamarkin said. Then he spent five years building it back up until Cruz's case, which had required absolute focus, late nights, and engagement with many lawyers and students. When he finally got a break, he suddenly felt profoundly sad. His regular life as a lawyer started to feel mundane and slow. Nothing interested him. "Here I am. Just won a case with national attention. I should be enjoying the limelight," he thought to himself.

Vanity Fair magazine asked him to appear in a photo spread with famous legal thriller author Scott Turow and other lawyers who had worked on the Cruz–Hernandez fight. Breen, who was not much of a magazine reader, had never heard of *Vanity Fair*; when he got to the shoot, stylists put makeup on him and tried to force him into a new shirt and tie. He left immediately. "It wasn't humility," he said. "It was foreign to me." CNN and FOX News were calling for interviews. Breen didn't call back. "I couldn't accept credit because I wasn't deserving of credit. Therein lies the Irish dilemma."

Breen stopped working. For two weeks he didn't feel like leaving the house. He saw a psychiatrist who gave him antidepressants that made him feel better. He talked about how guilty he felt regarding his success and about all the people he wasn't helping. Many lawyers did what he did every day, the good people of the public defender offices, but they never received accolades. Given his overall professional success, it seemed like he should have been able to deal with winning; but the experience of a mature adult life proved taxing to a man who had anesthetized himself with drink and then work for so long. "It's easier to deal with other peoples' problems than your own," he said.

■ ■ ■

Breen never mentioned the Cabassa case again to anyone. He assumed that Larry Marshall was working on it. In his heart, he prayed that his doubts were misplaced and that the two boys he had sent to jail all those years ago belonged there. Marshall had also received a spate of media attention after Cruz's exoneration and a deluge of requests from defendants desperate to have him take on their cases. Many of these came from death row inmates. Given the choices, he might have decided to forget about Breen's tip. But he didn't. "We didn't have any cases in which a prosecutor had approached us," so he kept it on his to-do list, and two years later began to work on it.

Marshall started by trying to find the court records. Unfortunately, the criminal court had lost almost all the files. He then began a series of conversations with Sam Adam, who thought he had stored his papers at his weekend farmhouse but was unable to locate them.

When Breen heard that Sam Adam couldn't find the files, he was pleased. It was comforting to know that Adam was doing nothing because it suggested he knew his client was guilty, as if perhaps at some point Michael had confessed to him in confidence. Adam kept looking for the files until he decided they had been destroyed. He had left them in a storage area in a barn, and, as he put it, "some squirrels got in there."

Marshall was getting nowhere. Every week at his legal clinic he announced that he had made no progress. "It was very painful," he said. In September 2000, five years after Breen had first mentioned the Cabassa case, Marshall delegated it to Karen Daniel, a Harvard Law School–educated attorney newly hired as an instructor at Northwestern's legal clinic and as a staff attorney at the center. She was, by all accounts, a straight shooter, and she had more time to attack the case. Daniel first wrote to Michael and Paul seeking their cooperation—an unusual step for the center, which had no shortage of convicts begging for attention. Paul, rarely communicating with anyone, never answered her letter. Michael, however, wrote back immediately. "I have always proclaimed my innocence," he said. "You have my fullest approval in whatever strategy you decide to take in my behalf regarding this wrongful conviction." He added Daniel and her students to his visiting list.

Then she turned to Michael's sister, Clare,[§] and his niece, Catherine,[§]

[§] Clare and Catherine asked to be given pseudonyms to protect their privacy.

asking them to come in to talk. As it happened, Clare and Catherine had been writing to the center for years, though Daniel knew nothing of their letters. The mother-and-daughter team had been working hard on their own innocence project since the day Michael was convicted. Catherine had witnessed his arrest. A kindergartner then, she had accompanied him to buy cheese for tacos. Suddenly, a van burst open. Two white men in long coats grabbed Michael and pushed her against a gate. She saw the van drive away. She ran home crying. Clare, her mother, rushed to the jail to bail him out. Michael had broken ribs and swollen lips and tears in his eyes. When he was convicted, Catherine, on her grandmother's lap, had said, "Don't worry, I am going to be a lawyer, I'll get him out of jail."

Shortly after Michael's sentencing, Clare got a job at the courthouse. She wanted to see how the system worked and maybe find someone who could help free her brother. Over the years, she was promoted. She became clerk supervisor and helped Catherine get a job as an intern during college. Eventually, Catherine herself became a full-time clerk.

However, neither woman ever said a word about Michael to anyone at the courthouse—not even to close friends, many of whom were prosecutors. Nobody knew that Catherine's uncle and Clare's brother was the Michael Evans who, according to the courts, had raped and murdered little Lisa Cabassa.

Catherine and her mother worked in secret. They wrote to the great criminal justice organizations and to famous lawyers like Barry Scheck, who had founded the Innocence Project at the Cardozo School of Law in New York City. They tried to track down Michael's records, which had mysteriously disappeared. At one point, they found a medical report on a man who, on the day of Lisa Cabassa's death, had entered Jackson Park Hospital and Medical Center at 6:46 p.m. and was released at 7:25. He had injured his penis, which was cut. In the report, an officer quotes a doctor saying, "There were no other injuries near the area or on the legs or inner thighs." The doctor "felt that this could have been caused by forcing himself on a small girl." If Januszewski had not changed the time she had left her office, the man might have been a suspect. Catherine and her mother developed theories but they always ran into dead ends, unable to find old witnesses.

They kept a paper trail of everything. Even with their connections, however, they never made any progress, and the effort was frustrating and upsetting on a daily basis. One of the hardest things for Catherine to bear was seeing Tom Breen joking around and making his dramatic arguments. She thought he was cocky. Over the years, she saw him change, yet her feelings remained the same. When I told Breen that Catherine had been watching him the whole time at the courthouse, joking around in his everyday work, he got up from behind his desk, sat in a chair near the window, and put his head in his hands. His face turned red. He said nothing.

Catherine and her mother never accepted the verdict or stopped trying to help Michael. For twenty-seven years, they set a place for him at family dinners and recounted details of the meal to him so he could feel as if he had been there. They spoke several times a day, spending thousands of dollars on phone bills, and they worked extra jobs to send him one hundred and fifty dollars a month. The money bought him a stereo, a hot pot, a coffee maker, gym shoes, cigarettes, a fan, a radio. Every six months, his prison-issued TV would short circuit and they would fork over another two hundred and fifty dollars. When Michael's father died, they paid two hundred and forty dollars to have him come to the funeral in shackles.

Catherine became so close to Michael that she visited him five times a month, even when he was sent to a prison six hours away. In one phone conversation, she thought she heard some men taunting him. After she hung up, her hand hurt. She didn't hear from Michael for two days, a rarity, and finally, when he called she learned that he had been put "in the hole" in solitary confinement. A gang of eight men had attacked him on his way to the commissary for being on the phone too long. He was new to the facility and didn't know the rules prisoners had established. He had thrown some hard punches and broken his hand. "We sensed things," Catherine said.

She planned her weekends around her two-hour visits. Because the state routinely transferred prisoners as a security measure, she would often journey hundreds of miles only to have missed him and be humiliated by the guards. She endured long waits and strip-searches. She opened her mouth to show she wasn't smuggling any foreign objects. She and her mother were "treated like prisoners," she said.

Inside, she always found Michael optimistic, almost to the point of absurdity. He seemed to grin for no apparent reason. In prison, he ate mainly bread and packaged food because the inmates regularly put rocks and glass in the cafeteria meals, urinated in the coffee, or poured disinfectant in the juice. During visits, when Michael had a chance to eat from the vending machines, he would gorge himself on four cups of coffee, three sandwiches, four candy bars, three ice cream bars. He would also smoke an entire pack of cigarettes.

Catherine tried to keep upbeat, even if she always wept on the way home. Come Monday, she'd be back at her desk as a clerk in the court system. Her coworkers criticized her for treating defendants' families too well. Whenever someone expressed horror at a crime committed by some defendant, Catherine would say the same thing: "Are you sure he did it?"

Now, with Karen Daniel by their side, it seemed as if the family might finally get justice. They turned over the police reports they had and all their correspondence with lawyers. But it wasn't enough. Daniel tried to find other records at the courthouse. She looked for the stenographer's notes and tried to track down the people who had recorded them.

However, the most important issue was the physical evidence, the semen. From the police reports, she knew that semen had been found on Lisa's body in the rectal area, and that there were swab samples. Daniel tried to track down the court evidence, which were supposed to have been kept in the criminal court building. Eventually, someone at the police department located some old ledgers from 1976. These led to a warehouse at the Chicago Police Department, where Daniel found a whole box of forensic samples. "It was pretty simple," Daniel admitted. "For a lot of these cases, the hard part isn't legal work. It's getting the agencies that have evidence to give it over. It's not rocket science."

One year after receiving the assignment, Daniel and her clinic students filed a motion asking for permission to test the swabs. Once the motion was won, she and the prosecutors negotiated for weeks over who would do the testing. Finally, the samples were tested, and in September 2002 the DNA evidence came back excluding Michael Evans and Paul Terry as possible sources of the semen found on the victim. Prosecutors responded by seeking additional testing. The state's attorney's office then compared the DNA evidence to samples from the other suspects. James Davis (mistakenly identified as Earl Jones), Keith Jones, Sam Parker, and Columbus Thomas were also cleared.

Karen Daniel saw Tom Breen at a dinner at Northwestern that November. As she told him the news, Breen seemed detached. The idea that he had engineered a "victory" that had ruined the lives of two young men was too much to bear. "I can't talk about it anymore," Breen told her. "It's making me feel too bad."

In May 2003, Judge Dennis J. Porter vacated Michael Evans's and Paul Terry's convictions and released them on their own recognizance. Daniel remembered Michael breaking into a huge grin that stayed on his face as he walked away. Paul didn't seem to know what was happening as his family, all wearing yellow T-shirts for solidarity, gave him one to put on.

The Cook County state's attorney proceeded to dismiss all charges in August 2003. In January 2005, Illinois Governor Rod Blagojevich granted the two men pardons based on actual innocence. It is as close as the legal system comes to an official apology. The state's highest elected official had in effect said, "These men are innocent," which brought a definitive end to the disgrace of imprisonment. A front-page story in the *Chicago Tribune* showed Breen looking tormented, eyes down. "Did I try to do it well? I did," he said, referring to the original conviction in 1977. "The system was different then. I was different."[48]

Governor Blagojevich said, "A pardon will help each of them rebuild their lives," calling the convictions "tragic."[49]

■ ■ ■

Like many people freed after a long prison sentence, Michael Evans found it difficult to set up a life. No one offered him a job. Donations were not forthcoming. Eventually, he found work as a cashier three days a week at a Harold's Chicken Shack, where his son was the assistant manager, and began to take a weekly writing class. He chose to live alone, apart from his family. "They've done enough for me," he said. He knows that his family's love made all the difference in getting him through prison. "Even though I couldn't have seen it," he said, "I believed justice could be done. . . . I didn't know if someone else would come forward or if I would get out through appeal. I believed that God would send me a savior. And he did. It was Karen Daniel. I think Tom Breen played a part in it, too . . . God worked through him. He knew deep in his heart he sent two innocent guys to prison." But for Michael, this was ancient history. "I hold no animosity in my heart. If God can forgive you, who am I not to forgive?"

Paul Terry fared much worse. Michael remembered seeing him during their first years in prison. "We both felt like sheep among wolves, being around hard, cold criminals," he said. Michael towered at six foot two; Paul was slight, only five feet nine. A gang jumped him early on, and he was hospitalized for his injuries. He came home after prison almost unrecognizable—skeleton-thin with his uncombed hair so long it stuck straight up in a messy bind. He had stopped bathing. Alone in his room, he muttered nonsense, talking to no one. "Bitch, get it up, just get up. Motherfucker, I'm going to beat your ass."

Paul had flashbacks and continued to be traumatized. "His whole body stiffens when he talks about what happened to him in prison," his sister Doris Johnson said. Over time he gained weight. He learned to play video games and make himself snacks with food he buys himself at a discount grocery store. His family will give him whatever he wants.

Nevertheless, after so many years of rationing his money, Paul is frugal. "My brother has the mind-set of a seventeen-year-old," his twin sister, Pam Hawkins, said, "and he is forty three years old."

Tom Breen is a mystery to Doris. "It is never too late to come forth to correct something you have done wrong. But when did he realize that these young men's cases needed to be corrected? What made him think of this case? Did he go to bed thinking about it? Did he think that they were locked up and wrongfully convicted? All these things had to have gone through his mind over the years." Catherine Evans asked the same questions, though to her, Breen's guilt was unequivocal. "They paint Tom Breen as a hero," she said with repugnance. But "it took him too long to admit it."

■ ■ ■

Where did the case of Lisa Cabassa's murder go wrong? Then and now, the prosecutors' faith in the case rested on Judy Januszewski's eyewitness testimony, which stank of lies and inconsistencies. Yet even after Breen had come forward, he continued to insist that she was a credible witness whom he was entitled to put on the stand. He emphasized the strength of her position: as a white woman in a changing or integrating neighborhood, she had felt threatened and wanted to protect her family. She had a sound reason for lying at first. She was scared, and there was proof she had been intimidated. If the police had hassled her, it was only to get results. Prosecutors understand that a witness won't just walk in and spill the goods. Further, he thought that Januszewski was telling the truth insofar as she believed what she was saying. "I am telling you, in her mind she was telling the truth," he said.

Breen didn't realize at the time, he said, what the perils were of resting an entire case on a single eyewitness who could accidentally get it wrong. He had clearly not taken into account what the U.S. Supreme Court had said about eyewitness identification as early as 1967: "The vagaries of eyewitness identification are well-known; the annals of criminal law are rife with instances of mistaken identification," Justice William J. Brennan Jr. wrote in *U.S. v. Wade*.[50] Today there's a canon of writing that holds out mistaken eyewitness identification as the most frequent single cause of wrongful convictions.[51] Investigators, under pressure to make an arrest, peg their case to an eyewitness and then go down the slippery slope of finding more evidence to support this mistaken identification (forcing the defendant to plead guilty, for example, or gathering junk science) all of which bolsters this original witness.[52]

In the criminal justice system, this tendency to "focus on a suspect, select and filter the evidence that will 'build a case' for conviction, while ignoring or suppressing evidence that points away from guilt" is called "tunnel vision."[53] Most inquiries into wrongful conviction cases cite tunnel vision as a cause, though they concede it can be unintentional: "Properly understood, tunnel vision is more often the product of the human condition as well as intuitional and cultural pressures, than of maliciousness or indifference."[54] Scholars have noted that even the most ethical prosecutors can fall prey to tunnel vision because of the perils of adversarialism. An overriding need to win in a contest causes them to look only for confirmatory evidence, ceding no ground.[55]

Breen still maintained that despite the pressure to win the Cabassa case, he would have asked a superior to drop the case had he had significant doubts at the time. Many former prosecutors echoed this sentiment, and recited the office's unofficial motto, "Do the right thing," meaning that they could drop a case if it were the ethical thing to do. Breen's boss, James M. Schreier, then chief of the felony trial division, could have easily given permission to do so. Prosecutors described Schreier as willing to take that course of action, even in the middle of a trial, if his lawyers didn't believe in the evidence. Schreier, now a judge, didn't remember the details of the Cabassa case, but he did emphasize that prosecutors can't always be convinced beyond a reasonable doubt that a defendant committed the crime before going to trial. "Prosecutors aren't walking lie-detector tests. People can be adept liars, including police. So you present the evidence you have."

Breen had been taught to follow a rule: let the jury decide a witness's credibility and a defendant's guilt. In so doing, he had delegated his own gut check, which many prosecutors feel is the threshold for taking a case to trial. A gut check, however, cannot be codified. On formal ethical and legal grounds, one needs only a small quotient of certainty to pursue a case. National standards say only that a prosecutor must have "admissible evidence," which the attorney "reasonably believes" shows that the defendant is guilty. The responsibility is on the jury to act as a "trier of fact."[56]

On the other hand, the responsibility to be morally sure of evidence is greater when dealing with emotionally explosive evidence before a jury. Studies show that a prosecutor can make an impact on a jury merely by deciding to prosecute. As Professor Bennett L. Gershman, a law professor at Pace Law School, writes:

> Juries trust prosecutors; they are impressed by the prosecutor's prestige and expertise. Indeed, jurors may reasonably assume that a case would not be brought in the first place if the prosecutor harbored any doubt, and may even assume that additional evidence probably exists to support the hypothesis of guilt. Two generalizations reinforce the danger of letting juries decide a questionable case: juries usually reach a verdict and that verdict usually is guilty.[57]

Jurors are also subject to their own pressures. The forewoman on the Cabassa case, Barbara Bartolotta, who was seventy-seven when I spoke to her by phone, said she had tried to persuade her fellow citizens that the prosecution had no case. "I reached a point where I thought I must be crazy. I must not have paid attention or something." So she eventually caved. "I didn't stick to my guns and honor my gut feeling," she said. "You know, we have been trained from childhood on to bow to the majority, that this is a democracy and the majority rules. I think this had to do with what I did." In the end, to Breen, the jury's guilty verdict justified his belief in Januszewski. "I am not critical of the jury," he said. "I had an absolutely unshakable witness. . . . There were all sorts of problems, and I am not suggesting there weren't," he added. "But I'm telling you, the bottom line was, she was unshakable."

Of course, we'll never know exactly when Breen realized that the "problems" with Januszewski's testimony collapsed his case against the two defendants. Memory and self-awareness are not reliable sources for this kind of information. But Sam Adam, at least, recalled a conversation with Breen during the trial that suggests he saw then just how weak his witness was. According to Adam, Breen reportedly said in one of the breaks, "If the jury convicts Paul Terry, there is no justice anywhere." (Indeed, the evidence against Paul was particularly weak—just Januszewski's identification from far away.) To Adam, the comment meant that Breen "knew at least one of them was innocent."

Sam Adam's memory of this comment and Tony Pinelli's recall of Breen's discomfort after the conviction are the only real evidence that Breen had any suspicion of the boys' innocence. It's not much. Breen insists that what he meant by his comment to Adam was that Januszewski had seen Terry so quickly and on such a dark night, he wouldn't have been "surprised nor disappointed that [Paul] would be found not guilty." Breen was still right, he thought, to prosecute him. "I felt that this would be a judgment call for the jury or the judge."

Januszewski was "not a villain," he insisted. And neither was Breen. He had done nothing wrong, he believed. And if he had, there were adversarial checks in place that should have fixed matters. As he put it, "She was brilliantly cross-examined" by Adam. If her testimony could not sustain the charges against the two boys, Adam was there to point that out.

Adversarialism, which is supposed to act as a check, can also encourage each side to rely on the other to catch mistakes as they are happening. In this way, a prosecutor can imagine that oversight exists so that he doesn't have to do the crucial, soul searching, inquiry himself. But the checks do not actually work this way since a zealous defense can't guard against the public's intense desire to protect its community. According to Larry Marshall, if there is one strain running through all the wrongful convictions, it is that jurors don't take seriously the presumption of innocence when it comes to heinous crimes. Letting someone off who may rape and kill again is intolerable and unrealistic, so jurors give the burden of proof a pass. "We may have undertaken an absurd model," Marshall said.

■ ■ ■

If Breen seemed disinclined to believe that he had ignored the weakness of Januszewski's testimony, his coprosecutor and investigators were even more resolute. Terry Ekl, then in private practice in suburban Clarendon Hills, with a glass elephant the Cabassa family gave him as a gift in a prominent place in his office, continued to defend his prosecution of the case. Despite the DNA evidence, Ekl took issue with the word "exonerated" to describe what the test results did for Michael and Paul. "Negative DNA doesn't mean they weren't involved. I am not contending they were. But the DNA doesn't conclusively prove they weren't." In other words, Evans and Terry could have been present at the scene as accomplices without leaving traces of sperm. Ekl had a point. The DNA from the semen was taken from an anal cavity, which meant only that Michael and Paul had not anally penetrated the child. Theoretically, a third participant could have done this, while Michael or Paul or someone else watched or performed a vaginal rape. But it is unlikely. As Breen points out, if one of the two men had actually committed the crime, and the other knew about it or participated in it, surely by now one would have ratted on the other.

Ekl was astounded by his old friend's change of heart. "Tom seems like a completely different person to me," he said of his former trial partner. The two men—athletic, aggressive, and ambitious—had played football and partied together. In the 1980s, Ekl represented Breen when he broke his nose in his car crash and sued the city for not properly warning drivers of the hole in the road. It was "twenty by fifteen feet," Ekl said, intimating that Breen should have seen it but that he had probably been drinking. Still, no evidence was admitted at that trial that Breen had been drinking, and he won one hundred thousand dollars with Ekl's help.

Professionally, they were at odds now. Ekl had agreed to represent one of the prosecutors, Thomas Knight, who had been charged with conspiring to frame and convict Rolando Cruz. Knight was eventually aquitted of the charges. During the trial, Ekl even insisted that Cruz was still involved with the crime—a hard-line position that made his case tougher to prove, since it went beyond whether the police and prosecutors had committed misconduct.[58] But it demonstrated his belief that even in the face of DNA and other evidence, his client, the prosecutor, still had the right guy. Ekl had much faith in the police. Breen "has a completely different perspective on a police officer's testimony. Instead of embracing the good, he focuses on the negative."

Ekl was not the only one who seemed to feel betrayed by Breen. A criminal justice reporter for the *Chicago Tribune*, Maurice Possley, noted, "There are people out there who want to kill him, really kill him. There is a brotherhood out there, a big umbrella of a club, and a lot of unspoken anger when people cross lines." Sam Adam agreed: "He is really despised. First of all, he is Irish . . . more so than other ethnicities there is a philosophical bond [with police] . . . He's Irish and with a father who is an FBI agent—you're not supposed to cross over the line."

Robert Egan, until recently deputy chief of the public interest bureau of the state's attorney's office, tried to describe why Breen rankled so many people. It had little to do with innocence or guilt. "Evans and Terry are kind of bit players in the whole drama," he said. Not too many people cared about them. The anger was rooted in something else. "You go along every day and think about your past and say, 'The past is past. There is nothing I can do about it, it's the way it goes.' We used to have an expression if we lost a case, 'We'll get him next time' . . . The people we failed to convict once would more than likely be involved in another prosecution in the future. Then Breen came along and questioned a case."

By speaking up, he challenged the they-would-have-ended-up-in-prison-anyway rationale. "The phenomenal part of what he did is he brought down all the mistakes from the past," Egan said. It made people in his office question themselves and whether they should be engaging in the same sort of "mental gymnastics." "Lawyers don't want to go there," he said. "The whole thing is really hard for a prosecutor to get around."

Lorna Propes, the former assistant state's attorney, agreed. "I think that those people who resent Tom's actions, who claim not to understand, are really acting out of defensiveness of him breaking the code. Maybe they're wondering about their own actions and whether they could be that courageous." She thought back to her experience. "I thought everyone we prosecuted was guilty. I believed what the police said."

No one was angrier than the police. They had the utmost confidence in their work and some felt deep hatred for Breen, especially two of the main officers in the Cabassa case, Anthony Katalinic and Fred Hill. Both are uniformly described as being some of the toughest, hardest working detectives in Area 2, which had come under attack in the early 1990s for accusations of torture.*[59] By the time I interviewed them, they had left Area 2 and were working as investigators for the state's attorney's office. They have since retired.

With regard to Paul and Michael, the two officers had no doubts. Both men believed that there was another person or group involved, but that Michael and Paul were also involved—they just didn't leave their semen. Katalinic insisted: "I think these guys are guilty. I think they were the ones responsible for the abduction." As for Breen, they felt betrayed by him, mostly because he hadn't come to them first. Now they couldn't trust him. "He is a goddamn liar," Hill went on. "He is the most despicable human being I know."

---

* Defendants from the 1970s to the early 1990s alleged that Area 2 officers had administered electric shocks to their testicles and other parts of their bodies from a small black box; suffocated them to the point of unconsciousness with plastic bags and a typewriter bag; and had used a cattle prod. A report by the Chicago Police Department's Office of Professional Standards concluded that abuse did occur and that it was "systematic." Commander Jon Burge, the lieutenant for most of the 1980s, was fired in 1993.

When special prosecutors issued a 2006 report, assessing one hundred and forty-six allegations of torture, they concluded that teams of Area 2 and 3 detectives had indeed engaged in decades of abuse but could not be prosecuted criminally because the statute of limitations had run out. In the report, Fred Hill was mentioned in an early allegation of abuse that involved Andrew Wilson, who was alleged to have been severely beaten and burned by cigarettes when he was taken to the stationhouse in connection with killing two police officers with his brother Jackie in 1982. One of the witnesses in Wilson's case testified in deposition that detective Hill repeatedly put a plastic bag over his head before he received blows to the head, chest, and other parts of his body. However, the special prosecutors found that the allegations against Hill didn't meet the burden of proof.

They learned about his change of heart from the *Chicago Tribune* and its huge photograph of Breen holding his head in his hands.[60] "It was the phoniest thing I had ever seen," said Hill. "He did it to ingratiate himself." The two detectives seemed truly confounded. "I have known him for thirty-something years and all of a sudden he concocted this," said Hill. "Why did he take all those years? Why did he suddenly change his mind? Why didn't he express any doubt to us?" True, Breen could have brought his doubts to the state's attorney. But the office doesn't have a good record of addressing its mistakes. The *Chicago Tribune* published a series of articles about prosecutorial misconduct in 1999, and one story detailed how dozens of former prosecutors who were criticized by appeals courts for breaking the rules of fair trial were subsequently promoted to become supervisors. Given the shelter the state's attorney's office provided to its prosecutors, it is understandable that Breen chose to confide in an outsider whom he knew would address the issue.[61]

Nevertheless, the detectives didn't think his coming forward was correct or ethical. "I would hate to see him painted as a knight in shining armor," said Katalinic. "He is not that."

Their wrath was perplexing. Breen had done little to overturn the case besides ask Larry Marshall to take a look at it. He had hardly gone on the warpath against his old office or called out poor police work. But even if he had, surely detectives who had been on the force for decades would concede that now and then mistakes get made. But they didn't. The police's inability to question their work amounted to "circling the wagons" to defend the group against outside attack.

Richard Hackman, a psychology professor and expert on team dynamics at Harvard University, calls the prosecutorial/police experience the "perfect example" of an "inter-group" relation in which moral standards get adjusted when the group encounters a threat. In this scenario, the prosecutors and police insist that they convicted the right guys, holding out against everyone else. A collective view of right and wrong gathers force, often at the expense of reason. "When you're in that inter-group situation, you have a demonstrable distortion of memory and distortion of perspective," said Hackman. The more individuals sacrifice for the group, the more difficult decisions are to undo, and thus the greater the individual's commitment to the collective belief. Even when faced with incontrovertible evidence that its beliefs are wrong, the group finds a way to consolidate its view. The group cannot tolerate error. Breen mentioned this often. "Before you joined an office, you were taught morals. When you join an organization, I don't care if it it's Enron or a prosecutor's office, you begin to think of the greater good of the organization. You get swept up in it. And the ends justify the means."[62]

In the case of police and prosecutors, sending an innocent man to prison for life is a supremely difficult decision to undo, both emotionally and practically. Group members preferred to declare that Breen had gone "to the dark side" and that Michael and Paul were guilty.

■ ■ ■

In 2004, Michael and Paul brought separate civil suits in federal court against the city and state for wrongful imprisonment. Paul's lawyers weren't happy with the judge he was assigned and decided to re-file in the Circuit Court of Cook County, where matters often proceed more slowly. Michael's case, however, heated up quickly against Hill, Katalinic, and eight other members of the Chicago Police Department. It charged that police, individually or conspiratorially, had concealed evidence that tended to exculpate Michael and therefore violated his due process rights under the Federal Civil Rights Act of 1871, commonly referred to as Section 1983. The suit also sought to prove that the four men in supervisory positions, as sergeants or higher rank, knew or turned a blind eye to the misconduct.[63]

Breen and Ekl weren't named as defendants in the suit, though this did not mean they had no hand in the miscarriage of justice. The U.S. Supreme Court has ruled that Section 42 U.S. Code 1983 gives "absolute immunity" for acts undertaken by a prosecutor in preparation for trial (though narrow exceptions exist).[64] The rationale is that making prosecutors liable would inhibit them from acting as zealous advocates; honest prosecutors would become entangled in litigation rather than in the business of fighting crime. Also, prosecutors are more likely to admit mistakes if no deterrent exists to their coming forward. Additional criminal and punitive remedies are available to wrongly convicted defendants, but only rarely are prosecutors actually sanctioned. If there's enough media attention, an overzealous prosecutor will get reprimanded (as in the case of Mike Nifong, the former district attorney in Durham, North Carolina, who was disbarred for misconduct in the way he prosecuted Duke University lacrosse players for rape in 2006). But this is the exception. Bennett Gershman based his book *Prosecutorial Misconduct* on hundreds of cases, "none of which, to [his] knowledge, resulted in punishment of the prosecutor by his superiors, to say nothing of punishment by courts or bar associations."[65]

Attorney Jon Loevy, who led the team of lawyers working on Michael's civil case, theorized that police misconduct had been so widespread, supervisors had to have known about it. "They seized on [Michael] as a suspect because they didn't have any suspects," Loevy said, describing the evidence at trial. "They disregarded all the evidence that . . . didn't point to their suspect. They crossed lines and fabricated evidence, evidence which wasn't true."

Loevy, who graduated from Columbia Law School in 1993 as a Kent scholar, an award given to the top one to three percent of the academic class, founded Loevy & Loevy with his father, Arthur, a labor lawyer. In the past twelve years, the firm has obtained jury verdicts totaling more than sixty million dollars (plus more in settlements), including six jury verdicts of more than a million dollars against the City of Chicago, according to Loevy.

Michael's legal team, which also included Karen Daniel, Locke Bowman of the Roderick MacArthur Justice Center (based at Northwestern University School of Law) and Flint Taylor of the People's Law Office (who spearheaded litigation against Area 2 cops and was also Paul's lead counsel in his civil case) faced a big challenge. The lawyers had to prove that police intentionally manipulated or withheld evidence from prosecutors, judges, and defense counsel, or created false evidence by means of coercion, manipulation, and fabrication. There

was not a single piece of paper or anything obvious to prove that police had done so. "There wasn't a smoking gun," admitted Bowman. In
fact, there was almost no paperwork at all, according to Frank Laverty,
a former detective whom Michael's lawyers depended on to explain
Area 2 practices, including a double filing system that hid exculpatory
information from the defense, which by law should have been turned
over.*[66]

For Michael's civil case, Laverty, extremely ill, testified by video
deposition and wrote a nineteen-page memo in which he evaluated the
files in the Cabassa case to see what investigative steps had or should
have been taken by police. Here are some issues he brought up:

1. A report on where and how Januszewski was interviewed and
   specifying which investigators were present would have indicated
   whether police thought she was initially credible. Either this report
   was never filed or it had gone missing. Also, information about the
   reward and why it wasn't collected was missing.
2. Details about the circumstances of Lisa's abduction—e.g., her activities on the day she disappeared, the separation from her brother,
   her habits and activities, names of people who lived in the house
   with Lisa, and the nature of the family's living arrangements—
   could have provided leads as to who else might have committed the
   crime. This information was never gathered or else it was missing.
3. Information about the time frame of Lisa's abduction and murder.
   A January 14 police report said Lisa had been abducted between
   six and six thirty, but a supplementary report cited eight p.m. No
   satisfactory explanation of the discrepancy was offered.

---

* Frank Laverty had blown the lid off the double filing system in the 1980s when he saw that reports he had written tending to exculpate the defendant in a rape and murder case were not introduced into the trial. It transpired that in Area 2, it was common practice to keep memoranda
separate from files turned over to the prosecution and, in turn, the defense. The separate sets of
records violated *Brady v. Maryland*, the 1963 U.S. Supreme Court Case that ruled that the prosecution has to turn over exculpatory evidence to the defense. The judge, upon learning about
the separate practice, threw out the case Laverty had worked on. A class action suit brought an
end to the separate memoranda practice.

4. Two investigators interviewed Michael on January 15, the day after the murder, but there is no record of this or why he was initially put aside as a suspect.

5. Januszewski testified that she had been held against her will on two different occasions. No reports are in the file of any extended questioning.

6. Januszewski also said she had several interviews with Area 2 detectives in the first six weeks after Lisa's death. No memoranda document these interviews, which could have given the defense a sense of whether she was being coerced.

"[T]he detectives knew from the beginning that Januszewski was incredible and lying about key events in the case such as the assertion that she witnessed the abduction," Laverty wrote. They hid relevant evidence in their separate files, he concluded. "These documents would have been necessary and essential for counsel for Michael Evans and Paul Terry to have in order for these defendants to receive a fair trial."

On the stand, Breen said he had no idea that Chicago police kept unofficial files until the story broke in the 1980s. Detective Hill testified that a "gigantic book" of tips and clues relating to the Cabassa murder investigation existed but couldn't be located now. Breen also testified that he didn't know about this, either. In an interview, he said he thought the cops had given him everything they had, that they had just typed their handwritten notes into a summary report. "Maybe we are all idiots, but we never thought there would be running notes," he said.

Each officer and superior denied knowing how the time frame of the murder got changed or why various witnesses were discounted. One seventeen-year-old, Brian Daniels, had testified to police that he and his four friends had seen Lisa with her brother at five or five thirty p.m. This was also left out of the police reports.

"Yes, it is a mistake," Katalinic admitted, regarding the failure to document the time change. But he "had nothing to do with it," he said in a response that was echoed by all his officers. "I can't see it as being intentional. I'm sorry." Lisa's brother Ricky and her mother, Carmen

Cabassa, were also brought in to shed some light on the subject, but their memories of the exact time that Lisa went missing were as fuzzy as they had been at the original criminal trial.

Nobody could say who had been the lead investigator on the case, though four officers seemed to have put in more work than the others (Katalinic, Hill, Tom McKenna, and Dennis Banahan). "There's no such thing as a lead detective on a case," said Richard O'Connell, a former sergeant, in a sentiment repeated by many (he also said that decisions about witness credibility were left to cops). Judge David H. Coar became furious on this point: "The police officers' testimony is so incredible with respect to that issue that it is to my mind boggling. If you believe the police officers' testimony in this case, then it was charitably a fire drill. Nobody was in charge."

The police also had to account for Michael's alleged confession. They never documented it, though officers insisted he had confessed. At the time, no detective questioned the authenticity of the confession or whether it had actually happened. Katalinic said the statement was given to Detective Duncan. Hill agreed. And yet Duncan was the only one of the officers who worked on the case who didn't get sued. "Because he's black," Katalinic said in a phone interview. Or because the civil lawyers needed Duncan as a witness for subsequent Area 2 litigation.

On the stand, Duncan refused to say he had received the alleged confession, though at the 1977 trial he testified that he had indeed taken the statement but never wrote anything up. "After a day or two I no longer was involved in that case at all," he said. However, he felt certain he would have remembered if he had essentially cracked the case with such a big piece of evidence. Still, Duncan didn't think the paperwork on the confession had been falsified. He trusted his fellow detectives not to lie: "I have confidence and faith in how we worked as a team in homicide and how [Katalinic] did the report." He then described the "excellent job" done by the people in the unit and how he did not see routine violation of rights.

Another witness in the civil trial was Thomas McCarthy, who in

1977 was an assistant state's attorney working for the felony review department, which looks at cases before approving the charges. The day of Michael's supposed confession (which McCarthy called "an oral admission"), he came down to Area 2 to make sure there was enough evidence to arrest him. He said he remembered Duncan going into the room where Michael was being held and then reporting that he had received a statement.

After that, McCarthy, only two years out of law school, along with Katalinic, asked Michael to confirm the verbal admission. Michael refused to repeat statements he had supposedly made just before. McCarthy then agreed to "a general discussion" about the murder, and proceeded with the bizarre interview in which the officers asked questions about whether Januszewski had "big tits." "He seemed very comfortable in that context," said McCarthy explaining why he used this language.

That McCarthy did not ask Michael about his confession is quite obviously strange, given that his job was to test police evidence before endorsing the boy's arrest. But he would not acknowledge this anomaly. Thirty years later, he still hesitated to challenge the police. He even refused to meet with Michael's attorneys before trial, which almost everybody else did, including Januszewski. "Well, as a state's attorney I was acting on behalf of the Chicago Police Department," he said when asked on the stand why he didn't want to meet the lawyers. Old allegiances die hard.

McCarthy's boss at the time of Lisa's death was Joe Urso. Now a judge, he said he would still have approved the charges against Michael whether the boy had confessed or not, which suggested there was enough other evidence to warrant the arrest, specifically Januszewski's eyewitness account.

Yet the supposed confession is precisely what police needed to convince Januszewski to testify at the first trial. Thirty years later, Januszewksi took the stand to say said she had never wanted to testify in the first place and had told police "many times" that she didn't want to provide the only piece of evidence. But she had been told that she was merely confirming other evidence. "They told me there was a confession," she said.

When she learned that her testimony was the sole piece of evidence she felt betrayed. After hearing the verdict, she claimed to have gone into a "very deep depression." By the second trial, Januszewski had accepted the relocation money and moved. Her husband had urged her to "let your friend the detectives take care of you." Once she had taken the money, she felt she had to go through with the second trial. It was her part of the bargain.

"If it would have been up to you, would you have testified?" asked Loevy.

"No," she said.

For Loevy's purposes, however, Januszewski was not a very helpful witness. In her early sixties, she seemed confused about details. She didn't remember whether she had ever spoken to Michael. She did not remember misleading the sketch artist or the notes on her calendar that marked the occasions on which Michael had harassed her at work. She did not recall seeing Michael pounding on the side of her house or that she had identified "Earl Jones." She did not recall something being shattered on the side of her home or the threatening notes (to this day no one ever found out where these came from). She did not even remember which officers she had talked to.

Perhaps these events had never happened, or perhaps the intervening years had addled her memory. In any case, she was no longer Breen's unshakable witness.

Loevy asked about how police had treated her. "They kept coming into the room saying, we need a name, we need a name, we need a name, correct?"

"Correct," she said.

"And you kept telling them, I don't know a name."

"Correct."

It was clear that the Area 2 detectives had stayed on her. They had her sit through a number of lineups. Then, on the day she fingered Evans, she was treated like a criminal. She was denied bathroom breaks and food. "I was feeling a lot of pressure certainly," she said. Sergeant Ferry told her they had "ways of making people talk." To eat, she was given only a hamburger from Burger King for the entire day. "I asked many times to be able to call my husband or to go home and they didn't allow me to do that," she said.

Gary L. Wells, professor of psychology at Iowa State University who testified as an expert in eyewitness identification for the plaintiff, said of the way police handled Januszewski, "Despite all of these years that I've been doing this kind of work, I've never seen, I guess, a more aggressive treatment of an eyewitness. Eyewitnesses are not suspects, and therefore the techniques that you use with eyewitnesses are interviews, not interrogations. . . . Interrogations by their very nature spill over into permitting high degrees of suggestion, placing the person in uncomfortable situations, and this is not the way that you're supposed to handle eyewitnesses."

So Januszewski was, in effect, interrogated, and in this context, nudged toward naming Michael Evans. His name didn't even come from her first. "They suspected that I knew who it was," she explained, "and I think they said it was 'Michael,' and I think I agreed to it at that particular time, yes."

By the end of the civil trial, Loevy thought he had aligned the evidentiary pieces of the puzzle just right. "This is one of the strongest cases I have ever had," he said. In his closing argument, he asked the jury for as much as sixty-four million dollars in damages (one to two million dollars in compensatory damages for each of the twenty-seven years that Michael was incarcerated, plus one million dollars against each officer in punitive damages).

According to Andrew Hale, then of Rock Fusco, which had been retained by the city to defend the officers, Michael rejected a $2.7 million settlement offer before the jury came back. Loevy refused to confirm the offer but did say that it had come too late. "The time of settlement would have been before [everyone] made this phenomenal investment," he said. The decision not to settle, however, turned out to have been a mistake. On August 8, 2006, after deliberating little more than one day, the jury returned a verdict in favor of all ten former Chicago Police Officers on all counts of the complaint. Loevy was shocked. "I have won a dozen cases that were far more challenging," Loevy said. He blamed an unsophisticated jury. "It was a law-enforcement leaning bunch," he said, adding that only a few had been to college.*

Since losing the civil case, Michael has been living with Wanda, his high-school girlfriend and the mother of his son. He did receive some money as part of his pardon from the state: $162,000 or $6,000 for each year he spent in prison. Within three years, the money was spent on rent, clothes, and food. Michael did, however, manage to get his GED high school equivalency diploma and in 2009, after years of looking, finally found part-time work stocking food in a school cafeteria in Chicago.

Breen was outraged that Michael's lawyers didn't insist he take the settlement offer for $2.7 million. "What does a forty-five-year-old, illiterate person do with fifty million dollars?" he said. Money was not going to buy him happiness; Michael just needed enough so he could grow old without having to worry. Fifty million dollars versus one million wasn't going to make a difference to him. "I am fully aware that money can't replace freedom," he added.

After Michael's loss, Paul decided to settle his case in state court. He and his family didn't want to risk an unfavorable verdict. Even if he did win at trial the city would probably appeal, which would take years, and Paul didn't want to relive the nightmare of his wrongful conviction and imprisonment any longer. The settlement with the city,

---

* One year after the trial, I placed calls to all nine jurors. I reached two. David Burke, whose uncle was a police officer, said he went in thinking that Michael "had quite a case," but as the trial went on, he didn't see proof that cops had set him up. He kept looking for police abuse but did not see it represented by any of the evidence. All but one juror was prepared to acquit the police on the first day of deliberations, but Olaseinde Sapara, a black juror, caved the next day. He said he was still unable to sleep. "I want to kill myself for not holding out longer. It has affected my life," Sapara said. He said he felt enormous pressure from his fellow jurors to end the trial. "I was stressed out. I was alone in the middle of the wilderness," he said.

reached in March 2009, amounted to $100,000 for each of his twenty-seven years behind bars—a total of $2.7 million. Sadly, Michael turned down such an offer and could not seek one again.

Had Michael's legal team won the case, the lawyers from Loevy's firm would have received a cut, as would Northwestern Law School's Roderick MacArthur Justice Center, whose attorneys say they disagreed with the risky strategy apparently adopted by Michael and his other lawyers. They wouldn't specify the agreement but standard fare is for attorneys to receive up to one-third of the damages in a civil case. For this reason, attorneys for the plaintiff have an incentive to gamble for big money damages rather than to settle. This in itself often leads to a kind of hyper-adversarialism, though it differs from the criminal context, where a conviction can bring a prosecutor power and prestige. But in both, the interests of the individual (plaintiff, defendant, or victim) get lost in the fervor to win.[67] That this fervor on the part of the Chicago police was just as strong, thirty years after the crime, indicates above all the powerful hold of the inter-group dynamic.

Thus Breen's decision to come forward is all the more remarkable. Even so, the conditions were right. Whistle-blower literature argues that people need the support of more than one person to nonconform.[68] In Breen's case, he had the assistance of his twelve-step program, which prescribed a course of honesty and making amends for past mistakes. He also had his new community at Northwestern's Center on Wrongful Convictions, which has since put him on its heavy-hitting advisory board. Finally, he had Jeanine Bell, the paralegal on the Cruz case, who advised him to speak up to Larry Marshall. The serendipity of her prodding Breen is just one of the things that joined them together. The two later married and had a son.

At the end of the day, however, Breen does not kick himself for not having seen the problems in the Lisa Cabassa case. Despite the wrath of his former colleagues, Breen still maintains that they all did a decent job, given what they knew then. If he had doubts at the time, he was also conditioned to accept the uncertainty that went hand-in-hand with the daily pressure on a prosecutor to make decisive calls of

judgment. The younger Breen was also probably able to compartmen-
talize any misgivings. If any one factor could account for Breen's
about-face seventeen years after the conviction, it would not be the sur-
facing of suppressed doubt or even his personal transformation. Most
important is that Breen had changed sides. In working for the defense
on some crucial innocence cases, he had acquired the capacity to see
situations from more than one perspective. No longer a prosecutor,
Breen was able to grasp how one could go too far in that role. In 1977,
the defendants in the Cabassa case were, as Egan had pointed out, almost bit players in the chase for justice; but now, having been close to
innocent people and having lived through his own travails, Breen
could not ignore Michael Evans's and Paul Terry's humanity and the
possibility that he had harmed them. Had he remained a prosecutor, it
is unlikely that Breen would have come forward.

Today, Breen could not be less of the prosecutor that he once was.
His separation from his former colleagues is clearly one of the things
that allowed him to speak up in the first place. "It's hard to rock the boat
when you're in the boat," he says. But if time could be turned back and
Breen was once again a young assistant state's attorney, it's not clear that
he would have made different decisions. At most, he might have
thought differently about the Cabassa case, knowing two facts he did
not know then: single eyewitness accounts aren't reliable and men generally don't commit pedophilia crimes in groups. But everything else
would have been the same: the public pressure to convict; the police's
emotional attachment to their theory of the case; Breen's regular inter-
actions with the police; a co-prosecutor who felt close to Mrs. Cabassa;
and a highly competitive office handling a case that could turn into a
problem for the boss come election time. Against these odds, what would
Breen have had to draw on against the impetus to convict? Just his instinct, his gut check—his, alone. One wonders whether, under that kind
of pressure, anyone would have acted differently.

CONCLUSION

I n the corner of my office, there are boxes of files containing police reports and court papers from the time I spent in Quitman County, Mississippi. For me, those files have come to symbolize the particular difficulty of documenting ordinary injustice: the mishandling of a single case can never capture the extent of the problem. Miss Wiggs, Quitman County's court clerk, had taped to her wall a list of cases not pursued by the prosecution. That list served as a roadmap, a guide to a large terrain of system failure, but Miss Wiggs herself could not have said what all the different cases had in common. She had neither the time nor expertise to look at the factual and legal merits of each individual situation and pluck out the common denominator. But she had nonetheless suspected something that many outsiders and the prosecutor had missed: a pattern of nonprosecution in the county's court.

Ordinary injustice often seems like an unfortunate collection of facts until an underlying pattern is revealed. Compounding the difficulty is the fact that the pattern is frequently invisible. The information in those file boxes, like the situations documented in this book, reveal not just what went on in court in Quitman County but what wasn't going on. Most people are in no position to do the tedious leg work necessary to find the pattern of ordinary injustice and show, for example, that a particular kind of crime is lost to follow up or that the accused is being denied an adequate defense. Proving mistakes, both visible and invisible, is very difficult in the criminal justice system, even for those who are insiders. Clare and Catherine Evans, both court clerks in Chicago, spent half a lifetime running their own covert investigation to prove the innocence of their beloved family member, Michael, who had been wrongfully convicted of rape and murder. Their efforts went nowhere.

For many, any intervention is already too late. Eleanor Johnson, whose daughter's case of sexual molestation had never been properly investigated, chided me in one of our last conversations. "You can write what you want," she said. "The truth isn't going to reverse time." And yet completing the untold stories may be the only way to weave together the patterns of lapses, which could compel the wider community to intervene and take responsibility for local courts. The patterns that emerge here show that American courts have inherent vulnerabilities. Wherever cases are pled, attorneys cut deals, and prosecutors act with unchecked discretion, the ground is fertile for ordinary injustice.

How does a community address ordinary injustice in its courts when the problem is so hard to identify for insiders and outsiders alike? Currently, there is no mechanism in place to keep track of the extent of ordinary injustice. In the adversarial system, professional discretion holds a highly privileged position at the expense of transparency. There is the appellate system, which can overturn individual verdicts, but it can do so only on the record presented; it cannot go beyond that to address the kinds of errors or failures detailed in this book. No office exists to perform routine surveillance of the state of law in the nation's courtrooms. Most academics and independent watchdogs don't methodically analyze the behavior of individual courts. Locally, there's too much deference given to the people who work in the system. Courts are public and anyone can drop in on these taxpayer-funded forums at any time of the day. But citizens rarely do. And when people do observe, as the court monitors did in Troy, they often are impressed with the trappings and ceremonies of justice, like the judge's demeanor and the orderliness of the proceedings, and miss the important problems that are present everywhere.

Those inside the system are generally unable to see their own errors, much less confront them. This blindness is a signature feature of ordinary injustice. The lapses might seem relatively harmless when the sentence is small, like a fine or community service, and so the erosion of rights accumulates unchecked. Proper procedure is worn away until the oversight becomes too egregious to ignore: a defense attorney sleeps through a death penalty trial or a prosecutor pursues a case despite evidentiary weaknesses. The point that is overlooked is that these outrages could not happen without the prior, long-standing, day-to-day erosion of the commitment to justice.

Without outside pressure on lawyers and judges, there is little chance for restoring adversarial vigor. In Chicago, Greene County, and Troy, it took the involvement of outsiders to identify the chronic systemic flaws. But in each context, the intervention was too circumstantial or arbitrary to ensure durable improvement. If in Chicago Tom Breen had not mentioned a troubling case to his friend, Larry Marshall of the Center on Wrongful Conviction, two men would likely still be in prison for a crime they didn't commit. And not every organization has a lawyer like Karen Daniel, who knew how to enlist police to search a warehouse stockpiled with decades-old evidence. Few are the rebel lawyers, like Steve Bright of the Southern Center for Human Rights in Georgia, who move through the courthouses seeking Constitutional violations and are willing to challenge them. And the odds are very slim that a group like the New York State Commission on Judicial Conduct would fish out a prisoner's letter from a pile of mail and decide to launch an investigation that took down a beloved but errant judge.

Furthermore, for all the valiant efforts of reformers, problems are often misdiagnosed. Removing an individual player (a rogue judge, a slipshod defense attorney, a sluggish or overzealous prosecutor) never ensures a systemic fix. In Greene County, the public defender who replaced Robert Surrency suffered from the same afflictions as his predecessor: too many cases, too little support, and the same players in a malnourished adversarial culture. "I felt like I was being held out as a poster child for all the things wrong in Georgia," said Surrency of the particular attention his performance received. In fact, the assistant district attorney was equally responsible—for hundreds of cases that hadn't been resolved. The defense and prosecution facilitated each other's bad habits, while the judges looked on, asking only for the orderly processing of cases.

On the other hand, what is widely visible are the relatively small number of trials that do take place. Here, there is enormous pressure to convict and a hyper-adversarial culture. These trials are the public's main window onto the courts, other than the mythic due process meted out in an endless succession of television legal dramas. The show trial reinforces this spectacular view of rigorous procedure. It is the arrests and prosecutions in these trials that, in the mind of the public, come to signify the health of the system. Consequently, prosecutors measure their success by the number of convictions they score.

In more routine cases, the absence of public records or laws that would require prosecutors to document their decisions make it easy for a prosecutor to discard cases without providing any legal rationale. The public does not have the means to follow court policies or track the decision-making in district attorneys' offices. Voters know almost nothing of the critical decisions related to plea bargaining and sentencing, and even less about the far more arcane process of charging defendants. Without information at their disposal, citizens are in no position to question the minor or even major lapses of prosecutors.

This lack of transparency is the central obstacle to change and will remain so as long as there is no constituency of users committed to improving the state's criminal trial courts. People in prison may have their families, who form support groups and organizations that try to challenge unfair treatment. But often they are poor and powerless, with limited time to pursue redress. Victims' rights advocates also lobby for change and have been quite successful in responding to individual acts of crime. But there is no group of citizens who consistently lobbies for the health of the courts as a whole in the way that parents lobby for good schools or the elderly for prescription drug reform. Who will rally for the courts when even those who have been injured by the system have given up or don't have the understanding or means to successfully challenge the system?

In Georgia, the light that Steve Bright and others managed to shine on the state's poor indigent defense practices has flickered off yet again. In 2005, the new statewide Georgia Public Defenders Standards Council went into effect, increasing the potential for quality public defense. But the legislature never fully funded the program. The indigent defense system ran out of money for death penalty defense three years in a row. Now politicians have reopened debate over the very legitimacy of the defense function and legislators are cutting funds. Attorneys have been fired and offices closed. And once again, the Southern Center for Human Rights is filing lawsuits against the state. The new system is crumbling (or has crumbled already depending on whom you ask) as if all the costly studies and time-consuming meetings and heavy media attention had never happened.

Citizens need an ongoing way to assess the performance of the courts so that invisible patterns of injustice can be identified and legislators cannot whimsically withdraw support for a solution once the problem has stopped attracting notice. A court, like a car, requires a warning light to alert the community of a flaw in the system's functioning. Sadly, it is not feasible to have a disinterested lawyer sitting both inside and outside the court, talking to the legal workers, following the defendants and victims through the system, and compiling a detailed survey of procedure. So the question becomes one of how we can devise a way of monitoring the courts that alerts the public when there is a need to take a closer look.

Social scientists, with expertise in measurement, working together with independent attorneys and court administrators, are in a position to create and implement yardsticks for the many facets of a court's performance.[1] The data they collect should focus on two different zones of interest. The first is the various areas of discretion allowed to legal professionals, such as a judge's decision to assign counsel and set bail, a prosecutor's choice to charge a defendant, and a defense attorney's distribution of time spent with clients and investigating cases. The second is the citizen-user's experience of the system, as in, for example, the timely assignment of court-appointed defense.

The information from such a court monitoring system would be collected and analyzed and the findings distributed to the community by a third party. The data should be presented publicly and in a format accessible to citizens who are not versed in the subtleties of legal procedure. A legislature could mandate that the figures be made widely available through regular updates on the Internet or in pamphlets. The release of the information could be timed to coincide with budget allocations and elections, thus holding court officials to more rigorous standards than simply their image as a crime fighter. Communities would become as accustomed to receiving and assessing data from their courts as they are to monitoring other parts of the infrastructure, like the quality of their schools or the state of their roads and bridges.

Such data would reveal patterns of misconduct similar to what transpired in Judge Bauer's court. His exorbitant bails, for example, would have been exposed in light of the overwhelming numbers of people held in jail as a result of those absurdly disproportionate sums. The percentage of defendants pleading guilty without attorneys—in Troy, throughout Georgia, and nationwide—should be a standard metric in every court, since it reflects the extent to which the abdication of rights is being tolerated. Other key information would reveal the length of a defendant's wait in jail without speaking to an attorney (average, median, longest) and the numbers of meetings a defendant had with counsel. Such a system would establish benchmarks across counties and states. In the end, taxpayers would be in a position to ask hard questions about whether tax dollars spent on indigent defense were producing a quality service, for example, or whether a court's function should be targeted for improvement based on how it ranked next to similar courts in neighboring counties.

As for prosecutorial discretion, it would be instructive to determine the percentage of cases that get thrown out in each county and to compare the rates to other courts in cities with similar demographics and rates of crime. One might also want to compile information about the ratio of people arrested to cases brought to grand jury. This data could show that a certain type of crime (domestic violence comes to mind) hasn't been prosecuted in a certain number of years, or that hundreds of cases have been left in limbo without a final disposition.

In addition, a prosecutor could be required to check off reasons why he decided to discard cases (such as an uncooperative witness or the defendant's mental health problems). In this way a pattern of defective operating procedures or the good judgment of a professional team would be revealed. Moreover, the guarantee of transparency would encourage prosecutors to question police more rigorously and use their discretion prudently. Similarly, closer scrutiny would predispose judges and lawyers to enforce and protect rights. And any citizen sensing a problem would have the numbers to back up further inquiry.

A public venue for complaints about the courts is another way to resolve problems in the system. The new public defender in Greene County, Georgia, knew that he was failing. He had been the subject of a rash of complaints to the bar. But complaints like these generally remain private. There needs to be a methodology to filter complaints, determine which ones are well informed, depersonalize them, and use them to improve performance. Gathering information in this way would force communities and professionals to begin to pay attention to the "no trials" as well as the "show trials." The principal scorecards would no longer be the quick disposal of a calendar of cases, an attorney's win-loss record, or the verdict in an attention-getting case.[2]

Transparency is not by itself a panacea. It is the starting point from which to drive the allocation of resources toward fixing the deficiencies and replicating excellence. The goal is to create a set of vital signs that record the vigor or torpor of the adversarial process. Of course, not all aspects of legal procedure can be quantified. In some cases there is no substitute for direct observation by a panel of qualified, disinterested peers. The most important work a defense lawyer does—persuading the prosecutor to make a reasonable plea offer, for example, and persuading the client to accept it—cannot be measured by statistics. It is the same with a prosecutor's decision to bring a case to grand jury. But the question of whether the vast majority of cases are within a minimally acceptable norm can be measured.

Lawyers will certainly fight over these metrics (they are, after all, trained in argument and have an enormous stake in the benchmarks that are chosen). Determining what qualifies as a good outcome (independent of a verdict) will be difficult, as will devising formulas that allow for meaningful comparisons across communities. How will we do this? Well, it's hard to think of another profession that doesn't tackle this challenge. Cardiac surgeons are graded and fight over the system on their report cards; teachers unions debate test scores as measures of their professional worth. Why not attorneys?

Some will argue that disclosure is an impractical first step because it is too costly and because citizens and professionals alike will never overcome their indifference to the state of our criminal justice system. But there is an inherent collective demand for justice, evident in the public's riveted attention on those few trials that do capture the national interest. Also, the exposure of adverse trial outcomes paves the way for change. In Illinois, the governor declared a moratorium on the death penalty in 2000 after thirteen people who had been sentenced to death were released based on findings of innocence. The exonerations in this state and others created a major shift in opinion about the inviolability of the justice system and the death penalty. This change demonstrates that citizens will not stand for deeply flawed courts, even if they themselves have never been victims or convicted of crimes.

Other critics will claim that professional monitoring generally makes little impact. Advocates for the poor will contend that the system is stripped to the bare bones as it is; any surplus money should go to the indigent defense attorney working with heavy caseloads and without the means for investigations. Judges and prosecutors will say that they themselves also lack the necessary resources to do their jobs.

All these criticisms have the power to shut down conversation. Albert O. Hirschman, one of the great thinkers on social change, writes that opponents of progressive reform often argue that attempts at social transformation will have no effect or are inept.[3] Hirschman condemns this "disabused and bitter" stance that does not allow for the possibility of "social learning or for incremental, corrective policy-making."[4] The debate over justice—that we don't have enough money for it and yet justice must be done—needs the opportunity to take hold. As of now, there is not even a starting point for communities to identify the kinds of legal errors that are taking place. Without this, we cannot even begin a discussion about how to create better local adversarial systems. Moreover, greater funding and more radical remedies don't stand a chance of success if there is no means of jump-starting and sustaining the political will.

Also, monitoring is far more practical than other suggestions for remedying the system (like eliminating plea bargaining or jury trials altogether, or making judges more like investigators than neutral arbiters). This book takes the adversarial system as found in our courts as its point of departure. Despite withering academic critiques and calls for dismantling it, adversarialism appears to be as fundamental to our legal culture as competition is to our partisan politics and market economy. Any proposal for reform has to take this into account.

In the absence of metrics, each single flawed case can be put down to he-said/she-said mismanagement. Jody Clifton's boyfriend beat her savagely with a tire iron and was never prosecuted for the crime. Law enforcement said she had lied about going back to live with him; she said they were trying to cover up their neglect of her case. When I last spoke to Jody, she learned that hers was not the only case to have been ignored. The district attorney hadn't prosecuted a single domestic-violence case in Quitman in more than twenty years. "Really?" she said. Her voice, normally flat, sounded astonished. "*Twenty years?*"

It does not have to be this way. Let us imagine a different scenario, one in which Jody Clifton had known that the treatment of her case was not exceptional but part of an epidemic of unprosecuted domestic-violence cases. Maybe she would have tried to confront the prosecutor or sought support for forcing him to act. Maybe law enforcement, knowing they were being watched, could have been shamed into action. Metrics would offer a mirror for people who work in the system, allowing them to see how their roles might have eroded at the expense of rights and public safety. Metrics alone are not an answer, but they could be the beginning of one. They are the tools we need to ask for the courts we deserve.

NOTES

Introduction

1. *Burdine v. Johnson*, 262 F.3d 336, 361 (5th Cir. 2001). The earlier Fifth Circuit decision can be found at *Burdine v. Johnson*, 231 F.3d 950 (5th Cir. 2000).
2. *Burdine v. Johnson*, 66 F. Supp.2d 854, 857–59 (S.D. Tex., 1999).
3. The Cruz case is discussed in chapter four but for a comprehensive study see Thomas Frisbie and Randy Garrett, *Victims of Justice Revisited*. (Evanston, Ill.: Northwestern University Press, 2005) as well as the coverage in the *Chicago Tribune*.
4. William Grady, "Prosecutors Blast Dugan's Claim That He Killed Jeanine Nicarico," *Chicago Tribune*, April 15, 1992.
5. Cruz was ultimately found not guilty and received a pardon based on innocence from the governor of Illinois in 2002. A grand jury later indicted four sheriff's deputies and three former county prosecutors for their roles in the case. They were acquitted. For a study of wrongful convictions, mostly in DNA cases, see Barry Scheck, Peter Neufeld, Jim Dwyer, *Actual Innocence: When Justice Goes Wrong and How to Make It Right* (New York: Signet, 2001), which discusses Rolando Cruz in pages 226–36.

Chapter One: "What's a Defense?"

1. Various national organizations, including the American Bar Association, have cited the 1973 National Advisory Commission on Criminal Justice Standards and Goals, which mandates the following limits on caseload: 150 felonies per attorney per year; or 400 misdemeanors (excluding traffic) per attorney per year; or 200 juvenile cases per attorney per year; or 200 mental commitment cases per attorney per year; or 25 appeals per attorney per year. National Advisory Commission on Criminal Justice Standards and Goals, *Report of the Task Force on Courts*, Chapter 13, "The Defense," (1973), 13.6. In 2001, Surrency was handling the maximum limit for both felonies and misdemeanors: 136 felonies (91 percent of the maximum); and 294 misdemeanors (98 percent of the maximum); plus 18 probation revocations, according to documents the clerk's office filed with the state.

2. The U.S. Department of Justice has published several reports showing the connection between criminal defendants and indigence. See, for example, *Indigent Defense Statistics*, "Summary Findings," U.S. Department of Justice, Office of Justice Programs, Bureau of Justice Statistics (Publicly financed counsel represented about 66 percent of Federal felony defendants in 1998 as well as 82 percent of felony defendants in the 75 most populous counties in 1996). These reports, as of January 2009, were available on the Bureau of Justice Statistics' Web site, http://www.ojp.usdoj.gov/bjs/id.htm. See also The Spangenberg Group, *Contracting for Indigent Defense Services: A Special Report*, U.S. Department of Justice, Bureau of Justice Assistance (2000): 3 ("It is widely estimated that 60 to 90 percent of all criminal cases involve indigent defendants"). Available at http://www.ncjrs.gov/pdffiles1/bja/181160.pdf.

3. Charles Fried, "The Lawyer as Friend: The Moral Foundations for the Lawyer-Client Relation," *Yale Law Journal* 85 (1976): 1071.

4. Robert E. Surrency (Office of the Public Defender), memorandum to the Greene County Commissioners, January 11, 2000.

5. For a discussion of the ethics' codes failure to define ethical obligations see Fred C. Zacharias, "Structuring the Ethics of Prosecutorial Trial Practice: Can Prosecutors Do Justice?" *Vanderbilt Law Review* 45 (1991); for an elaboration of the dilemma a prosecutor faces see Vanessa Merton, "What Do You Do When You Meet a 'Walking Violation of the Sixth Amendment' if You're Trying to put that Lawyer's Client in Jail?" *Fordham Law Review* 69 (2000).

6. Zacharias, "Structuring the Ethics of Prosecutorial Trial Practice," 73.

7. Ibid., 70 ("Prosecuting weakly, however, does not repair the defects in adversarial justice; it eliminates adversariness altogether").

8. Merton, "What Do You Do," 1023.

9. The last survey conducted by the U.S. Department of Justice Bureau of Justice Statistics on indigent defense systems was by Carol J. DeFrances, "Indigent Defense Services in Large Counties, 1999" *Bureau of Justice Statistics Bulletin*, (November 2000): 1. The report details the methods by which criminal indigent defense systems are delivered in the nation's one hundred most populous counties. It found that public defenders handled about 82 percent of the 4.2 million cases received by the providers, assigned counsel 15 percent, and contract attorneys about 3 percent.

10. The three types of systems are described in Robert L. Spangenberg and Marea L. Beeman, "Indigent Defense Systems in the United States," *Law and Contemporary Problems* 58 (1995): 32–41.

11. The Spangenberg Group on behalf of the American Bar Association Standing Committee on Legal Aid and Indigent Defendants, "Indigent Defense in Virginia, Assigned Counsel," *A Comprehensive Review of Indigent Defense in Virginia* (January 2004): 40.

12. Editorial, "Overdue Relief on Attorney Fees," *Virginian-Pilot*, March 1, 2007.

13. The Spangenberg Group, *A Comprehensive View of Indigent Defense in Virginia*, 50.

14. The Spangenberg Group, *Status of Indigent Defense in Georgia: A Study for the Chief Justice's Commission on Indigent Defense—Part I* (2002), quoting Superior Court Judges George F. Nunn and Edward D. Lukemire, letter to the Houston County Board of Commissioners, January 29, 2002. This report is available at http://www.georgiacourts.org/aoc/press/idc/idc.html.

15. Ibid.

16. American Bar Association, Criminal Justice Section, Standing Committee on Legal Aid and Indigent Defendants, *Report to the House of Delegates* (February 1985). Available at http://www.abanet.org/legalservices/downloads/sclaid/110.pdf.

17. The Spangenberg Group, *Contracting for Indigent Defense Services*, 10.

18. *Report of Chief Justice's Commission on Indigent Defense—Part I*, Georgia Supreme Court (2002): 2, http://www.georgiacourts.org/aoc/press/idc/idc.html.

19. The Spangenberg Group, *Status of Indigent Defense in Georgia*, 20.

20. American Bar Association, Standing Committee on Legal Aid and Indigent Defendants, *Gideon's Broken Promise: America's Continuing Quest for Equal Justice* (December 2004): 14. Available at http://www.abanet.org/legalservices/sclaid/defender/brokenpromise/fullreport.pdf. The annual appropriations to state and local law enforcement, including the information cited here about the Edward Byrne Memorial Justice Assistant Grant Program in 2008, Public Law 110-161, can be found on the Library of Congress Thomas Web site: http://thomas.loc.gov.

21. American Bar Association, *Gideon's Broken Promise*, 14 (citing testimony of Gary Windom, chief public defender, Riverside County Public Defender Office, Riverside County, California).

22. The Spangenberg Group, *50 State and County Expenditures for Indigent Defense Services FY 2002* (September 2003). Available at http://www.abanet.org/legalservices/downloads/sclaid/indigentdefense/indigentdefexpend2003.pdf.

23. American Bar Association, *Gideon's Broken Promise*, 13–14 ("The U.S. Department of Justice's *Sourcebook of Justice Statistics* reports that in 2001, nearly $5 billion was being spent in prosecuting criminal cases in state and local jurisdictions").

24. Dan Christensen, "Broward PD Says No to Instant Plea Deals," *Broward Daily Business Review*, June 6, 2005.

25. Anthony G. Amsterdam, *Trial Manual 5 for the Defense of Criminal Cases* (Philadelphia: American Law Institute, 1988), 1:§ 184, at 320.

26. Rule 5.5(a) of the *Georgia Rules of Professional Conduct* states: "A lawyer shall not practice law in a jurisdiction in violation of the regulation of the legal profession

in that jurisdiction, or assist another in doing so." Available at http://www.gabar
.org/handbook/rules_index/.

27. State Disciplinary Board, "Guidelines for Attorneys Utilizing Paralegals," Advisory
Opinion No. 21 (September 16, 1977). Available at the Georgia State Bar Web site:
http://www.gabar.org/handbook/state_disciplinary_board_opinions/adv_op_21/.

28. Boswell's concerns were relayed in Michael B. Shapiro (executive director of the
Georgia Indigent Defense Council), memorandum to Greene County File, September 16, 1999.

29. Michael B. Shapiro (executive director of the Georgia Indigent Defense Council)
letter to Marie Boswell, clerk of Greene County Superior Court re: meeting of
May 10, 2000, undated.

30. For the events leading up to the passage of the legislation and the efforts of the
state bar, I am grateful to the reporting in the *Fulton County Daily Report*, especially the work of Rachel Tobin Ramos and Trisha Renaud. Bill Rankin of the *Atlanta Journal-Constitution* also did remarkable reporting over the years.

31. Rachel Tobin Ramos, "Indigent Bill Beats Long Odds, Speaker's Inexplicable
Turnaround Cleared the Way for Public Defender Law," *Fulton County Daily Report*, December 3, 2003.

32. Trisha Renaud, "Bar Group: Indigent Reform Plans Stay, Advisory Committee
Rejects Opposition to Proposals for Improving Defense," *Fulton County Daily
Report*, July 25, 2001.

33. Ibid.

34. Trisha Renaud, "Indigent Reform: Now or Later? New Litigation Coming to
Courthouse Near You, Bright Tells Gathering," *Fulton County Daily Report*, September 18, 2002.

35. Trisha Renaud, "Newsmaker of the Year: Stephen B. Bright: Angry Man of Indigent Defense," *Fulton County Daily Report*, December 3, 2003.

36. *Luckey v. Harris*, 860 F.2d 1012 (11th Cir. 1988).

37. Bill Rankin, "Coweta Settles Suit on Indigent Defense," *Atlanta Journal-
Constitution*, March 9, 2003.

38. Sara Rimer, "Suspects Lacking Lawyers Are Freed in Atlanta," *New York Times*,
June 4, 2002.

39. Bill Rankin, " 'I Felt Like I Was Just Nothing'; Suspect Held Months After
Charges Dropped," *Atlanta Journal-Constitution*, December 20, 2003.

40. U.S. Constitution, amend. 6.

41. *Powell v. Alabama*, 287 U.S. 45, 60 (1932).

42. John H. Langbein, *The Origins of Adversary Criminal Trial*, rev. ed. (2003; repr.,
New York: Oxford University Press, 2005), 2–3.

43. Ibid., 76–77.

44. Lawrence M. Friedman, *Crime and Punishment in American History* (New York:
BasicBooks, 1993), 72.

45. *Powell v. Alabama*, 65.

46. Akhil Reed Amar, *The Bill of Rights* (New Haven: Yale University Press, 1998), 116.

47. Dan T. Carter, *Scottsboro: A Tragedy of the American South*, rev. ed. (1974; repr.
Baton Rouge: Louisiana State University Press, 1994), 18.

48. Carter, *Scottsboro*, 19–22.

49. *Powell v. Alabama*, 60; Carter, *Scottsboro*, 23.

50. *Powell v. Alabama*, 65; Carter, *Scottsboro*, 48.

51. *Powell v. Alabama*, 57.

52. Ibid., 71.

53. Carter, *Scottsboro*, 249.

54. *Powell v. Alabama*, 67.

55. Historian Lawrence M. Friedman theorized as to why the U.S. Supreme Court got involved: "[The justices] read the newspapers; they must have known something about the background of this notorious case." *Crime and Punishment*, 299.

56. For a history of plea bargaining there is a plethora of material but I found two works especially helpful: Allen Steinberg, "From Private Prosecution to Plea Bargaining: Criminal Prosecution, the District Attorney, and American Legal History," *Crime and Delinquency* 30 (1984): 584, available at http://cad.sagepub .com/; and George Fisher, *Plea Bargaining's Triumph: A History of Plea Bargaining in America* (Stanford: Stanford University Press, 2003).

57. Lynn Mather, "Prosecutors," in *Encyclopedia of the American Judicial System: Studies of the Principal Institutions and Process of Law*, ed. Robert J. Janosik (New York: Charles Scribner's Sons, 1987), 671; Steinberg, "From Private Prosecution," 569.

58. Steinberg, "From Private Prosecution," 580.

59. Mather, "Prosecutors," 672.

60. *Johnson v. Zerbst*, 304 U.S. 458, 463 (1938), quoting *Powell v. Alabama*, 64.

61. Ibid., 467.

62. *Betts v. Brady*, 316 U.S. 455 (1942).

63. David Cole, *No Equal Justice: Race and Class in the American Criminal Justice System* (New York: The New Press, 1999), 66.

64. Richard Kluger, *Simple Justice: The History of Brown v. Board of Education and Black America's Struggle for Equality* (New York: Vintage Books, 1977), 660.

65. These cases include *Miranda v. Arizona*, 384 U.S. 436 (1966) (requiring that a suspect be allowed to see an attorney before being interrogated); *Mapp v. Ohio*, 367 U.S. 643 (1961) (upholding the Fourth Amendment right to be free from illegal searches and seizure and to have any illegally seized evidence excluded from criminal trials); *Malloy v. Hogan*, 378 U.S. 1 (1964) (finding a Fifth Amendment privilege against self-incrimination); and *In re Gault*, 387 U.S. 1 (1967) (guaranteeing minors the right to a lawyer).

66. *Griffin v. Illinois*, 351 U.S. 12, 19 (1956).

67. Ibid., 19.

68. Anthony Lewis, *Gideon's Trumpet*, rev. ed. (1964, repr. New York: Vintage Books, 1989).

69. *Gideon v. Wainwright*, 372 U.S. 335, 344 (1963).

70. Since *Gideon,* the U.S. Supreme Court has struggled to define the class of cases in which the Constitution mandates the appointment of counsel, including *Argersinger v. Hamlin*, 407 U.S. 25, 37 (1972), holding that "absent a knowing and intelligent waiver, no person may be imprisoned for any offense, whether classified as petty, misdemeanor, or felony, unless he was represented by counsel at his

trial," and more recently, *Alabama v. Shelton*, 535 U.S. 654 (2002), in which a divided Court held that counsel must be provided for the accused in order to impose a suspended prison sentence.

71. *Strickland v. Washington*, 466 U.S. 668, 689 (1984).

72. Ibid., 669.

73. Ibid., 679.

74. Ibid., 707–8.

75. *Burdine v. Johnson*, 262 F.3d 336, 361 (5th Cir. 2001). The earlier Fifth Circuit decision can be found at *Burdine v. Johnson*, 231 F.3d 950 (5th Cir. 2000).

76. The Court of Criminal Appeals of Texas recently upheld the death penalty conviction of George McFarland, whose attorney slept during McFarland's death penalty trial. The court based its finding on the fact that a second attorney was present and an active advocate at all times. *Ex parte McFarland*, 163 S.W.3d 743 (Tex. Crim. App. 2005).

77. American Bar Association, *Gideon's Broken Promise*, 38.

78. American Bar Association, *ABA Standards for Criminal Justice: Prosecution and Defense Function* (3d ed., 1993). Available at www.abanet.org/crimjust/standards/dfunc_toc.html.

79. Renaud, "Angry Man of Indigent Defense."

80. Ibid.

81. All quotations from Mark Straughan come from his February 12, 2002, testimony to the Georgia Supreme Court Commission on Indigent Defense. Available at http://www.georgiacourts.org/aoc/press/idc/idchearings/021202.TXT.

82. In a description of the role of criminal defense attorneys in a totalitarian society (prior to reforms of the past decade) lawyers are depicted as "servants of the state" who do not investigate, cross-examine, or call witnesses to figure out whether the client is guilty. Defense attorneys don't meet with their clients, either. "There was no need to talk to them," lawyer Ma Rongjie explained. "The police and the prosecutors worked on the case a very long time, and the evidence they found which wasn't true they threw away." Likewise, a Bulgarian attorney noted that "[i]n a Socialist state there is no division of duty between the judge, prosecutor, and defense counsel . . . The defense must assist the prosecution. . . . " Monroe H. Freedman, "Our Constitutionalized Adversary System," *Chapman Law Review* 1(1998): 59–61.

83. Bill Rankin, "Defending the Poor: Part Two: A Cheap Dose of Due Process in Dodge," *Atlanta Journal-Constitution*, April 22, 2002.

84. Bill Rankin, "Indigent Defense Rates F," *Atlanta Journal-Constitution*, December 12, 2002.

85. Testimony of Robert Surrency, public defender for Greene County, before the Georgia Supreme Court Commission on Indigent Defense, March 22, 2002. Available at http://www.georgiacourts.org/aoc/press/idc/idchearings/032202.TXT.

86. Ibid.

87. Ibid.

88. Bill Rankin, "Three Systems: Is One Superior?" *Atlanta Journal-Constitution*, April 21, 2002.

89. *Report of Chief Justice's Commission on Indigent Defense—Part I*, 44.

90. The Spangenberg Group, *Status of Indigent Defense in Georgia*, 95.

91. *Report of Chief Justice's Commission on Indigent Defense—Part I*, 69.

92. Ibid., 59.

93. Ramos, "Indigent Bill Beats Long Odds."

94. Ibid.

95. Ibid.

96. Renaud, "Angry Man of Indigent Defense."

97. Ben Mitcham retired in 2007. Since then, he has been working for the public defender in a nearby county and is hoping to open his own private practice.

98. While Mitchell's client might be able to get his right to appeal reinstated through a writ of habeas corpus (a civil proceeding against the warden that questions the constitutional integrity of the conviction), there is no right to counsel in habeas corpus cases in Georgia. See *Gibson v. Turpin*, 270 Ga. 855 (1999), which held that an indigent death-row inmate with the same lawyer at trial and on direct appeal has no constitutional right to state-funded lawyer upon habeas corpus, despite claim that it was his first opportunity to raise Sixth Amendment claim of ineffective assistance of counsel; and *Shirley v. State*, 188 Ga. App. 357 (1988), which found that a trial court can grant directly, on motion, a client's right to appeal if it is satisfied that the failure to pursue an appeal wasn't the defendant's fault, though again, an indigent defendant has to do this without counsel. Also, in *Pennsylvania v. Finley*, 481 U.S. 551 (1987), the U.S. Supreme Court held that states have no obligation to provide post conviction relief for collateral attack upon judgment, and when they do, fundamental fairness mandated by due process does not require them to supply a lawyer.

99. The Spangenberg Group, *Status of Indigent Defense in Georgia*.

100. The Fall 2001 Grand Jury General Presentments and Report (filed in Superior Court of Houston County on December 20, 2001), at 2.

101. Charlotte Perkins, "Grand Jury Recommends Study of Public Defender System," *Houston Home Journal*, January 10, 2002.

102. Terry Everett resigned after eighteen years as the public defender in 2007, at the age of fifty-eight. "I basically got tired of always fighting with the commissioners for budget and trying to manage a staff with less resources," she wrote in an e-mail. "I had practiced law for thirty-four years with only an occasional week's vacation. I was beginning to think that I might be part of the problem rather than part of the solution and that's not a place I was comfortable being." In 2009 she was still the chairperson of the indigent defense committee for the Georgia Association of Criminal Defense Lawyers and a member of the indigent defense committee for the Georgia Bar. She spends her time volunteering as a disaster relief worker and helping local charities that aid the poor, elderly, and incarcerated.

103. Carolyn Hall (chief assistant public defender, Dublin office), memorandum to the Georgia Public Defender Standards Council, May 21, 2005.

104. Meredith Hobbs, "At Overloaded PD Office, Chief Steps Down as Charges Fly," *Fulton County Daily Report*, May 15, 2006.

105. ABA Committee On Ethics and Professional Responsibility, *Ethical Obligations of*

Lawyers Who Represent Indigent Criminal Defendants When Excessive Caseloads Interfere with Competent and Diligent Representation, Formal Op. 441 (2006).

106. Erik Eckholm, "Citing Rising Workload Public Lawyers Reject Cases," *New York Times*, November 9, 2008.

Chapter Two: A Troy Champion

1. For historical information about Troy I drew upon W. Conrad Holton, "Rediscovering Troy," *Pennsylvania Gazette*, June 1988, and Thomas Phelan and P. Thomas Carroll, *Hudson Mohawk Gateway: An Illustrated History* (Simi Valley, California: American Historical Press, 2001), 84, 105.

2. Mary Proctor and Bill Matuszeski, *Gritty Cities* (Philadelphia: Temple University Press, 1978), 210. Phelan and Carroll, *Hudson Mohawk Gateway*, 148, 154–55.

3. The U.S. Department of Justice's Bureau of Justice Statistics publishes information about offenses reported by different police departments. Sourcebook for Criminal Justice Statistics, Uniform Crime Reporting System. Troy City Police, Offenses Reported, 1990 through 2005 (Albany, 2005).

4. David Kocieniewski, "Crime in City Down in '97 by 9.1 Percent," *New York Times*, January 3, 1998.

5. George L. Kelling and James Q. Wilson, "Broken Windows," *Atlantic Monthly*, March 1982: 34.

6. *Bauer v. McGreevey*, 147 Misc.2d 213, 216 (Rensselaer S. Ct. 1990).

7. For the history of judicial elections I rely heavily on Steven P. Croley, "The Majoritarian Difficulty: Elective Judiciaries and the Rule of Law," *University of Chicago Law Review* 62 (1996): 689, n.3. Croley puts the American judicial election system into perspective this way: "Many constitutional democracies—Australia, Austria, Belgium, Canada, France, Germany, Japan, India, Ireland, Italy, Norway, Portugal, Spain, and Switzerland . . . have judicial review, but none has anything like the institution of elective judiciaries that some American states have. Indeed, elective judiciaries would contravene the continental conception of law. So far as I am aware, only Japan and Switzerland have anything that remotely resembles the elective systems that some states have."

8. Ibid., 716.

9. Ibid., 715.

10. Ibid., n. 107 (quoting Roscoe Pound's 1906 "The Causes of Popular Dissatisfaction with the Administration of Justice," reprinted in *Baylor Law Review* 8 [1956]: 23).

11. Ibid., 724. In 2009 the U.S. Supreme Court found that judges must disqualify themselves from cases involving people who contributed outstanding amounts of money to help put them on the bench. Case number 08-22, *Caperton v. Massey Coal*, involved a chief executive of a mining company who spent three million dollars to help unseat an incumbent on the West Virginia Supreme Court in 2004. When a case involving his company came before the court, the judge he supported went on to join the 3-to-2 majority that threw out a fifty million–dollar jury verdict against his business. At issue was whether a judge's failure to recuse himself from the case, in which he received substantial campaign donations from one of the parties, violates the due process rights of the other party.

12. Tim O'Brien, "Battle Turns Bitter in Troy Judgeship Race," *Albany Times Union*, November 5, 1994.

13. Bauer had 2,491 new cases in 1994, the year he came into office, as opposed to 3,244 in 2003 during his last full year in office, according to *The New York State Unified Court System Report of Action in City and District Courts Outside NYC.*

14. A report from New York State Bar Association reviews findings about recidivism, barriers to re-entry, and consequences that stem from conviction, as well as the issues of employment, education, benefits, financial penalties, housing, family, civic participation and immigration. New York Bar Association, Special Committee on Collateral Consequences of Criminal Proceedings, *Re-Entry and Reintegration: The Road to Public Safety* (May 2006) (adopted as official NYSBA policy November 2006). Available at http://www.reentry.net/link.cfm?9285.

15. Jeremy Travis, "Invisible Punishment: An Instrument of Social Exclusion," in *Invisible Punishment: The Collateral Consequences of Mass Imprisonment*, eds. Mark Mauer and Meda Chesney-Lind (New York: The New Press, 2003), 18. Travis also asserts that thirteen million Americans have been convicted of felonies, more than six percent of the adult population. "The proportion of felony convictions among African-American adult males is even higher," he writes.

16. Milton Heumann, "Plea Bargaining," in *Encyclopedia of the American Judicial System: Studies of the Principal Institutions and Processes of Law*, Volume IV, ed. Robert J. Janosik (New York: Charles Scribner's Sons, 1987), 891. The American Bar Association has issued standards describing the responsibilities of judges. According to Standard 14—3.3, the responsibilities of the judge are as follows:

   (a) The judge should not accept a plea of guilty or nolo contendere without first inquiring whether the parties have arrived at a plea agreement and, if there is one, requiring that its terms and conditions be disclosed.

   (b) If a plea agreement has been reached by the parties which contemplates the granting of charge or sentence concessions by the judge, the judge should:

      (i) order the preparation of a preplea or presentence report, when needed for determining the appropriate disposition;

      (ii) give the agreement due consideration, but notwithstanding its existence reach an independent decision on whether to grant charge or sentence concessions; and

      (iii) in every case advise the defendant whether the judge accepts or rejects the contemplated charge or sentence concessions or whether a decision on acceptance will be deferred until after the plea is entered and/or a preplea or presentence report is received.

   (c) The judge should not through word or demeanor, either directly or indirectly, communicate to the defendant or defense counsel that a plea agreement should be accepted or that a guilty plea should be entered.

   (d) A judge should not ordinarily participate in plea negotiation discussions among the parties. Upon the request of the parties, a judge may be presented with a proposed plea agreement negotiated by the parties and may indicate whether the court would accept the terms as proposed and if relevant, indicate what sentence would be imposed. Discussions relating to plea negotiations at which the judge is present need not be recorded verbatim, so long as an appropriate record is made at the earliest opportunity. For good cause, the judge may order the record or transcript of any such discussions to be sealed.

(e) In cases where a defendant offers to plead guilty and the judge decides that the final disposition should not include the charge or sentence concessions contemplated by the plea agreement, the judge shall so advise the defendant and permit withdrawal of the tender of the plea. In cases where a defendant pleads guilty pursuant to a plea agreement and the court, following entry of the plea, decides that the final disposition should not include the contemplated charge or sentence concessions, withdrawal of the plea shall be allowed if:

(i) the judge had previously concurred, whether tentatively or fully, in the proposed charge or sentence concessions; or

(ii) the guilty plea is entered upon the express condition, approved by the judge, that the plea can be withdrawn if the charge or sentence concessions are subsequently rejected by the court.

In all other cases where a defendant pleads guilty pursuant to a plea agreement and the judge decides that the final disposition should not include the contemplated charge or sentence concessions, withdrawal of the plea may be permitted as set forth in standard 14–2.1.

17. Tom Goldstein, "Judge's Distaste Worth $141,000 to Coffee Man," *New York Times*, July 21, 1977.

18. U.S. Constitution, amend. 8.

19. Alfredo Garcia, "Practice of Bail," in *The Oxford Companion to American Law*, Kermit Hall and others, eds. (New York: Oxford University Press, 2002), 51.

20. Friedman, *Crime and Punishment in American History*, 74.

21. *Stack v. Boyle*, 342 U.S. 1, 4–5 (1951).

22. Ibid., 4.

23. Ibid., 6.

24. There is, however, no automatic right to bail. A judge can always deny it altogether.

25. *McKinney's Consolidated Laws of New York Annotated*, Criminal Procedure Law, § 510.30 (West 2006).

26. This isn't to say that preventative detention can never be an issue when setting bail. Many states allow the danger a defendant poses to the community to be a consideration in accordance with a 1987 case *U.S. v. Salerno*, 481 U.S. 739 (1987), where the court refused to strike down the Federal Bail Reform Act of 1984, which permitted pretrial detention for those charged with serious crimes.

27. John H. Langbein, "Historical Foundations of the Law of Evidence: A View from the Ryder Sources," *Columbia Law Review* 96 (1996): 1168–69, 1199.

28. For a full discussion of the judicial role in England versus the United States see Gordon Van Kessel, "Adversary Excesses in the American Criminal Trial," *Notre Dame Law Review* 67 (1992): 403, 426.

29. Albert W. Alschuler, "Mediation with a Mugger: Concerning the Shortage of Adjudicative Services and the Need for a Two-Tier Trial System in Civil Cases," *Harvard Law Review* 99 (1986): 1808, 1824.

30. Robert A. Kagan, *Adversarial Legalism: The Way of American Law*, rev. ed. (2001, repr. Cambridge: Harvard University Press, 2003), 83.

31. Alschuler, "Mediation with a Mugger," 1824.

32. Kagan, *Adversarial Legalism*, 83, quoting Thomas Weigend, "Continental Cures for American Ailments: European Criminal Procedure as a Model for Law Reform," *Crime and Justice* 2 (1980): 411.

33. Daniel Meador, "Criminal Procedure," in Hall and others, 649. For an explanation of the judge's role in plea bargaining in the United States see Ofra Bikel's video *The Plea, MacNeil/Lehrer News Hour*, PBS, June 17, 2004, which can be viewed or obtained by going to http://www.pbs.org/wgbh/pages/frontline/shows/plea/.

34. The sign stated: "I have asked the Troy police to arrest anyone found trespassing on/in the property. I have made it clear that if a person is not a tenant, or a guest or invitee thereof, his/her presence on/in the property is unauthorized, and he/she should be arrested for trespassing."

35. Bauer also said that while Bobo had no prior warrants or holds on her, she was consorting with other criminals and had a prior record of misdemeanors and felonies with Troy Police Court. However, he knew this only "generally." "I didn't have a criminal history in my hand, but she was a known person to the county," whom he could incarcerate because she could receive a maximum sentence of fifteen days in jail and a $250 fine.

36. Robert Axelrod, *The Evolution of Cooperation* (New York: Basic Books, 1984), 61.

37. The Fund for Modern Courts, *Capital District Court Monitors: Report On the Troy City Court*, March 1998.

38. A city court clerk couldn't confirm the dismissal because it is a completed case with a "sealed" record.

39. The commission ultimately did not sustain the excessive bail charge involving Chris Cruz. It didn't give a reason why and commission members and staff wouldn't comment, but conceivably Cruz's criminal history and/or the allegations of loitering for buying drugs justified the sum. As for the issue of Cruz's right to counsel, the commission never asserted a violation, presumably because Bauer had indeed assigned a lawyer, who had been late.

40. Alschuler, "Mediation with a Mugger," 1825.

41. New York law relating to counsel can be found at *McKinney's Consolidated Laws of New York Annotated*, Criminal Procedure Law, § 170.10(3) and § 180.10(3) (West 2006). The U.S. Supreme Court recently held that a defendant's initial appearance before a magistrate judge marks initiation of adversary proceedings that triggers the Sixth Amendment right to counsel. The Court found that the federal government, including the District of Columbia, as well as forty-three states, take the first step toward appointing counsel before, at, or just after initial appearance. *Rothgery v. Gillespie County, Texas*, 128 S.Ct. 2578, 2586–87 (2008). Also, before police officers may question a suspect, they are required to advise the suspect of a right to counsel under *Miranda v. Arizona*, 384 U.S. 436 (1966).

42. *McKinney's Consolidated Laws of New York*, Vehicle and Traffic Law, § 1800 (penalties for traffic infractions), § 1236(a) (lamps on bicycles), § 1236(b) (bells/signal device on bicycles), § 1234 (riding on roadways) (West 2005).

43. Defendants can waive counsel and proceed pro se in accordance with *Faretta v. California*, 422 U.S. 806 (1975).

44. Stephanos Bibas, "Plea Bargaining Outside the Shadow of Trial," *Harvard Law Review* 117 (2004): 8.

45. Kagan, *Adversarial Legalism*, 84.

46. Malcolm Feeley, *The Process is the Punishment: Handling Cases in a Lower Criminal Court*, rev. ed. (New York: Russell Sage Foundation, 1992), 30.

47. *Brady v. United States*, 397 U.S., 742, 751 (1970).

48. Feeley, *Process is the Punishment*, 283–84.

49. Ibid., 24.

50. Ibid., 33.

51. Ibid., 35.

52. Albert W. Alschuler has written many articles condemning the practice of plea bargaining, including "The Changing Plea Bargaining Debate," *California Law Review* 69 (1981): 652, in which he urges the abolition of plea bargaining. In an earlier piece, "The Defense Attorney's Role in Plea Bargaining," *Yale Law Journal* 84 (1975): 1179, he argues that plea bargaining is inherently corruptive of the attorney-client relationship; and in "Plea Bargaining and Its History," *Law and Society Review* 13 (1979): 211, he challenges the historical justification for plea bargaining. Also, in "The Prosecutor's Role in Plea Bargaining," *University of Chicago Law Review* 36 (1968): 50, he provides anecdotal evidence that suggests that plea bargaining induces innocent defendants to plead guilty. Another scholar, Stephen J. Schulhofer, has theorized that abolishing plea bargaining is a real possibility in "Is Plea Bargaining Inevitable?," *Harvard Law Review* 97 (1984): 1037.

53. John H. Langbein, "Torture and Plea Bargaining," *University of Chicago Law Review* 46 (1978): 3–22.

54. Ibid., 21.

55. *North Carolina v. Alford*, 400 U.S. 25, 28 n.2 (1970).

56. *Santobello v. New York*, 404 U.S. 257, 260 (1971).

57. John Caher, "Troy Judge Faces Accusations at Judicial Conduct Commission in Public Hearing," *New York Law Journal*, July 29, 2003.

58. *Albany Times Union*, "A Judge on Trial" August 2, 2003.

59. Associated Press, "Peace T-Shirt Leads to Arrest at New York Mall," *Seattle Times*, March 5, 2003.

60. Alan Wechsler, "Mall Protest Hits Highway," *Albany Times Union*, April 1, 2003.

61. The New York State Commission on Judicial Conduct's decision *In the Matter of the Proceeding in Relation to Henry R. Bauer* was decided on March 30, 2004 and is available on the commission's Web site http://www.scjc.state.ny.us/Determinations/all_decisions.htm.

62. *Matter of Aldrich*, 58 N.Y.2d 279, 283 (1983).

63. New York State Commission on Judicial Conduct, *In the Matter of the Proceeding in Relation to Henry R. Bauer*.

64. Several dissenting judges saw little wrong in what Bauer had done. In the Court of Appeals' decision, *In the Matter of Henry R. Bauer, Judge of the Troy City Courts, Rensselaer County v. State Commission on Judicial Conduct*, 785 N.Y.S.2d 372 (2004),

three judges argued in two separate dissents that Judge Bauer deserved censure only. In a joint dissenting opinion, judges Victoria A. Graffeo and Susan Phillips Read agreed that while the right to counsel violations "could not be condoned," the judge himself said he had changed his practices somewhat. Moreover, the commission's examination had been mere "snap-shots" that weren't necessarily representative of the whole, noting that, for the violations of right to counsel, "nineteen sustained charges, which occurred during two years of a ten-year judicial career" didn't merit his removal. For bail, the commission found twenty-six violations. "There is no way to discern whether these cases are exceptions to, or representative of, petitioner's general conduct on the bench," they found. The remaining errors seemed to be "not knowing acts of judicial misconduct." Another dissenter, Judge Robert S. Smith felt that Judge Bauer's "most unfortunate" response to the charges—his "outraged defiance"—didn't outbalance the mitigating fact that Judge Bauer "has been, in many important respects, quite a good judge," and didn't warrant removal from the bench. Judge Smith didn't think that Judge Bauer had repeatedly denied counsel to poor defendants and taken advantage of their lack of representation to jail them with excessive bail. "If I thought that this had occurred, I would vote for removal," Smith wrote. "I am convinced, however, that this impression is incorrect." Smith added that the judge's misconduct "was somewhat less serious than it appears at first glance." He seemed to posit that lawyers didn't, in any case, make a difference in the process. "I see no indication in the record that any defendant who was remanded for failure to post bail would have avoided incarceration, or would have been released sooner, if he or she had had a court-appointed lawyer."

65. James V. Franco, "Court of Appeals Calls for Judge's Removal," *Troy Record*, October 15, 2004.
66. James V. Franco, "Judge Booted from Troy Bench: State's Highest Court Suspends Bauer, But He'll Still Receive $113,000-per-year Salary," *Troy Record*, May 12, 2004.
67. "Sound Off: We Don't Need This Now," *Troy Record*, May 28, 2004.
68. "Reader Mail," *Troy Record*, April 20, 2004.
69. Frank Grasso letter to Judge Henry Bauer, April 24, 2003 (on file with the author).
70. Editorial, "Despite Conduct, Judge Bauer Still a Troy Champion," *Troy Record*, October 10, 2004.
71. Part 100.1 of the Rules Governing Judicial Conduct states, "A judge shall uphold the integrity and independence of the judiciary," and further specifies that, "An independent and honorable judiciary is indispensable to justice in our society. A judge should participate in establishing, maintaining and enforcing high standards of conduct, and shall personally observe those standards so that the integrity and independence of the judiciary will be preserved. The provisions of this Part 100 are to be construed and applied to further that objective." The rules are promulgated by the chief administrator of the courts, with the approval of the court of appeals and are available at http://www.scjc.state.ny.us/Legal%20Authorities/rgjc.htm.

Chapter Three: Miss Wiggs's List

1. Kenneth Culp Davis, *Discretionary Justice: A Preliminary Inquiry*, rev. ed. (1969, repr. Chicago: University of Illinois Press, 1977), 207–8. For a general discussion

of the steps in the process to prosecute see Wayne R. LaFave, Jerold H. Israel and Nancy J. King in their text *Criminal Procedure* 2nd ed. (St. Paul, Minn.: West Group, 2004), 7–20, 685–86.

2. Douglas McCollam, "The Ghost of 'Gideon': It's Been 40 Years Since Arnold & Porter Fought at the Supreme Court for Counsel for the Poor. Now the Firm is Fighting Again," *The American Lawyer*, March 4, 2003.

3. Carr v. State, 873 So.2d 991, 995 (Miss. S. Ct. May 20, 2004); Adam Liptak, "County Says It's Too Poor to Defend the Poor," *New York Times*, April 15, 2003.

4. *Quitman County v. State*, 910 So.2d 1032, 1037 (Miss. S. Ct. 2005).

5. For a historical perspective on the Delta, see James C. Cobb, *The Most Southern Place on Earth: The Mississippi Delta and the Roots of Regional Identity*, rev. ed. (1992, repr. New York: Oxford University Press, 1994), 255.

6. Ralph David Abernathy, *And the Walls Came Tumbling Down: An Autobiography* (New York: HarperCollins, 1991), 413, 506.

7. The Bureau of Justice Statistics has conducted a bi-annual report on data collected from a representative sample of felony cases filed in the nation's seventy-five largest counties since 1990. The report cited here, Tracey Kyckelhahn & Thomas H. Cohen, "Felony Defendants in Large Urban Counties 2004," Department of Justice, Bureau of Justice Statistics (April 2008), can also be found at http://www.ojp.usdoj.gov/bjs/pub/pdf/fdluc04.pdf.

8. Daniel S. Medwed, "The Zeal Deal: Prosecutorial Resistance to Post-Conviction Claims of Innocence," *Boston University Law Review* 84 (2004): 152.

9. As Professor William T. Pizzi explains: "Prosecutorial discretion in the American legal system must be seen as part of a political tradition that is built on a preference for local control over political power and on an aversion to strong centralized governmental authority and power. There is no better example than our federal system in which each state retains the power to make its own criminal laws and even to determine its own system of criminal procedure, consistent with the U.S. Constitution. This aversion to strong centralized governmental power runs deep in the American political tradition." "Understanding Prosecutorial Discretion in the United States: the Limits of Comparative Criminal Procedure as an Instrument of Reform," *Ohio State Law Journal* 54 (1993): 1342.

10. Brooklyn Law School professor Daniel Medwed wrote that, "Candidates vying for the office of chief prosecutor typically campaign on a general tough-on-crime platform, strewn with references to their overall win-loss record and reminders about specific successes in high-profile cases." "The Zeal Deal," 182. Georgetown University Law School professor Abbe Smith comes to a similar conclusion: "In view of the institutional culture of prosecutor's offices and the culture of the adversary system generally, it is perhaps inevitable that the overriding interest of prosecutors would be winning. This is so notwithstanding the prosecutor's ethical obligation to embrace justice over winning, or the ambiguity of what it means to 'win.' " "Can You Be a Good Person and a Good Prosecutor?" *Georgetown Journal of Legal Ethics* 14 (2001): 388–89.

11. Medwed, "The Zeal Deal," 153.

12. For the details in this paragraph, I am grateful to the reporting of Emily Le Coz

NOTES 281

in "Acquittals Trouble D.A.: 'Juries Don't Respond the Way they Used To,'"
Clarksdale Press Register, March 29, 2003.

13. Daniel Richman, "Institutional Coordination and Sentencing Reform," *Texas Law Review* 84 (2006): 2061.

14. LaFave, Israel, and King, *Criminal Procedure*, 407–8, 741; Akhil Reed Amar, *The Bill of Rights* (New Haven: Yale University Press, 1998), 84–85.

15. The Fifth Amendment provides, in part, "No person shall be held to answer for a capital, or otherwise infamous crime, unless on a presentment of indictment of a grand jury, except in cases arising in the law or naval forces, or in the Militia, when in actual service in time of war or public danger. . . ."

16. LaFave, Israel, and King, *Criminal Procedure*, 743.

17. The eighteen states that require grand jury indictments are Alabama, Alaska, Delaware, Georgia, Kentucky, Maine, Massachusetts, Mississippi, New Hampshire, New Jersey, New York, North Carolina, Ohio, South Carolina, Tennessee, Texas, Virginia, and West Virginia. LaFave et al., *Criminal Procedure*, 19, 745. Mississippi's requirement originates in Article 3, section 27 of the state Constitution, which provides: "No person shall, for any indictable offense, be proceeded against criminally by information, except in cases arising in the land or naval forces, or the military when in actual service, or by leave of the court for misdemeanor in office or where a defendant represented by counsel by sworn statement waives indictment; but the legislature, in cases not punishable by death or by imprisonment in the penitentiary, may dispense with the inquest of the grand jury, and may authorize prosecutions before justice court judges, or such other inferior court or courts as may be established, and the proceedings in such cases shall be regulated by law."

18. LaFave, Israel, and King, *Criminal Procedure*, 19, 745.

19. The advisory opinion, Miss. Att'y A.G. No. 2005–0314 (July 1, 2005) can be found on the Office for the Attorney General for the State of Mississippi's Web site: http://www.ago.state.ms.us.

20. National District Attorneys Association, *National Prosecution Standards*, 2nd ed. (Alexandria, Va.: National District Attorneys Association, 1991). These standards are available free on the Web site of the NDAA.

21. *National Prosecution Standards*, "42.8 Defense of Decision," 127 ("The prosecutor should promptly respond to inquiries from those who feel aggrieved by the screening procedure and decision").

22. For example, many states have laws against minors having sex with each other, a crime which most prosecutors wouldn't touch since it happens thousands of times a day.

23. For example, a defendant is charged with resisting arrest and a prosecutor has to decide whether it is acceptable to resolve the case by dropping the charge so long as the defendant agrees to not pursue a potential civil action against the police and prosecutor. One prosecutor mentioned the importance of using this remedy carefully so as not to "continually whitewash police abuse."

24. *National Prosecution Standards*, "42.4 Factors Not to Consider," 125–26.

25. Ibid., "42.7 Record of Decision," 127; and "42.5 Information Sharing" and "42.6 Reconsideration of New Information," 126.

26. David James eventually filed a civil suit seeking to be reinstated in his old job as an investigator and requesting three million dollars in compensatory and punitive damages in federal court in the Northern District of Mississippi. The complaint charged that Mellen violated his right to free expression (under the Fifth and Fourteenth Amendments) in deciding James couldn't do his job and run for office at the same time; the suit also alleges that Mellen had previously permitted white employees to run for office but disallowed James, who is black, thus discriminating against him in violation of § 1983 and Title VII of the Civil Rights Act. David James's claims were denied by the federal district court and the Fifth Circuit U.S. Court of Appeals.

27. *Wayte v. United States*, 470 U.S. 598, 607 (1985).

28. LaFave et al., *Criminal Procedure*, 687.

29. Reva B. Siegel, "The Rule of Love: Wife Beating as Prerogative and Privacy," *Yale Law Journal* 105 (1996): 2118.

30. Ibid., 2139.

31. Ibid., 2120.

32. Ibid., 2153 (citing *State v. Hussey* 44 N.C. (Busb.) 123, 126–27 (1852), which held that wives were incompetent to testify against husbands in all cases of assault and battery, except where permanent injury or great bodily harm was inflicted).

33. For a discussion of the Civil Rights Remedy of the Violence Against Women Act, see Elizabeth M. Schneider, *Battered Women & Feminist Lawmaking* (New Haven: Yale University Press, 2000), 188.

34. In 2008 the *Chicago Tribune* reported that only 17 percent of domestic violence cases in Cook County, Illinois, resulted in a conviction, a rate that shows no improvement, despite concrete efforts to make prosecution easier for victims. Liam Ford, "Courts Are Failing Battered Women," *Chicago Tribune*, October 10, 2008.

35. While these policies have quelled some criticism, one analysis explains: "To date, however, there is little evaluation data that can be brought to bear on the wisdom of no-drop policies." Robert C. Davis, Barbara E. Smith & Heather J. Davies, "Effects of No-Drop Prosecution of Domestic Violence Upon Conviction Rates," *Justice Research and Policy* 3.2 (2001): 2–3.

36. These jurisdictions were Omaha, Nebraska; Everett, Washington; Klamath Falls, Oregon; and San Diego, California. The first three received special grants for no-drop prosecutions from the Office of Justice Programs. Barbara E. Smith, Robert Davis, Laura B. Nickles, and Heather J. Davies, *An Evaluation of Efforts to Implement No-Drop Policies: Two Central Values in Conflict*, Final Report (Washington, D.C.: U.S. Department of Justice, National Institute of Justice, 2001).

37. National District Attorneys Association, "Policy Position on Domestic Violence," Adopted October 23, 2004 by the Board of Directors in Monterey, California, 10, is available on the organization's Web site http://www.ndaa.org/newsroom/resolutions_policy_position_papers.html.

38. Barbara Hart, "Battered Women and the Criminal Justice System," *The American Behavioral Scientist* 36 (1993). For a discussion of the debate surrounding no-drop policies, see Cheryl Hanna, "No Right to Choose: Mandated Victim Participation in Domestic Violence Prosecutions," 109 *Harvard Law Review* (1996): 1863–64.

39. National District Attorneys Association, "Policy Position on Domestic Violence," 10.

40. Jody Clifton and her mother, Sara, say Jody stayed several days longer than the report states.

41. In *Payne v. Tennessee*, the court held that the heinousness of a defendant's crime, viewed in terms of the character of the victim, is "surely relevant in determining a [defendant's] blameworthiness." 501 U.S. 808, 817 (1991).

42. Michelle Oberman, "Turning Girls into Women: Re-Evaluating Modern Statutory Rape Law," *DePaul Journal of Health Care Law* 8 (2004); and Michelle Oberman, "Regulating Consensual Sex with Minors: Defining a Role for Statutory Rape," *Buffalo Law Review* 48 (2000).

43. Oberman, "Turning Girls into Women," 120–33.

44. For illuminating the historical context of statutory rape law I relied on the scholarship of Michelle Oberman, as well as Frances Olsen, "Statutory Rape: A Feminist Critique of Rights Analysis," *Texas Law Review* 63 (1984): 404; and Jane E. Larson, " 'Even a Worm Will Turn at Last': Rape Reform in Late Nineteenth-Century America," *Yale Journal of Law and the Humanities* 9 (1997): 1.

45. Larson, "Even a Worm," 4.

46. Ibid., 8.

47. Oberman. "Turning Girls into Women," 130–32.

48. Kit Kinports, "Sex Offenses," in Kermit L. Hall and others, eds., *The Oxford Companion to American Law* (New York: Oxford University Press, 2002), 737.

49. The revised law regarding statutory rape, drugging, and spousal rape can be found at *Miss Code Ann,*. § 97–3-65 (West 2007).

50. Cassia Spohn, Dawn Beichner, and Erika Davis-Frenzel, "Prosecutorial Justifications for Sexual Assault Case Rejection: Guarding the 'Gateway to Justice,' " *Social Problems* 48 (2001): 208. This article cites two other works on the way culpability of the offender is assessed: Darrell Steffensmeier, Jeffery Ulmer, and John Kramer, "The Interaction of Race, Gender, and Age in Criminal Sentencing: The Punishment Cost of Being Young, Black, and Male," *Criminology* 26 (1998):763–68; as well as Darnell Hawkins, "Causal Attribution and Punishment for Crime," *Deviant Behavior* 1 (1981): 207–30. For further reading on the extent to which prosecutors' determinations in statutory rape cases are informed by their personal prejudices, see Kay L. Levine, "The Intimacy Discount: Prosecutorial Discretion, Privacy, and Equality in the Statutory Rape Caseload," *Emory Law Journal* 55 (2006): 732–37.

51. According to a study, Mississippi had the highest birthrate in the nation for teenage mothers and Quitman County had a higher-than-state-average birthrate for teenage mothers. Brian W. Amy, Peter Fos, and Claudia Dvorak, *Quitman County Health Profile* (Jackson, Miss.: Mississippi State Department of Health, 2003), 16.

52. Spohn et al., "Prosecutorial Justifications," 233.

53. For a general description of the insanity defense and the reasoning behind it see Lawrence M. Friedman, *Crime and Punishment in American History* (New York: BasicBooks, 1994), 143–48.

54. The Mississippi Supreme Court has held that prosecution of attempted theft

required "a direct ineffectual act toward its commission." *Burney v. State*, 515 So.2d 1154, 1158 (Miss. 1987).

55. In 2002 the state legislature specifically targeted the theft of anhydrous ammonia in the criminal code. The relevant Mississippi statute, § 41–29–313 (Precursor chemicals or drugs; presumption of unlawful manufacture of controlled substances; offenses; penalties) makes it "unlawful for any person to knowingly or intentionally steal or unlawfully take or carry away any amount of anhydrous ammonia or to break, cut, or in any manner damage the valve or locking mechanism on an anhydrous ammonia tank with the intent to steal or unlawfully take or carry away anhydrous ammonia."

56. James Jennings, "Man, 25, Found in Car, Dies at Hospital," *Clarksdale Press Register*, December 31, 2003; Molly Grantham, "Reader Opinions," *Clarksdale Press Register*, January 14, 2004.

57. The continuing education requirement for Mississippi municipal police chiefs and officers is contained in § 45–6-19 of the Mississippi Code of 1972, as amended in 2004. For information about police officer employment requirements I relied on pages vi–vii of the 2005 version of the *Reciprocity Handbook* published by The International Association of Directors of Law Enforcement Standards and Training (IADLEST) which is located in Albion, Michigan.

58. Richman, "Institutional Coordination and Sentencing Reform," 2060.

59. Linder & Associates, *Toward a Fully Integrated Criminal Justice System* 109 (New Orleans, La.: Orleans Parish District Attorney's Office, 2005), 109.

60. Ibid., 49.

61. Chief Doyle says this exchange was taped, but the Lambert police department has no record of it.

62. Under statutory rape law in Mississippi, sexual intercourse is specifically defined as the "joining of the sexual organs of a male and female human being in which the penis of the male is inserted into the vagina of the female." However, the state is absolved of the need to prove penetration in cases involving victims under the age of sixteen where the evidence establishes that the genitals, anus, or perineum of the child is torn or lacerated as a result of the attempt to have sexual intercourse with the child. Miss. Code Ann. § 97–3-65 (2008).

Chapter Four: Show Trial

1. Philip Wattley, "$5,000 Reward is Offered for Killer of Lisa Cabassa," *Chicago Tribune*, January 17, 1976.

2. Lee Strobel, "Convict Teen in Killing as Lisa's Mom Sobs," *Chicago Tribune*, June 18, 1976; Daniel Egler and Michael Hirsley, "Killing of Girl: Neighbor Jailed in Liza, 9, Death," *Chicago Tribune*, February 27, 1976.

3. Maurice Possley and Ken Armstrong, "The Flip Side of a Fair Trial," *Chicago Tribune*, January 11, 1999.

4. Robert H. Jackson, "The Federal Prosecutor," *Criminal Law & Criminology* 31 (1940), 6. Cited in Bennett L. Gershman, "The Prosecutor's Duty to Truth," *Georgetown Journal of Legal Ethics* 14 (2001): 350.

5. Bennett L. Gershman, a professor at Pace Law School and former prosecutor, ex-

plains: "A prosecutor's moral courage to judge the truthfulness of a witness may be influenced by institutional considerations that discourage either critical evaluation or the ability to take appropriate action. Prosecutors' offices that are heavily influenced by conviction statistics—both to project a tough law-and-order image and for leverage in budget negotiations—will probably maintain close supervision over individual decision making by assistants, and principled decisions that might be perceived as inconsistent with a strong crime-fighting image may be discouraged. It is much more likely in such a setting that a possibly innocent defendant will be required to accept a generous plea offer on the eve of trial rather than that the prosecutor will dismiss a case in which he lacks confidence." Gershman, "The Prosecutor's Duty to Truth," *Georgetown Journal of Legal Ethics* 14 (2001): 350.

6. This scene is recalled in both Possley and Armstrong, "The Flip Side of a Fair Trial" and Steve Bogira, *Courtroom 302: A Year Behind the Scenes in an American Criminal Courthouse*, rev. ed. (2005, repr. Vintage Press, 2006), 69.

7. Maurice Possley and Steve Mills, "After 25 Years, DNA May Clear 2 of Death, Rape; Interviews Show Conviction Based on Bad Testimony," *Chicago Tribune*, January 22, 2003.

8. Lee Strobel, "Judge Hits Cop Handling of Rape-Murder Suspect," *Chicago Tribune*, June 8, 1976.

9. In *Brady v. Maryland*, 373 U.S. 83 (1963) the court held that the prosecution's withholding evidence from the defendant violates the due process clause if it is material to either guilt or punishment.

10. William Griffin, "Rules Prosecution Withheld Evidence," *Chicago Tribune*, September 28, 1976.

11. Philip Wattley and Jay Branegan, "Teen Led to New Lisa Suspects," *Chicago Tribune*, November 10, 1978; Lee Strobel, "Witness in Lisa Slaying Recants; State's Case Ruined," *Chicago Tribune*, December 17, 1976.

12. Philip Wattley and Jay Branegan, "Four More Charged in Slaying of 9-Year-Old Lisa," *Chicago Tribune*, November 19, 1976.

13. Lee Strobel, "Witness in Lisa Slaying Recants; State's Case Ruined," *Chicago Tribune*, December 17, 1976.

14. "Lisa Slaying Witness Not Coerced: Official," *Chicago Tribune*, December 18, 1976.

15. Edmund J. Rooney, "Woman: I'll Testify Again in New Lisa Murder Trial," *Chicago Daily News*, September 28, 1976, and Editorial, "Leave Lisa's Case Alone," *Chicago Daily News*, September 29, 1976.

16. *United States v. Young*, 470 U.S. 1, 18–19 (1985).

17. David Jackson, "Tearful Juror Calls the Lisa Verdict 'Fair,'" *Chicago Daily News*, April 29, 1977.

18. Jay Branegan, "We Know Why Lisa Figure Feared: Juror," *Chicago Tribune*, April 29, 1977.

19. "Lisa Jury Misled, Foreman Says," *Chicago Tribune*, May 17, 1977.

20. The U.S. Supreme Court reinstated the death penalty six months after the commission of the crime against Lisa Cabassa in *Gregg v. Georgia*, 428 U.S. 153 (1976). At the time of the Cabassa crime, the country was still operating under

the 1972 U.S. Supreme Court decision of *Furman v. Georgia* 408 U.S. 238, which had imposed a de facto moratorium on capital punishment.

21. The opinion of the Appellate Court of Illinois can be found at *People v. Evans*, 399 N.E.2d 1333, 1343–44 (Ill. App. Ct. 1979).

22. Keith A. Findley and Michael S. Scott, "The Multiple Dimensions of Tunnel Vision in Criminal Cases," *Wisconsin Law Review* (2006): 309.

23. United Press International, "10 Acquitted in Illinois In Killings in Prison Riot," May 10, 1981.

24. Barry Scheck and Peter Neufeld describe the work of their Innocence Project, including Dotson's exoneration, in Barry Scheck, Peter Neufeld, and Jim Dwyer, *Actual Innocence: When Justice Goes Wrong and How to Make It Right*, rev. ed. (2000, repr. New York: Signet , 2001), 51.

25. Civia Tamarkin and Rob Warden, "Born to Lose: The Gary Dotson Story You've Never Heard," *Chicago Magazine*, January 1988, 130–31, 164.

26. Ibid., 164.

27. Ibid., 165. This article mentions that the governor's intervention followed a badly mismanaged outbreak of salmonella that had infected more than fifteen thousand residents of Illinois and surrounding states.

28. Philip Lentz and Ann Marie Lipinski, "Dotson Hearing May Be the Ticket," *Chicago Tribune*, May 8, 1985.

29. Tamarkin and Warden, "Born to Lose," 164.

30. Hanke Gratteau and John Kass, "Dotson Sentence Commuted But Conviction Was Correct, Governor Says," *Chicago Tribune*, May 13, 1985.

31. Tamarkin and Warden, "Born to Lose," 166.

32. Center for Wrongful Convictions, "The Illinois Exonerated: Gary Dotson," Northwestern University School of Law, Bluhm Legal Clinic, http://www.law .northwestern.edu/wrongfulconvictions/exonerations/ilDotsonSummary.html.

33. Ibid.

34. Larry Green, "12-year Legal Nightmare at an End; Recanted Testimony, High-Tech Help to Clear Gary Dotson," *Los Angeles Times*, August 15, 1989.

35. *Los Angeles Times*, "Dotson, Cleared of Rape but Rejailed, to Be Freed," December 24, 1987 ("If he [Thompson] had not done anything, Dotson faced the possibility of staying in prison until at least 2008, and the governor felt that was too stiff a sentence for a parole violation," an aide said).

36. Center for Wrongful Convictions, "The Illinois Exonerated."

37. Sharon Begley, "Leaving Holmes in the Dust," *Newsweek*, October 16, 1987.

38. Green, "12-year Legal Nightmare at an End."

39. Ibid.

40. Maurice Possley and Rick Kogan, *Everybody Pays: Two Men, One Murder and the Price of Truth*, paperback ed. (2001, repr. New York: Berkley Books, 2002) 253.

41. Ibid., 268

42. For the details about the Cruz case included in this chapter, I have relied on the in-depth reporting of Thomas Frisbie and Randy Garrett in their book, *Victims of Justice*, which follows Cruz and his co-defendants from the day of the crime to

the day of his vindication. Frisbie and Garrett, *Victims of Justice Revisited*, rev. ed. (1998, repr. Evanston: Northwestern University Press, 2005), 94.

43. Ibid., 45.

44. Ibid., 121.

45. Ibid., 124.

46. Samuel R. Gross, professor of law at the University of Michigan Law School, writes in the "Risks of Death: Why Erroneous Convictions Are Common in Capital Cases," *Buffalo Law Review* 44 (1996): 495–96 that "In a close criminal case the jury is supposed to release a defendant who is in their opinion, probably guilty. This is a distasteful task under any circumstances, but it becomes increasingly unpalatable—and unlikely—as we move up the scale from non-violent crime, to violent crime, to homicide, to aggravated grisly murder."

47. Frisbie and Garrett, *Victims of Justice*, 344. Charges were later dropped against Hernandez. Brian Dugan has yet to be tried for the murder of Jeanine Nicarico, though it is set for trial in 2009, according to newspaper reports.

48. Steve Mills and Maurice Possley, "Former Foe Having 2nd Thoughts," *Chicago Tribune*, January 22, 2003.

49. Maurice Possley and Steve Mills, "4 Men Get Pardons, Clean Slates; After Serving 10 to 27 Years, All Cleared by DNA Tests," *Chicago Tribune*, January 7, 2005.

50. *U.S. v. Wade*, 388 U.S. 218, 228 (1967).

51. See, for example, Samuel R. Gross et al., "Exonerations in the United States 1989 Through 2003," *Journal of Criminal Law and Criminology* 95 (2005): 542 (finding eyewitness error in 64 percent of the cases identified the study of three hundred and forty wrongful convictions between 1989 and 2003).

52. Scheck, Neufeld, and Dwyer, *Actual Innocence*, 352, recommend that police and prosecutors be trained about the risks of providing corroborating details that might disguise doubts a witness may hold.

53. Dianne L. Martin, "Lessons About Justice from the 'Laboratory' of Wrongful Convictions: Tunnel Vision, the Construction of Guilt and Informer Evidence," *University of Missouri–Kansas City Law Review* 70 (2002): 848.

54. Findley and Scott, "The Multiple Dimensions of Tunnel Vision," 292.

55. Professors Findley and Scott explain: "While the role of the prosecutor is often described as that of 'minister of justice,' in reality that idealized role often conflicts with the prosecutor's rough-and-tumble role in the adversarial process . . . Evidence that institutional and cultural pressures in prosecutors' offices contribute to conviction psychology can be seen in empirical data showing that it increases over time; the more experience a prosecutor has, the more likely he or she is to express an interest in obtaining convictions over an interest in doing justice." "Multiple Dimensions of Tunnel Vision," 328–29.

56. Prosecutors receive guidelines for ethical conduct from the Model Rules of Professional Conduct and standards put forward by the American Bar Association. See, for example, Model Rules of Professional Conduct Rule (1995) 3.8(a) ("The prosecutor in a criminal case shall: refrain from prosecuting a charge that the prosecutor knows is not supported by probable cause"); ABA Standards 3–3.9(a)

("A prosecutor should not institute, or cause to be instituted, or permit the continued pendency of criminal charges when the prosecutor knows that the charges are not supported by probable cause").

57. Gershman, "The Prosecutor's Duty to Truth," 341.

58. Frisbie and Garrett, *Victims of Justice Revisited*, 192.

59. For journalistic accounts of the Area 2 torture see John Conroy, *Unspeakable Acts Ordinary People: The Dynamics of Torture* (New York: Knopf, 2000), 21–26, 60–87, and Steve Bogira, *Courtroom 302*, 174–81. Information specific to Fred Hill can be found in a deposition of Donald G. White in *Andrew Wilson v. City of Chicago* (N.D. of Ill. July 14, 1989), 21. The special prosecutor's report which discusses and then dismisses the Area 2 allegations is Edward J. Egan and Robert D. Boyle, *Report of the Special State's Attorney*, July 19, 2006.

60. Mills and Possley, "Former Foe Having 2nd Thoughts."

61. Ken Armstrong and Maurice Possley, "Break Rules, Be Promoted," *Chicago Tribune*, January 14, 1999.

62. For a fascinating study on a group's inability to admit wrong in the face of contrary evidence, see Leon Festinger, Henry W. Riecken, and Stanley Schachter, *When Prophecy Fails: A Social and Psychological Study of a Modern Group that Predicted the Destruction of the World* (New York: Harper & Row, 1956).

63. Phone calls to the other defendants went unreturned. According to Andrew Hale, who represented them as well as the city, they had been advised not talk to the press until the litigation brought by both Michael and Paul had been completed. The settlement of Paul's case was announced as this book was going to press.

64. In 1976, the court decided *Imbler v. Pachtman*, 424 U.S. 409, which established that a prosecutor is absolutely immune from a civil suit for damages under 42 U.S.C. section 1983 for alleged deprivation of the accused's constitutional rights. However, the court left open for debate what prosecutorial acts would fall in the scope of a prosecutor's duties. The court revisited the issue in 1992 in *Burns v. Reed*, 500 U.S. 478 (1991) where it held that absolute immunity for damages did not apply to the prosecutor's act of giving legal advice to the police. Then, in *Buckley v. Fitzsimmons*, 509 U.S. 259 (1993), a case that arose out of a lawsuit by Stephen Buckley, one of the defendants in the Jeanine Nicarico murder, the U.S. Supreme Court held that prosecutors may be sued for damages under 42 U.S.C. section 1983 for their participation in the investigative phase of a criminal case.

65. Bennett L. Gershman, *Prosecutorial Misconduct*, ed. (Thomson West, 2008), §14:1, n.5.

66. For more on Frank Laverty see Bogira, *Courtroom 302*, 151 as well as John Conroy, "Detective Frank Laverty Did the Right Thing—and Paid for It for Years," *Chicago Reader*, January 5, 2007.

67. At times civil litigation makes an enormous difference in public policy. In 2003, for instance, Governor Ryan commuted the death sentences of all one hundred and sixty-three men and four women on death row to life in prison after thirteen people on death row were exonerated in prolonged legal battles. It is doubtful that such a change would have happened without the "cause lawyers" who hurled lawsuits against the city and state demanding large money damages.

68. David B. Greenberger, Marcia P. Miceli and Debra J. Cohen, "Oppositionists and Groups Norms: The Reciprocal Influence of Whistle-blowers and Co-workers," *Journal of Business Ethics* (1987): 537 (discussing research that "oppositions would be most successful when the whistle-blower minority contains more than one" and "the influence of the minority is greater when the minority includes at least two members").

Conclusion

1. "Courts are the most understudied major public institution in terms of organizational culture and performance," according to an important recent book which uses ideas of business school scholars to assess how judicial bodies operate. Brian J. Ostrom, C. W. Ostrom Jr., R.A. Hanson, and M. Kleiman, *Trial Courts as Organizations* (Philadelphia: Temple University Press, 2007), 7. For other studies on court organization and criminal courts, The National Center for State Courts provides an invaluable resource. Many of the Center's projects can be found on its Web site: http://www.ncsconline.org/. Finally, academics have been looking at courtrooms as organizations for decades and Ostrom et al. provide an excellent bibliography, but the earlier works I found particularly helpful deserve mention: Abraham Blumberg, "The Practice of Law as a Confidence Game: Organizational Cooptation of the Profession," *Law & Society Review* 1 (1967): 15–29; James Eisenstein, Roy Fleming, and Peter Nardulli, *The Contours of Justice: Communities and Their Courts* (Boston: Little Brown, 1987); James Eisenstein and Herbert Jacob, *Felony Justice: An Organizational Analysis of Criminal Courts* (Boston: Little Brown, 1977); and Lawrence B. Mohr, "Organizations, Decisions, and Courts," *Law & Society Review* 10 (Summer 1976): 621–42.

2. A report by the Vera Institute of Justice in New York favors ongoing, routine interviews of victims, defendants, attorneys and others who work in the justice sector. This should not be an expensive or complex system, just consistent check-ins about quality. Vera Institute of Justice, *Measuring Progress Toward Safety and Justice: A Global Guide to the Design of Performance Indicators Across the Justice Sector,* November 2003, http://www.vera.org/publication_pdf/207_404.pdf.

3. I refer here to the "futility thesis," which is one of three categories of justification described in Albert O. Hirschman, *The Rhetoric of Reaction: Perversity, Futility, Jeopardy* (Cambridge, Mass.: Belknap Press, 1991); the other two categories, perversity and jeopardy, refer more to unintended consequences.

4. Ibid., 80, 78.

ACKNOWLEDGMENTS

First and foremost, I must thank those who entrusted me with their experiences in America's courts. A work of nonfiction of this scope would not be possible if citizens from all walks of life had not shared their private and public travails.

Most of the victims and defendants had long given up on the promise of justice for themselves, but remained committed to the possibility of justice for others. This book is a tribute to their hope.

It was Tom Breen who suggestively handed me the Theodore Roosevelt quotation saying it "is not the critic who counts," that the "credit belongs to the one who is actually in the arena . . . who spends himself in a worthy cause," and if he fails "at least he fails while daring greatly." I took these words to heart, and now I must thank the men in the arena. By daring to let me into their professional lives the four main characters have shown how vulnerable even the most well-intentioned among us are when outmatched by the status quo. I see hope for a more just America in Robert Surrency's perseverance, Hank Bauer's resilience, Laurence Mellen's authenticity, and Tom Breen's introspection.

In each of the four locales several individuals made singular contributions. Cathy Crawford knows her way around the criminal courts. The untold stories of her relentless quest to aid the less powerful deserve a book of their own. In Troy, Jonathan Gradess offered thoughtful perspective on New York courts. Spending months in Mississippi on a modest budget was possible because of Shay Youngblood, then the John and Renee Grisham writer in residence at the University of Mississippi at Oxford. She supplied not only shelter, but a creative home that enabled the reporting to flourish. In Quitman County, Butch Scipper, the county treasurer (among other titles) opened doors to a tight-knit community. Steve Bogira and John Conroy gave helpful guidance on the Chicago chapter, as did Eric Herman, who pointed me toward invaluable sources. I am grateful to Larry Marshall not only for his example but for introducing me to Tom Breen.

At Metropolitan Books, Sara Bershtel recognized the urgency of improving our courts and became an instant advocate of this project at its earliest stages. My editor Riva Hocherman's rigor, intelligence, narrative sensibility, and enormous raw talent helped transform years of reporting into a book. Thank you, Riva. I would also like to thank everyone at Metropolitan and Henry Holt who worked to make this book happen, including Melanie DeNardo, Grigory Tovbis, and Rita Quintas.

My agent Sarah Chalfant of The Wylie Agency has the rare gift of being ultra-efficient, totally enthusiastic, and bighearted. She has been there no matter the hour—a true champion. Edward Orloff, who works with Sarah, also deserves praise for his skill, competence, and for introducing me to the meticulous Brian Gallagher, who helped with fact checking.

The seeds for this project were planted during my first year of study at Yale Law School as a Knight Foundation Fellow. That fellowship aimed to unite the fields of journalism and the law; this book tries to make good on that generous opportunity. I went on to finish my J.D. at Stanford Law School, where I gained not just the legal skills necessary to do this work but the inspiration that can only come from master professors. I especially want to thank Barbara Babcock for a dazzling experience in criminal procedure, Deborah Rhode for a seminar on "gender law," and Kathleen Sullivan for making me talk in class. Kate Stith, my Constitutional law professor at Yale, provided invaluable support and advice that greatly influenced my career path. And it was the courage that I witnessed after law school as a clerk for the honorable Rosemary Barkett of the Eleventh Circuit Court of Appeals that set the standard for commitment to equal justice under the law.

In terms of journalism, often in my mind's eye were some people who haven't been with me for a long while, but the lessons they taught and their example have long served as guides. Steve Brill, for whom I worked in the early 1990s at *The American Lawyer* magazine, modeled excellence in reporting on the legal profession. He attracted the most talented people and I learned from them, including: Andy Court, Joan Friedman, Olga Georgevich, Gay Jervey, Robert Safian, and Nicholas Varchever. The all-nighters I spent at 195 Angell Street, the home of the *Brown Daily Herald*, helped me discover the joy of journalism in the first place.

The work began to take shape at the Radcliffe Institute for Advanced Study. There, Drew Faust, Judith Vichniak, and their staff provided this freelance journalist a berth in one of the world's foremost incubators of thought. My colleagues there provided fellowship and brilliant advice: Susanna Blumenthal, John Comaroff, Susan Eckstein, Caroline Elkins, Jane Gaines, Jacquelyn Dowd Hall, Soledad Loaeza, Cindi Katz, and Senam Okudzeto. My partner in research Kate Romatowski did excellent work. Also, dear "aunt" Betty Vorenberg, a longtime champion of the disenfranchised, gave home-cooked meals and wonderful conversation. A second year spent as a fellow at Harvard Law School's Human Rights Program led by Jim Cavallaro and Henry Steiner helped situate the problems observed in the United States in a global context.

At Harvard I attended a class taught by Richard Hackman, an expert in organizational psychology. His innovative scholarship helped me think through the basic thesis of this work. Several conversations with professors at Harvard Law School stood out: Jody Freeman on administrative transparency; Randall Kennedy on unequal protection; Carol Steiker on the role of the criminal courts.

Chris Stone, at the Kennedy School of Government, reinforced the importance of performance measurement in the criminal justice system. His fellow researcher, Todd Foglesong, provided further help on several occasions from abroad. The creative leadership of several court administrators and their staffs, especially Margaret Gressens of the North Carolina Court System's Office of Indigent Defense Services, and the cutting-edge research of prominent scholars from different disciplines—Brian J. Ostrom, Charles W. Ostrom Jr., Roger Hanson, and Matthew Kleiman—offered critical guideposts for ways to understand and improve our courts. The renowned Robert Spangenberg provided assistance and historical perspective in efforts to assess justice programs.

Gerald Gamm, who chairs the political science department at the University of Rochester, kindly offered me the opportunity to teach a seminar based on this book. His thoughtful leadership allowed this work's concepts to be explored by a diverse group of bright, probing undergraduates whose queries brought this book into sharper focus: Amanda Burns, Daniella Calenzo, Samantha Carr, Jessica Fydenkevez, Jason Gershowitz, Alex Gurevich, Aalok Karambelkar, Jason Novak, Michael Potere, Laura Richenderfer, Adam Rose, Angad Raj Singh, Anita Sun, Mien-Too Wesley, Molly Williams, Mark Williams, and Ben Wittwer.

At Yale I first met and was inspired by the work of Steve Bright. From him, I learned about the Southern Center for Human Rights. I would call on Steve again when I received a fellowship to write about civil rights from the Nation Institute. The institute, under the leadership of Hamilton Fish, appointed me the Hayward Burns Memorial Fellow. That support enabled me to sit in courtrooms across the United States and write a series of articles that became the impetus for this book. With brainpower and politesse, Katrina vanden Heuvel nurtured the stories that first appeared in *The Nation*. Betsy Reed, the magazine's gifted executive editor, brought my reporting into focus.

Crucial support came from the Open Society Institute that funded the initial travel with a Soros Justice Media Fellowship. The Fund for

Investigative Journalism provided resources for a last round of follow-up interviews. I owe a debt to both.

In the middle of writing this book I moved to the extraordinary community of Rochester, New York. The remarkable company of Deborah Ronnen and Sherm Levey has enriched my life in this splendid city. Sherm arranged for office space at his law firm Boylan Brown while I completed the manuscript. I am thankful to his colleagues at the firm for their support. Many friends in Rochester have been a blessing: Andrea Allen, Vee and George Angle, Kimm and Andrew Branch, Laureen Burke and Scott Forsyth, Bob Dworkin and Sharon Gordon, Giuseppe Erba and Mark Pierzynski, Luzmilla and Hossein Hadian, Gretchen Helmke and Mitch Sanders, Cort and Jackie Johnson, James Mackey and Brett Danielson, Mary and Ned Nicosia, Allyson and Webster Pilcher, Joanna and Bernard Ravina, Coral Surgeon, as well as Cyndi Weis. To the creative genius of Tom Johnson, I owe a huge debt for his warmth, intelligence, and the desk he designed.

Many thanks to those who commented on sections or chapters at different stages, helped create the title, and provided counsel: Pam Bernstein, Joanna Blattberg, Locke Bowman, Bob and Holly Carter, Catherine Cerulli, Lori Chajet, Marion Chartoff, Bennie Crenshaw, Courtney Dickinson, David Feige, George Fisher, Bennett Gershman, Dave Grayzel, Linda LaBranche, John Langbein, George Kendall, Jonny King, Norm Lefstein, Lynn Levey, Jennifer Long, Joan Loughnane, Santi Lyon, Lynn Mather, Robert McDuff, Vanessa Mobley, Siddhartha Mukherjee, Michelle Oberman, Marcy Phillips, Jay Postel, Howard Relin, Connie Rosenblum, Michal Safdie, Paul Schectman, Sy Schwartz, Andrew Shapiro, Chris Slobogin, Laurie Stein, Mike Tein, Eliot Thompson, Rob Warden, Stephanie Kuduk Weiner, and Rachel Yassky.

In helping me conceive this project, I am grateful to Mark Weiner, a gifted writer, author, and law professor, who has been a most encouraging force in my life. Kate Frucher has the best judgment on matters of love as well as business. And one of my husband's dearest friends, the physician Emanuel d'Harcourt, brought his vast experience in the world of public health to bear on an early draft of this book; his cogent notes served as a roadmap for major revisions. Tom Newman provided wonderful comments and gave me words to explain to everyone else why this book was taking so long. Ben Herman and his wife Cara Drinan read several different sections—once on date night. Sayres Rudy is gifted in so many ways, but for the tender way he parcels out his incisive criticism he deserves an award. The amazing Hillary Schrenell read this book in a crude form and gave assiduous attention to the details. I met Hillary, and too many other brilliant folks, through my friendship with Samantha Power. Samantha's example is as powerful as they come; through her work she encouraged me to tackle entrenched problems. I wish I could adequately convey the debt I owe Fiona Maazel. There is not a page that has not benefited from her intellectual honesty and narrative skills.

Even before this book was conceived, a cadre of lifelong friends helped me to the place where I could simply start this journey and then walked alongside the entire way. No one would begin anything unless one person at the very start was there saying you can do this. That voice is Sylvia Olarte and it has stayed with me. During the long trips away when the work became exciting and often confusing, the courageous Laura Pitter was my lifeline. Of course, there is Alexa Albert who has mastered the fine art of wringing the most out of life; she is the best friend. And Lisa Cohen has given tremendous help in so many realms, but always with wit and the deep understanding that can only be forged in the crucible of high school. The amazing Emma Daly has an ability to remain cool that should be bottled and sold in stores. Time and again Sharon Dolovich channeled ideas and questions from her deep reservoir of intellectual curiosity into this book. Whatever Sharon does or says has the magical effect of making me sit down and write. Finally, there is no human being quite like Elizabeth Rubin. She is the utterly talented journalist who understands so much about people, institutions, and matters of the heart and has the words to explain it to the rest of us. Her bold influence is seen throughout these pages.

During the final writing of this book I gave birth to a son, Leopold Bach Markman. I never could have imagined a child could be so lovely.

Finishing a book and having a baby don't necessarily go together, but the work of Eday John Baptiste made it possible. My mother-in-law, Muriel Gleichenhaus Markman, always seems to know exactly what is needed. She is a force.

My home team has always been there to buoy me: my sister Nancy with her bright spirit and constant flow of little thoughtful packages; my brother-in-law, Vic, whose easy laugh and helping hands lighten everyone's load; my mother Bonnie whose long-standing commitment to criminal justice reform was passed on to me—I am, in the end, my mother's daughter; and my father, Gil, who at several low moments promised that the light would shine in. My dad is many things to me, but first and foremost, he is a source of light.

There are three who I wish could be here. My father-in-law Dr. Ira Markman pre-sold many copies of this book explaining this project to his urology patients. I can only imagine how proud he would be to know that it was done. My grandmother Frances Lessall too wanted nothing more than to see this book, but she died at the age of 95, a great believer in the project. And Eleanor Smalls Quailey of Beaufort County, South Carolina, is clearly a presence in this book. All are missed.

And very last is John Markman, whom I met and married during the course of the reporting and writing. John has one of the most versatile minds I have ever encountered. He blanketed it around this project. This book talks about the importance of having a mirror so that errors can be seen. John reflected this work, and me, so well. He took me out to the shed on more than one occasion (please finish!) and then led me back to my desk, providing endless optimism, humor, and compassion, always imagining the difference that a book on ordinary injustice could make. So much of what is here is us. For John, I am truly grateful.

INDEX

ABOUT THE AUTHOR

AMY BACH, a member of the New York State Bar, has written on law for *The Nation*, *The American Lawyer*, and *New York* magazine, among other publications. For her work in progress on *Ordinary Injustice*, Bach received a Soros media fellowship, a special J. Anthony Lukas citation, and a Radcliffe Fellowship. She lives in Rochester, New York, and has taught legal studies at the University of Rochester.